The Internet
& World Wide Web

THE ROUGH GUIDE

by

Angus J. Kennedy

Contents

The Internet

& World Wide Web

THE ROUGH GUIDE

There are more than 100 Rough Guide travel,
phrasebook, and music titles, covering
destinations from Amsterdam to Zimbabwe,
languages from Czech to Thai, and musics
from World to Opera and Jazz.

To find out more about Rough Guides, and to
check out full text of a dozen of our titles (from the US
to India), get connected to the Internet
with this guide and find us on the Web at:

http://roughguides.com/

Rough Guide to the Internet Credits

Text editor: Mark Ellingham

Design and lay-out: Henry Iles

Production: Susanne Hillen, Judy Pang

Proofread by Rosemary Morlin

This book is dedicated to A Certain Surprising Intimacy

This third edition published Nov 1997 by Rough Guides Ltd
1 Mercer St, London WC2H 9QJ
375 Hudson Street, New York 10014
Website: http://roughguides.com
Email: mail@roughguides.co.uk

Distributed by The Penguin Group

Penguin Books Ltd, 27 Wrights Lane, London W8 5TZ

Penguin Books USA Inc., 375 Hudson Street, New York 10014

Penguin Books Canada Ltd, 10 Alcorn Avenue, Toronto, Ontario MV4 1E4

Penguin Books Australia Ltd, PO Box 257, Ringwood, Victoria 3134

Penguin Books (NZ) Ltd, 182–190 Wairau Road, Auckland 10

Printed in the United Kingdom by Cox & Wyman Ltd (Reading)

The publishers and author have done their best to ensure the accuracy
and currency of all information in The Rough Guide to the Internet;
however, they can accept no responsibility for any loss or inconvenience
sustained by any reader as a result of its information or advice.

© Angus J. Kennedy, 1997

464 pages; includes index

A catalogue record for this book is available from the British Library

ISBN 1-85828-288-8

Read Me

There's nothing worse than feeling left behind – when everyone is talking about something, but it just doesn't gel. The Internet's had this effect over the last few years. Everything you pick up. Internet this, cyber that. But, unless you've been connected, you're still in the dark. Getting to grips with the Net can be daunting, but it's a short (if steep) learning curve, and the basics don't take long to master. This small guide is crammed with nuggets of practical advice, trouble-shooting tips, step-by-step tuition, and addresses of the places you'll need to go. We'll make you a Net guru in the shortest possible time. Guaranteed!

Internet books mostly fall into two categories: the brick-sized volumes that tell you far more than you want to know in unimportant areas and not enough on shortcuts; and the patronizing simplistic ones, that make it look easy in the bookstore with cute icons and catchy titles, but aren't much use once you start having problems. And, if they're written before mid-1997, they should be filed under ancient history. The truth is you don't need a fat book to get started on the Internet. It's too much work. And boring.

This Rough Guide gives it to you straight. In plain English. We think the Net is a pushover. If you can figure out how to use a word processor, you'll master the Net. Sure, you'll have teething troubles, but we show you how to solve them and where to go for help. Rather than compile everything there is to know about the Net, we give you the basics and show you how to use the Net itself to find out more. Since the Net and its associated technology changes almost daily, it's wiser to get your information from where it's always fresh.

What's more, we'll show you how to: get the best deal on Internet access, send messages across the world instantly for the price of a local call, find all the software you'll ever need free, become an expert in the most important Internet programs, and locate anything, anywhere, on the Net without having to learn any difficult commands. Or, if you're really impatient, you can wing it and go straight to our listings chapters to explore the weird, wild, and wonderful World Wide Web, or get those nagging questions off your mind in one of the special interest newsgroups. Who knows, you might even make a few friends along the way.

Well, what are you waiting for?

PART ONE

---

basics

Frequently Asked Questions

Before getting into the nitty gritty of what you can do on the Internet – and what it can do for you – here are some answers to a few Frequently Asked Questions (or FAQs, as acronym-loving Net-heads call them).

So what's this Internet good for?

The Internet is a real bag of tricks. Some say it's like having 30 million consultants on your payroll – that you don't have to pay. You can look for answers to every question you've ever had, send messages and documents across the world in a flash, shop in another continent, sample new music, visit art galleries, read books, play games, chat, read the latest news in any language, meet people with similar interests, grab free software, bet on the stock market, or just fritter the hours away surfing through mountains of visual bubble-gum.

It's also an invaluable business tool for everyday correspondence, marketing products, providing support, inviting customer feedback and publishing. Indeed the Net is fast becoming as integral to business as the telephone and fax machine.

Sounds like fun, but what is it exactly?

It's getting tougher to pin down the Internet – it's changing that quickly. Once it was simple. You could just explain that the Internet was an **international network of computers** linked up to exchange information. The word Internet is a contraction of international and network.

The core of this international network consists of computers permanently joined through high-speed connections. To get on the Internet, you simply connect your computer to any of these networked computers via a Service (or Access) Provider. Once you're online (connected) your computer can talk to any other computer on the Internet whether it's in your home town or on the other side of the world.

That's plain enough, but if you want to be picky you have to consider it's not just the computers hooked up by fancy telephone wires that make up the Internet. It's what it's used for as well. Mostly, that's the transfer of **electronic mail** (**email**), and electronic publishing on the **World Wide Web**. So when people say they found something on the Internet, they didn't find it randomly zipping around the wires hooking up the computers, they either retrieved it from where it was stored on a computer connected to this international network, or someone sent it to them by electronic mail.

But most importantly, the Internet is not really about computers. It's about people, communication, sharing knowledge. It's about overcoming physical boundaries to allow like minds to meet. And that's why you want it.

What's electronic mail, again?

 Electronic mail or **email** is a method of sending text files from one computer to another. You can send messages across the world in seconds using Internet email.

Hang on, who pays for the international calls?

The Internet is barely affected by political boundaries and distance. For example, suppose you're in Boston, and you want to buzz someone in Bangkok. Provided you both have Net access, it's as quick, easy, and cheap as sending a message across the street. You compose your message, connect to your local Internet provider, upload your mail and then disconnect.

Your mail server will examine the message's address to determine where it has to go and then passes it on to its appropriate neighbor, which will do the same. This usually entails routing it toward the backbone – the chain of high-speed links that carry the bulk of the Net's long-haul traffic. Each subsequent link will ensure that the message heads towards Bangkok rather than Bogotá or Brisbane. The whole process should take no more than a few seconds.

Apart from your Internet access subscription, **you pay only for the local phone call**. Your data will scuttle through many different networks, each with its own methods of recouping the communication costs – but adding to your phone bill isn't one of them.

Then how does the pricing model work?

Once you're on the Net itself, most of what's there is free. But unless you can get free access at work, school or wherever, you'll need to pay for the privilege of being connected. That means paying an **Internet Service Provider** to allow you to hook into its network. Depending on where you live, that could be a set price per month or year, or an hourly rate. Then on top of that, you'll have some sort of **telephone, ISDN, or cable charge**.

It's possible – indeed probable – that none of this money will ever go to the people who supply the content you'll be viewing. It simply goes toward maintaining the network. This suggests that eventually not everything will be free for ever and in the future it's likely that many publications (or sites) will charge a subscription for entry. As yet, that's still rare, other than for technical and financial publications, so enjoy it while it lasts.

What's the difference between the Internet, the Web, AOL, CompuServe, and the Microsoft Network?

The **World Wide Web** (or Web) is a user-friendly point-and-click way of navigating data stored on the Internet. CompuServe, AOL, and the Microsoft Network are called **Online Services**. They plug in to the Internet, and thus form part of the Internet, but each also has exclusive services and content available only to their members and not the general Internet public. You'll find more about them in "Online Services" (see p.45), and more on the Web in "Surfing the World Wide Web" (see p.105).

So who's in charge?

Well, technically no-one, though a number of powerful commercial players such as **CompuServe, Microsoft, Cisco, MCI, UUNet,** and **Netscape** have played major roles in putting the framework in place, and there are various bodies concerned with the Net's administration. Foremost among the latter are the **Internet Network Information Center (InterNIC)**, which registers domain names, the **Internet Society** which, amongst other things, acts as a clearing house for technical standards, and the **World Wide Web Consortium**, which discusses the future of the Web's programming language.

No-one, however, actually "runs" the Internet. As the Internet is, in effect, a network of networks, most responsibilities are contained within each local network. For instance, if you have connection problems, you would call your connection supplier. If you object to material located on a server in Japan or Ireland, say, you'd have to complain to the administrator of that local server.

While it certainly promotes freedom of speech, **the Internet is not so anarchic** as some sections of the media would have you believe. If you break the laws of your country while using the Net, and you're caught, you're liable to prosecution. For example, suppose you publish a document in the US outlining the shortcomings of a military dictator in Slobovia. It might not worry the US authorities, but it could be curtains for any Slobovian caught downloading the document. The same applies to other contentious material such as pornography, terrorist handbooks, drug literature, and religious satire. The Internet is not an entirely new planet.

But isn't it run by the Pentagon and the CIA?

When the Internet was first conceived 30-odd years ago, as a network for the American Defense Department, its purpose was to act as a nuclear attack resistant method of exchanging scientific information and intelligence. But that was then.

In the 1970s and 80s several other networks, such as the **National Science Foundation Network** (NSFNET), joined, linking the Internet to research agencies and universities. It was probably no coincidence that as the Cold War petered out, the Internet became more publicly accessible and the nature of the beast changed totally and irreversibly. These days, intelligence agencies have the same access to the Internet as everyone else, but whether they use it to monitor insurgence and crime is simply a matter for speculation.

So, is this the Information Superhighway?

Only buffoons refer to the Internet as the Information Superhighway. But, it is the closest thing we have to a prototype of Al Gore's vision as talked up by Bill Gates and associates. It has huge capabilities for cheap, global, and immediate communication; it may grow to dominate areas of **publishing, news, and education**; it is already providing an alternative **shopping mall**; and it will almost certainly make major inroads into **banking and customer services**.

Nonetheless, to get services like video on demand, we'll need a much faster network than today's Internet. Right now the Net's already straining under the pressure of new users, and it might even get worse before it gets better. Although with new **digital alternatives** such as ADSL, cable, and satellite links looming daily, the future is starting to brighten. However, the real digital "revolution" is still very much on hold.

And what about Intranets?

The mechanism that passes information between computers on the Internet can be used in exactly the same way in a **local network** such as in an office. When this is not publicly accessible, it's called an **Intranet**. Many companies use Intranets to distribute internal documents – in effect publishing Web pages for their own private use.

What's full Internet access?

You can access the Internet – and send email – through several channels, so long as you have a computer and a modem (the device that links your computer to the phone line). But not all channels will let you do everything. The **World Wide Web**, **IRC**, **FTP**, and **Telnet** – key areas of the Net which we'll deal with later in this book – require **"full Internet access"**.

You can get full Internet access through an **Online Service** like CompuServe or America Online, or with what's called an **IP (Internet Protocol)** account from any **Internet Service Provider (ISP)**. You'll encounter a range of IP accounts, which may include **SLIP** (Serial Line Internet Protocol) and **PPP** (Point to Point Protocol) for standard modem dial-ups, ISDN, and cable. Regardless of what grade IP access you choose, you'll be able to do the same things, though perhaps at different speeds.

What's bandwidth?

A higher (or fatter) **bandwidth connection** means the capacity to carry more data at once – just as a thicker pipe means you can pump more water. But unlike water, where pressure can increase, data is limited by electron speed. When a connection is at full capacity, it can't be pushed faster, so data goes into a queue – thus forming a bottleneck that slows things down. So even if you have a high bandwidth connection to the Internet, you could be impeded by insufficient bandwidth between you and your data source.

What are IP addresses?

Every computer which is permanently connected to the Net has a 32-bit unique **IP (Internet Protocol) address**, so other Internet computers can find it. A typical address looks like this: 149.174.211.5 (that is, four numbers separated by periods).

Your computer will be allocated an IP address when you get full Internet access. If it's dynamically allocated, it means it will change each time you log in. That's usual with a PPP (Point to Point Protocol) connection. SLIP (Serial Line Internet Protocol) connections tend to use a fixed address. The good news is that, other than when you first get connected, you'll probably never have to use these numbers. Why? Because there's a different system for humans called the **Domain Name System**.

Okay, then, what's the Domain Name System?

People don't like using numbers. Isn't it easier to remember a name than a telephone number? So, the Internet uses the **Domain Name System (DNS)** parallel to the IP number system. That way you have the choice of using letters or words, rather than numbers, to identify yourself online and in your email address.

Domain names can be scary at first sight, but they'll grow on you. Indeed, you can often tell a lot about who or what you're connecting to from the address. For example, consider the email address: sophie@thehub.com.au

As all Internet **email addresses** are in the format user@host (the host being your access provider), we can deduce that the user's name or nickname is Sophie while the host is thehub.com.au The host portion breaks down further into the subdomain, domain type, and country code. Here, the subdomain is thehub (an Internet Service Provider), its domain type com means it's a company or commercial site, and the country code au indicates it's in Australia.

Every country has its own distinct code, although it's not always used. These include:

au Australia
ca Canada
de Germany
fr France
jp Japan
nl Netherlands
no Norway
se Sweden
uk United Kingdom
tw Taiwan

If an address doesn't specify a country code, it's more than likely, but not necessarily, in the USA.

Domain types are usually one of the following:
ac   Academic (UK)
com Company or commercial organization
co   Company or commercial organization (UK)
edu Educational institution
gov Government body
mil Military site
net Internet gateway or administrative host
org Non-profit organization

What are hosts, servers, and clients?

In Net-speak, any computer that is open to external online access is known as a **server** or **host**. The software you use to perform online operations such as transfer files, read mail, surf the Web, or post articles to Usenet, is called a **client**.

A Web client is more commonly called a **Web browser** – a field dominated by **Netscape** and **Microsoft (Internet**

Explorer). A **Web server** is a machine where Web pages are stored and made available for outside access.

What is a BBS?

Once upon a time **BBSs (Bulletin Board Services)** were like computer clubs, where you could dial in to post messages and trade files. However, these days the definition is far fuzzier. All Online Services, such as CompuServe and America Online, are technically BBSs. That is, they have a private network or file area which is set aside out of the public domain of the Internet. The big Online Services are not what most people refer to as BBSs, though. The term is usually taken to mean a small network which primarily acts as a place to download and trade files.

There are well over 100,000 private BBSs in the USA alone, most often devoted to particular or local interests, and in some cases access is free. They customarily have areas to play games, chat, use email, post messages, and sometimes get limited access to the Internet through their own private network connections.

Where do I get an email address?

You should always get at least one email address thrown in by your Internet provider with your **access account**. Many providers supply five or more addresses – enough for the whole family. The only problem with these addresses are that they tie you to that provider. If you want to switch provider, you either have to negotiate a mail-only account or obtain an address that can move with you (see p.178). So choose your provider with care.

If you already have an email address, say at work or college, but want a **more personal or funky sounding**

address, ask an access provider for a POP3 mail only account, or sign up to a Webmail service (see p.179). That way you get to choose your address but still access mail through your regular connection.

Can I rely on email to get there?

In general Internet email is considerably more reliable than the postal service. It's rare, but not unheard of, for mail to go astray. However during 1997, AOL and Microsoft Network – to name just the big players – had severe mail outages resulting in the delay, and in some cases loss, of email. And many corporate mail servers have had growing pains, too, experiencing holdups and the odd deletion. On the whole though, you can assume email will arrive.

If you don't get a reply within a few days, of course, you can always send your message again. At worst, it will act as a reminder. If you find your mail regularly takes more than a few minutes to arrive, you should seriously consider switching your provider.

Can I shop online?

It won't be long before you can buy almost anything you want via the Internet. There are already thousands of **online stores** but Net shopping has yet to take off in a big way. It suffers from the usual reticence people feel toward mail order, as well as much publicized (and frankly, inflated) concerns about credit card security. Netscape and Microsoft Web browsers already provide adequate security, so it can only be a matter of time before Net shopping gains mainstream acceptance.

Can I make money out of the Internet?

Yes, no, maybe – perhaps it's better to ask yourself the question "Can I continue to make money without the Internet?" The last few years have seen a gold rush in the computer hardware, software, training, and publishing industries. Some, who got in early, made a killing getting businesses on the Web – the Net's "commercial zone." Today, it's settled down somewhat. Web page designers are commonplace, and can no longer charge extortionate rates unless they're tied in with a major agency. However those with serious technical and programming skills are still in high demand.

If you're wondering whether to throw the Internet into your existing **marketing mix** to help boost sales, the answer's probably yes. But rather than use it to try to attract customers, it's better to think of it as a place to post in-depth product literature, provide customer support, and canvass feedback. Not too many companies are making money from **direct sales** – though that's improving, particularly for specialist products, such as oddball CDs and rare books.

Another way to profit is by charging others to **advertise on your Web page**. Of course, they'll only want to do that if your site's popular. So you're commonly paid according to the number of times visitors pursued links from your site to your sponsor's. Alternatively if your site generates heavy traffic and looks promising, someone may want to buy you outright.

Advertising on the World Wide Web is perfectly acceptable but you should forget traditional direct response methods through email. If you try scattergunning **junk email** or peddling wares in non-commercial areas, you'll get cyber-assassinated – or **"flamed"** as it's called on the Net. If you want to see what that means, try posting an urging advertisement in Usenet, or to a mailing list – and wait for the response!

So is the Net still basically a geek hangout?

 There's no doubt about the Internet's geek-pulling power. There's stuff for Star Trek geeks, investment geeks, political geeks, hip hop geeks, movie geeks, health geeks, gardening geeks, sporting geeks, and every other sort of geek imaginable. Geek's where it's at.

Okay, but what about deviants?

These days just about anyone who's anyone has a Net account. Celebrities – rock stars and actors especially – often look themselves up to see what's said about them and join discussions. Doctors, lawyers, journalists, and scientists use the Net to trade knowledge with their peers. Students use it for research and to hand in assignments. It's something different for everyone. So sure, there may also be perverts, gangsters, and con artists, but probably no more than you mix with every day in "real life".

But is it yet another male-dominated bastion?

Well, there are reckoned to be more than twice as many men as women online, but for no particularly good reason. Some argue that women, more than men, are daunted by the technological hurdle and expense involved in getting online, others that women have less of men's "hobbyist" and "listing" obsessions. Whatever. That's still a lot of women and the percentage appears to be growing.

In theory, the Net is really as level as playing fields get – and its usage is likely to become little different from the phone, fax, and home video. After all, it's meant for communication and entertainment, and no-one can stop you, your views, your work, or your peers from getting online.

Will I make friends on the Internet?

It's easy to meet people with common interests by joining in **Usenet (newsgroup) discussions**. And being able to discuss sensitive issues with strangers while retaining a comfortable degree of anonymity often makes for startlingly intimate communication.

Translating email pen pals into the real world of human contact, or even romance, is another thing. You won't be able to tell your new e-pal Alex's age, sex, appearance, or motives at first glance. And there's nothing stopping anyone from assuming the name of their pet, town, fantasy, or idol as an email user name or IRC nickname. Or from re-inventing themselves. So if you find yourself in private council with a "Prince", don't swoon too soon.

What do I do if I'm harassed by another user?

It's possible to be harassed on the Internet by someone sending you unwelcome email, posting hostile replies to your comments in a Newsgroup, pestering you in a Chat/Internet Phone channel or publishing something on a Web page. The simplest thing to do is ignore them. If you've provoked the harassment, then you'll just have to deal with it and take it as a lesson. If it goes beyond that, forward the messages or **pass their details to your Internet Access Provider**. Even if your harasser has masked their identity, they're probably still traceable.

Your provider should contact their provider, who'll most likely warn them or kick them offline.

It's not easy to seriously harass someone via the Net and get away with it. After all, it generates evidence in writing. There have already been convictions for relatively mild threats posted to Usenet. Apart from the nature of the harassment, whether you have a case for action will depend on where you're both based. For example, across US state lines it becomes an FBI matter. Internationally, you might have no recourse other than to appeal to their access provider. For more, see http://www.cyberangels.org

Is there a lot of really weird stuff on the Net?

Yes, lots. Just like in real life, except it's easier to find.

What if children discover pornography or drugs?

Children tend to find what interests them and the deeper it's hidden, the harder they'll look. After all, didn't you? And even the bitterest old prude surely couldn't blame them for being curious. Face it, they're the Quake generation. Still, there is some undoubtedly rough material on the Net and it's beginning to be countered. Several educational bodies have taken steps to limit access to contentious matter, and there are a number of **programs** on the market designed to deny access to material containing sexually explicit, violent, or drug-related key words. Microsoft, notably, has already built **customizable censoring control** into its Web browsers, which gives parents or employers discretion over such material. (For more on this see p.124.)

For all their efforts, it's impossible to filter the Net completely, and perhaps just as well, because it's not the Internet's place to preach morals. You might also reflect on the idea that children exposed to the Internet might mature faster and learn to think more freely and independently. What they see of things like drugs, sex, and religious cults will be through first-hand interactive debates and discussions. If someone posts an article in a newsgroup advocating crack as an easy way to make money and friends, it might attract twenty negative postings in response. By following these **"threads" of responses**, children can understand reasoned argument, and form their own opinions based upon evidence rather than fashion and dogma. Maybe.

Will being on the Internet put me at risk?

It's unlikely that someone is so interested in you that they could be bothered trying to worm their way into your PC to read or interfere with your files. So it's more a hypothetical question of whether it's possible for someone to break in. Security is tightening all the time, but yes, although highly unlikely, it's not entirely impossible. Nonetheless, the truth is **it's easier to break into your house** – and burglary is harder to trace.

For paranoids, it's maybe worth pointing out that Web sites produce routine check files called "cookies" which may contain information on your browsing activities. If that bothers you, and it shouldn't really, you can just switch them off.

What about viruses?

You are far more likely to catch a virus from a corporate network or a friend's floppy disk than the Internet. Still, it pays to run a **virus check** regularly and keep your virus checker's signature file up to date.

It's almost unheard of to get a virus from downloading programs from a reputable site. Sure, there are regular scares that controls embedded into Web pages could exploit browser security flaws and harm your PC. But fixes generally appear days later. And these flaws are rarely exploited at any rate. The two highest risk areas are decoding unknown programs posted to **Usenet Newsgroups**, and running programs sent to you via **email**. The biggest culprits are word processing documents with malicious macros. For more on this, if you're running Microsoft Office, read http://www.microsoft.com/office/antivirus/

Will I need to learn any computer languages?

No. If you can work a word processor or spreadsheet, you'll have no difficulty tackling the Internet. You just have to get familiar with your Internet software, which in most cases isn't too hard. The biggest problem most people have is **setting up for the first time**, but it's becoming less of an issue as most Internet providers supply start-up kits that make it easy.

Once online, most people access the Internet through **graphical "icon-based" software**, with a similar feel to most Macintosh and Windows programs. And on the World Wide Web – the most popular part of the Net – **you hardly even need to type**: almost everything is accessible by a click on your mouse.

The one time you might need to use UNIX commands – the Internet's traditional computer "language" – is if using Telnet to remotely log on to a UNIX computer. And that's something most of us can avoid.

Can I use the Internet if I can't use a computer?

As mentioned above, even if you can't type, you can still use the World Wide Web – all you have to do is **point your mouse and click**. That's about as far as you'll get though. If you've never had any contact with computers, consider the Internet your opportunity. Don't think of computers as a daunting modern technology. They're just a means to an end. The best way to learn how to use a computer is to grab one and switch it on.

How do I get connected?

Good question and worth a whole chapter. Read on.

Getting Connected

There are all kinds of ways to access the Internet. Within the next year, you'll probably come in regular contact with a Net-connected terminal. Maybe at your work, college, school, local library, or even your local coffee shop. But if you're not in that position already, you needn't wait. It's possible to get everything you need to be up and running within a few days. The good news is it's no longer expensive nor complicated, and it's getting cheaper and easier by the day.

You don't need to be a computer expert

The most common barrier to getting connected is technophobia, or more specifically fear of computers. That's understandable, because the Internet could draw you into an intimate relationship your computer. However, it doesn't have to be that demanding. In fact, most people find it absorbing, maybe even obsessive, once they've started. In general using the Internet is simpler than using a word processor. And definitely a lot more fun. But even if you've never used a computer, you should be able to figure out how to surf the Web within a matter of minutes. Finding your way around is another matter, but you're at an advantage – you have this guide.

Although it's mostly relatively simple, you will strike the odd hitch. So be prepared for a period of modest confusion. Everyone goes through it, but you'll soon learn the ropes. And the online community is always willing to help, as long as you direct your queries to the right area. Before long, you'll be sharing your new-found expertise with others.

What you'll need

Before you can get connected, you'll need three things: a **computer** with enough grunt to handle the software, an account with an **Internet Service Provider**, and a hardware device – usually the fastest **modem** you can afford – to connect your computer to the Internet. How you connect to the Internet can make the difference between pleasure and frustration. You don't necessarily need state of the art computer gadgetry, but no matter what you have, you'll find a way to push it to the limit.

Computer firepower

It's possible to access the Net in some way with almost any machine you could call a computer, but if you can't run your Web browsing and mail software together without a lot of chugging noises coming from your hard drive, you're going to get frustrated.

To drive browsing software comfortably, you'll need at least a **486 SX25 IBM-compatible PC**, or a **Macintosh 68030** series, equipped with **8Mb RAM**. This won't be enough to run the latest resource hungry software, but you'll be able to get by at a pinch if you stick to the old versions. And while you can also connect to the Net with Ataris, Amigas, PCTVs, Psion Organizers, Palmtops, and even the Nokia 9000 cellular phone, you'll be severely restrained by the lack of software. If you want to do more than send email, you'll be far happier with something faster and more versatile.

To listen to music samples and sound effects, or use Internet telephony, you'll also need an **internal sound card, microphone, and speakers or headphones**. Macs come with reasonable sound capability, but with PCs it's usually an extra. Unless your primary purpose is to create professional quality music, buy a Sound Blaster compatible card as it will work with almost everything.

With standard **video hardware**, you'll be disappointed with the Web's short movies as they might only appear matchbox-size on your screen. If you'd like to improve the drawing time, quality, and size of your downloaded images and movies, you should consider graphic upgrade options such as accelerator cards, RAM additions, MPEG movie cards, and 3D accelerator cards. But it's not necessary.

If you can afford it and want the most out of the Net, the **ideal entry computer package** would be a fast Pentium MMX Processor, 32+Mb RAM, 1+Gig hard drive, 32 bit sound card with wavetable synthesis, hex speed CD-ROM, and as your operating system **Windows 95**, **NT 4.0** or later. There's nothing wrong with **Power Macs** either, as any of their loyal (and productive) users will attest, except that most of the interesting software comes out for PCs first, and sometimes never makes it to Mac. But if you'd exchange user-friendliness for the cutting edge and you're more into art and publishing than twiddling, you might be happier with a Mac.

There's a lot to be said, too, for buying the same set-up as a friend, so you have someone to turn to for help.

Note: If you're on a network at work or college, don't attempt to connect to the Net without your systems manager's supervision. Networked PCs and Macs can use the same software listed later in this book, but may connect to the Net differently.

Connecting your computer to the Net

A powerful computer won't make up for a slow link to the Internet. Get the fastest connection you can afford. Unless you're hooked up through a network, you'll need a device to connect your computer to the telephone line or cable. There'll be a similar device at the Access Provider's end. This device will depend on the type of Internet account. The two main types are **Leased Line** and **Dial-up**. Leased Lines are expensive and aimed at businesses that need to be permanently connected. Dial-up suits the casual user. Investigate the Net through a Dial-up account before contemplating a Leased Line.

Modems – the plain vanilla option

 The cheapest, most popular, but slowest, way to connect is by installing a modem and dialing up through the standard telephone network. Modems come in three flavors: internal, external, and PCMCIA. Each has its advantages and disadvantages.

The cheapest option is usually an **internal modem** – unless you have a portable, for which internal modems are often comparatively pricey. It plugs into a slot inside your computer called a bus. It's not a difficult job, but does require that you take the back off your computer and follow the instructions carefully (or get your computer store to do it). Because they're hidden inside your computer, internal modems don't take up desk space, clutter the back of your computer with extra cables, or require an external power source. They do, however, generate unwanted heat inside your computer, place an extra drain on your power supply, and lack the little lights to tell you if or how the call is going.

An **external modem** is easier to install. Depending on

the make, it will simply plug straight in to your computer's serial, parallel, or SCSI port, making it easily interchangeable between machines (and simple to upgrade). External modems require a separate power source, maybe even a battery. And they usually give a visual indication of the call's progress through a bank of flashing lights (LEDs).

The credit card-sized **PCMCIA modems** are a mixture of both. These fit internally into the PC Card slots common in most modern notebooks and remove easily to free the slot for something else. They don't require an external power source, but are expensive and sometimes fragile.

Whatever type you choose, the major issue is **speed**. Data transfer speed is expressed in bits per second or bps. It can take up to ten bits to transfer a character. So a modem operating at 2400 bps (2.4 kbps) would transfer at around 240 characters per second. That's about a page of text every eight seconds. At 28.8 kbps, you could send the same page of text in two-thirds of a second.

A 14.4 kbps (V.32) modem is considered entry level for the World Wide Web. But if you can afford it, get a **56.6 kbps** or better. They're a little more expensive, but they will reduce your online charges, and give you more for your money. That's if your provider supports this speed. At the time of writing many providers are still struggling to upgrade from 28.8 kbps to 33.6 kbps, let alone to 56.6 kbps. If you're restricted to 28.8 kbps, don't be too bothered – it's fast enough for most purposes.

Finally, **make sure whatever you buy will work with your computer**. PCs need a high-speed serial card with a 16550 or 16650 UART chip to process any more than about 9.6 kbps reliably. Most modern PCs have them as standard, but check anyway. They're not an expensive upgrade.

Faster ways to connect

What's good about modems is that they are the right-here right-now accepted standard everywhere in the world and work over the standard telephone system without any excess charges. But they are also slow and unstable, compared to what's around the corner.

The next immediately available option is **ISDN**. This provides three channels (1x16 kbps and 2x64 kbps) which can be used and charged for in various ways. ISDN Internet accounts don't usually cost more but, depending on where you live, the line connection, rental, and calls can cost anywhere from slightly to outrageously more than standard telephone charges. That's up to your telco. With ISDN, rather than using a modem, you'll need a slightly more expensive device called a Terminal Adapter, plus appropriate software, and possibly an upgrade to your serial card. For details on how to install ISDN under Windows 95 see: http://www.microsoft.com/windows/getisdn/

ISDN is a vast improvement on modem technology, not just for speed, but for superior line handling and almost instantaneous connections. However, just as it's gaining acceptance, several other copper-wire technologies promise to bring far higher bandwidths into homes at a fraction of the cost. One is the possibility of getting access, perhaps even a cheap permanent connection, bundled with a **cable TV** connection. This is already being trialed and rolled out commercially in some areas. But you can only get it if you have cable down your street and if that cable company is offering Internet access. Cable potentially offers very high speed access without call charges, but suffers because you have to share the line. It's certainly worth investigating, so ask your local cable company.

Also on the horizon is **ADSL**, which promises to deliver up to 6 Mbps in to, and 640 kbps out of, the home over the standard telephone cables via yet another type of adapter. It looks great, but so far seems to be all talk with little commercial action.

But if you need superfast delivery and you need it now, your best choice could be via **satellite**. You receive from the satellite, and send through a standard dial-up or leased line account with an access provider. So although you might be able to receive data at up to 10 Mbps, you can only send at a standard modem rate. Then, of course its also limited by the speed of the Net itself. For more, see http://www.direcpc.com And be sure to watch the press and ask around, because access to these sorts of speeds will make the Internet a whole new playground.

Satellite is not the only wireless access, though it is the fastest. For starters, there's NewsCatcher (http://www.airmedia.com), an odd black Bakelite pyramid that receives Net broadcasts, including email alerts, by air and pushes them into your serial port. That means no telephone charges, just a subscription fee. And Metricom's Ricochet Wireless Modem access (http://www.ricochet.net) serves duplex 28.8 kbps via an unrestricted radio channel, direct to the ISP. Again no telephone charges, but not exactly high speed.

So, how do I get a connection?

To connect to the Internet, you'll need someone to allow you to connect into their computer, which in turn is connected to another computer, which in turn . . . that's how the Internet works. Unless you have a working relationship with whomever controls access to that computer, you'll have to pay for the privilege.

A firm in the business of providing Internet access is known as an **Internet Access Provider (IAP)** or **Internet Service Provider (ISP)**. Once, Internet access was available only to the echelons of research and defense. Now, it's a highly competitive business, with companies offering free trial periods and software to attract your custom. However if your provider goes broke you might be left without access and lose your email address. So choose your ISP carefully.

One alternative to the dedicated IAPs and ISPs is to subscribe to one of the major **Online Services** – such as **CompuServe**, **America Online**, or **Microsoft Network** – which offer full Internet access at increasingly commercial rates. Most of these commercial giants offer two separate services: access to the Internet proper and access to their own private network. On the Internet front, they can be appraised in the same way as any other ISP, and are reviewed in the following chapter.

How much is it going to cost?

Since the gates to the Net are in the hands of small as well as large business, there's a highly confusing array of Access Providers (and pricing structures).

The biggest issue is whether you have time charges. Where local calls are fixed or free, as in North America, Asia, and Australasia, providers began by either restricting the number of access hours included in the monthly charge or charging by the minute. The idea being to discourage line hogging. So in the US, typical charges were $20.00 per month for the first 40 hours access and then $2.00 per hour thereafter. However, due to fierce competition most US providers switched to "all you can eat" accounts for a single monthly fee, usually $20.00. Now, many are in the process of switching back to timed charging, because single users did sit on the line all day. In countries, notably the UK, where local calls are timed, lengthy connections mean hefty phone bills. So line hogging is not an issue. In the UK it's common just to pay a single monthly fee of as little as £8.00 or an annual fee of £90.00.

If you're planning to connect into the Net through a telephone line, then it's crucial to choose a provider with a local dial-up number. And, if you travel, a range of access numbers. Otherwise you can run up some serious phone bills. These numbers are called **Points Of Presence (POPs)**. Often, in the US, if you need to call your provider from outside the state, it may offer a free 1-800 number with a flat fee of about 15¢ per minute including the call. If you have free local call access, then make sure your provider has a POP in your local zone. In the UK, unless you restrict your access to nights and weekends, your phone bill will usually outweigh your Internet access bill.

Wherever you're based, it pays to shop around and look for the optimum combination of price, service, availability, and extra features. To help with your quest, we've printed a list of providers at the end of this book. Inevitably, given the huge number of operators, it's far from complete (and no guarantee of quality), but it will get you started – and you can always change later on, exploring the Net itself to see what's on offer in your area. You could also check the computer classifieds in one of the proliferating Internet magazines. Many offer guides comparing local providers' prices, services, and points of presence.

In general, the best idea is to get started with someone who will give you all the start-up software and cheap access for the first month. Ring several Freecall numbers and ask for their latest information packs and access software. Alternatively, look in at your local computer store and pick from one of the packages offering easy-to-install software pre-programmed with a call-up to a local provider.

What to ask

Choosing an Access Provider is the single most critical part of getting connected. The simplest way is to ask around, read magazine reviews, and see what others recommend. If you have to do your own research, look for answers to the following questions. It might seem laborious but it's nowhere near as painful as being stuck with poor access.

Can I access for the price of a local call?

If you have to pay long-distance rates, it's going to cost you more. Many providers give you the option of dialing a toll-free national number and charging you back. Get a local provider if possible. Ask if it has multiple points of presence (POPs).

Do you use POP3 for email?

POP3 is superior. It enables you to pick up your mail from a cybercafé, at work, or wherever you can get online. If a provider doesn't use it, ask if there's a way to pick up mail remotely. For example, you can pick up AOL(America Online) mail by logging in over the Net with its software. But that can be a pain.

What are your support hours?

It's not essential to have 24-hour support, but it's a bonus to know someone will be there when you can't get a line on the weekend or at 11pm.

Can you send me a copy of your network map?

A quality provider should be proud to provide you with a topology map of its peer connections. What you are really asking is from whom it buys its connection, with whom it exchanges data, and the size of its internal network. It's easier to get it as a map so that you can compare it with others at your leisure. You have to try to figure out whether its network is fast and reliable. Good signs are its own transcontinental and international links, close proximity to the backbone, multiple routing options, and high-speed connections. Of course, none of this matters if it's overloaded with traffic. A lot of people balk at this question but next to a reliable mail server, it's actually what matters most.

What is your start-up cost?

Avoid paying a start-up fee if possible – though if it includes a decent start-up kit with a copy of Netscape 4.0 or Internet Explorer 4.0, it could be worth the savings in download time and bother.

What software do you supply – is it 32 bit, and does it work with Netscape or Microsoft Internet Explorer?

Likewise avoid paying for start-up software. Some providers recommend commercial packages, others provide their own. Whatever you're getting, if it doesn't work with Netscape or Internet Explorer, forget it – and if you're running Windows 95, you don't want 16 bit software. If you are reasonably confident with your computer try a free software alternative first. Spending more money is no assurance of long-term higher standards or simplicity.

What are your ongoing monthly charges?

Most providers charge a monthly fee, with some that's your only cost. This is common in the UK where local calls are charged by time. Elsewhere it often forms a base rate with certain time constraints.

What are your usage time charges?

In most countries where local calls are free or untimed, you'll be charged for the amount of time you're connected. In many cases your monthly charge will include a number of free hours per month or day. Find out if unused hours can be used as future credits.

Are there any premium charges?

Premium charges are one of the main drawbacks with the Online Service giants such as CompuServe, which provide quality commercial databases as well as Internet access. But having to pay extra to use certain services is not necessarily a bad thing, as you don't want to have to subsidize something you don't use.

Is it cheaper to access at certain times?

In an effort to restrict traffic during peak times, providers may offer periods with reduced or no online charges. Think about when you're most likely to use your connection. Try during the cheap period. If you can't connect, it's slow, or you'd rarely use it at that hour, then it's no bargain.

Can you support my modem type and speed?

Modems like talking to their own kind. When modems aren't happy with each other, they connect at a slower rate. It's not much use if your 56.6 kbps modem can only connect at 28.8 kbps. Ask what connection speeds your provider supports. If it's lower than your modem's top speed, look elsewhere.

Do you offer high-speed access such as ISDN or ADSL?

If the answer's yes, find out the cost all up, including the hardware, wiring, rental, and call charges. If it's affordable, ask for installation contacts. In some parts of the US, for example, installation is only about $20.00, and thereafter costs the same as a telephone.

Do you carry all the newsgroups in Usenet? If not, how many do you carry and which ones do you cut?

Usenet has more than 25,000 groups and it's still growing. That's 95% more than you'll ever want to look at in your lifetime. Most providers carry only a portion, but it's still usually over 60%. The first ones to be axed are often the foreign language, country specific, provider specific, and the adult (**alt.sex** and **alt.binaries**) series. If you particularly want certain groups, your provider can usually add them, but if it has a policy against certain material it may refuse. Unless you're concerned that particular groups could have a negative influence on whomever is using your connection, get as many groups as you can. You never know what you'll uncover.

What will my email address be, and how much do you charge to register a domain name?

You usually have the option to choose the first part of your email address. You might like to use your first name or nickname. This will then be attached to the provider's host name. Check if your name's available and what the host name would be. You don't want a name that could reflect badly on your business plans. For instance, if you register with the UK Service Provider Demon, your email address will end with **demon.co.uk** – perhaps not the ideal choice for a priest (although one vicar who used the first edition of this book reckons it's a conversation point). If you want your own domain name, a provider should be able to register your choice for you. For instance, if John Hooper trains ducks to use computers, he could register duckschool.com and give himself the email address **john@duckschool.com**. Then it would be easy to remember his address, just by thinking about who he is and what he does. Expect to pay an extra $200.00/£150.00 per year, or more, for this privilege.

How much does it cost for personal Web page storage?

Many providers will include a few megabytes of storage free so you can publish your own Web page. In general, if you go over that megabyte limit there'll be an excess charge.

How long have you been in business, who owns the company, and how many subscribers do you have?

You need to know who you're dealing with. Big operators may offer certain advantages like national and even global dial-up points, security, guaranteed access, stability, and close proximity to the high-speed backbone. However, they can be slow to upgrade because of high overheads and may have dim support staff. Small younger providers can be more flexible, have newer equipment, more in-tune staff, cheaper rates, and faster access, but conversely may lack the capital to make future critical upgrades. There aren't any rules, it's a new industry and all a bit of a long-term gamble.

Once you've done your calculations, drawn up your shortlist of providers, and received your start-up software, you should be ready to dial your provider of choice. If you've done your research well you should have come across at least one free introductory period. These can be worth having – but be wary. You'll often have to supply your credit card details and join before they'll let you in. Make sure the offer really is free, has no hidden costs, and check your statement if you cancel. Certain major online services have been notoriously slack in the accounts department.

Connection Software: TCP/IP

 It's standard practice for Access Providers to supply the basic connection software – usually for free. However, because the Internet is constantly evolving, no matter how good the starter kit, you'll soon want to replace or add components.

The basic kit

What you get from a provider, or from buying a start-up kit or disk in a computer store, varies from the bare minimum needed to dial in and establish an IP connection, to a full Internet toolkit.

At the heart of every package is the **TCP/IP** software, known as the **stack** or in Windows as the **winsock**. It enables the computer to talk the Net's language. It needs to know your IP address and the address of the server your provider uses to convert domain names into IP addresses and thus connect you. All your Net software, such as your newsreader, Web browser, and mail client, relies on it to converse.

Once this TCP/IP software is correctly configured to your provider's details, you can pick and choose all the other components as you see fit. If you switch providers you just have to alter a few details in the TCP/IP configuration. Your provider will have no problem telling you what to change or will supply you with the TCP/IP already configured.

Windows 95, OS/2, OR Mac?

If you're running **Windows 95**, IBM's **OS/2 Warp**, or Macintosh **System 7.5**, you already have all the TCP/IP software you need to get started. Your provider will either supply you with the configuration settings on a file or give you written instructions on how to set up. Failing that, get someone to walk you through it over the phone. Once that's done the rest is easy.

Earlier systems

If you're using an **earlier version of Windows**, or a **pre-System 7.0 Mac system**, you'll need to either upgrade your operating system or obtain a TCP/IP program.

Of the several **TCP/IP programs** for Windows 3.x, the most popular is Trumpet Winsock. It's available freely on the Internet and used as the core of many ISPs' Windows 3.x bundles. It's not actually free, though. If you want to use it after a trial period, you are requested to pay the author. Its dial-up scripting takes a while to figure out, but once you have it going it's rock solid and works with everything.

Macintosh users need look no further than MacTCP, or its successor Open Transport, which can be obtained separately from most Access Providers or from your Apple dealer as part of the Apple Internet Connection Kit.

Dialing different providers

Once your connection software is set up you should be able to forget about it, unless you have to **dial a different provider**. It's simple to set up Windows 95 to handle multiple providers, you just start a new account under Dial-up Networking. However, if you've installed a Windows 3.x ISP bundle, under any version of Windows you might encounter conflicts. When you install Windows 3.x TCP/IP software, it deposits its own version of a file named winsock.dll into your system path. If you install two TCP/IP packages you could have two such files in different directories, but both in your system path, or one could overwrite the other. Make sure this doesn't happen. Just plain don't install an ISP kit under Windows 95 that isn't specifically designed for it.

If you **change providers** and you already have a TCP/IP program on your machine, or if you are running Windows 95, OS/2 Warp, or a Macintosh, ask your new provider's advice on configuration.

Dialers

The other essential piece of connection software is the **dialer**. It is often integrated into the same software that enables the TCP/IP connection. The dialer is the place to enter your user details, password, and your provider's telephone number. After it's configured all you should ever have to do is click on "connect", or something similar, to instruct your modem to dial.

If it might be useful to you, get a dialer that enables you to enter several providers' details and alternative phone numbers. **Windows 95** handles this supremely through a combination of its Dial-up Networking, Dial-up Scripting, Internet Connection Wizard, and Internet Explorer. Microsoft has been continually upgrading its Internet connectivity in Windows 95. If you have a brand new build of Windows 95, it should incorporate Dial-up Scripting and the Internet Connection Wizard. If not, your access provider should be able to supply you with enough to get you online. Then drop into Microsoft's home on the World Wide Web (http://www.microsoft.com) and download all the upgrades. (You'll find them in the Products section under Windows and Internet.) Another way to do this is by installing the latest version of its World Wide Web browser, **Internet Explorer**. If you decide not to use Internet Explorer, at least grab the latest ISDN Accelerator Kit and dial-up add-ons. They'll improve performance and add several new and useful features.

Did you get all that TCP/IP stuff?

If you didn't understand a bar of the last couple of pages on getting connected, don't worry! Internet connection and TCP/IP configuration is your Internet Access Provider's specialty. It's in their interest to get you up and running, so if things go haywire, or you're just plain confused, do things the easy way – give them a call. After all, if you can't get connected, they're not going to get paid.

Right – is that it, or do I still need more software?

The TCP/IP and dialer combination is enough to get you connected to the Net. But you'll need more software to get to the Net's various areas. That should initially come from your access provider.

The one thing you absolutely definitely need is an **FTP program**, so you can download all the best Internet software from the Net itself, for free. It's highly likely you've been given a Web browser, preferably Netscape or Internet Explorer. If so, you're set. Both will do fine for FTP – and just about everything else. Otherwise you'll need a dedicated program like CuteFTP or Fetch. Use that to get yourself a browser. You'll find addresses in the "Software Roundup" (p.369) or better still ask your provider's support where to get one. They should point you to the location that's closest and quickest.

Once you have a browser you can surf around for the latest programs to send mail, read news, chat, and whatever else you desire. Don't worry, they're not hard to find with the whole Internet at your disposal – and they needn't cost a penny. For more on how to do it, just read on.

CONNECTING FOR THE FIRST TIME

 The best exercise for your very first connection is to get onto the World Wide Web. First, install or configure your **TCP/IP, dialing,** and **mail software** to your provider's specification. If your provider has done its job properly and supplied you with clear instructions, this shouldn't be too hard. You'll also need a Web browser which shouldn't require configuration, although you might like to add your mail details if it doubles as your mail program.

Next, connect your modem (or terminal device) to the phone line, and instruct your dialer to call. It will make all kinds of mating noises while connecting, like a fax machine. Once the connection's negotiated, these sounds will cease. At some stage

---

you'll have to enter your user name and password. This will be a one-off event if it's incorporated into your scripting, otherwise you'll have to do it every time. Keep this password private – anyone could use it to rack up your bill or, perhaps worse, read your mail (although you may be issued with a separate password to retrieve mail).

Now start your **Web browser** – hopefully that will be Netscape or Internet Explorer, and try accessing a few of the addresses from our Web Guide (p.195). You'll find instructions on how to use the Web in "Surfing the Web" (p.105). If you're able to log into the sites, you're off the mark and its close to plain sailing from now on. Otherwise you'll need to find out what's wrong.

If you've been given a program called **Ping** as part of your software package, you can use it to verify that you have an IP connection by contacting another computer. Just open up **Ping** and key in any domain name such as www.microsoft.com or www.ibm.com If **Ping** fails to convert the domain name into an IP address on both attempts, you've either incorrectly configured your TCP/IP settings, your provider's Domain Name Server is not working, or you've failed to achieve an IP connection. Log off, recheck your settings, and try again. If you can't get it to work, ring support and ask for help. If you haven't been given Ping, skip that test and try sending mail to yourself and picking it up again see "Email" (p.58). Again, if that fails, call for help.

If you haven't been given a browser, only an FTP program, the same applies except rather than surf the Web, try downloading something from an FTP site. A browser would be the obvious choice. See "FTP" (p.77).

Once you've successfully verified it works, you're ready to launch into everything else the Net has to offer. Give yourself a pat on the back – the hardest part's over.

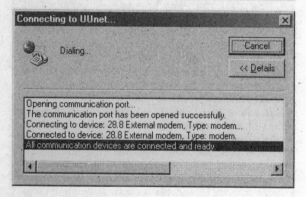

Okay, I'm connected – but it's very slow, or I keep getting a busy tone

This is an all too common lament. The Net can suffer badly from overload and transfer rates will slow down due to **bottlenecks** between the computer where a file or Web page is stored and your computer. However, if transfers are slow from everywhere, the problem lies closer to home. It could be that your provider has too many users online, or accessing its Web area from outside, and the jam is forming between it and the Net. In this case your provider needs to increase its bandwidth to the Net. It could also be a general Internet backbone overload, which is outside your provider's control. ISPs tend go through cycles of difficult traffic periods. If they have the resources and the foresight to cope with demand, you won't notice. But as it's such a low margin business, they're more likely to stretch things. It should be in the constant process of upgrading, especially bandwidth. If not, move on.

Another common bugbear is striking a **busy/engaged tone** when you dial in, especially at peak hours like the end of the working day. Keep trying until you get in: even though you dial a single number, there are several modems at the other end. If it happens often, complain, or get a new provider.

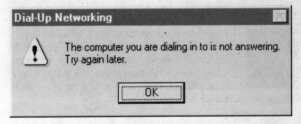

Occasionally you might be **able to connect, but not actually get on to the Net**. This could be due to several things, such as a malfunctioning DNS server, incorrectly configured TCP/IP, failure to get an IP address, or a temporary outage. If you specify a few DNS servers in your configuration, the first won't occur. If you've already succeeded in getting on the Net and you haven't meddled since, your configuration should be all right. But check it anyway. If you can pick up your mail, and access local Web sites, but not others, there'll be an outage somewhere. Report it, and try later. If it's intermittent, chances are you're not getting an IP connection every time. Apart from dialing again, all you can do is complain or change providers. But if you'd really like to know what's going on in the network, install NetMedic (http://www.vitalsigns.com). It can tell you exactly where its breaking down, and whether your provider is falling short.

Always call your provider when you have complaints with its service. You'll get to know what's going on and where it's headed. If you're not treated with respect, no matter how trivial your inquiry, take your money elsewhere. There's a prevailing arrogance within the computer industry. Don't tolerate it. You're the customer; they're not doing you a favor.

The single best piece of advice

 If you know someone who's a bit of an Internet guru, coax them over to help you hook up for the first time. Throw in enough pizza, beer, and compliments about their technical prowess, and you'll have an auxiliary support unit for life.

Online Services

AOL, CompuServe, Line One, Microsoft Network (MSN), and Prodigy provide Internet access to their subscribers but are commonly called Online Services rather than Internet Service Providers (ISPs). That's because they supply more than just Internet access. Each offers subscribers private, customized content, either on a network separate to the Internet (and only available to members), or in a password-protected Web site. They tend to be more expensive than a regular ISP but are worth considering as they are well organized operations – secure, regulated, easy to navigate, simple to install, and come with loads of free Web space. AOL and CompuServe, in particular, score in maintaining some excellent discussion forums, and international reach, offering a broad range of local numbers (Points of Presence) to dial in. If you want to pick up mail on your travels, this can be a big plus – see our section "On The Road" (p.176).

Following are brief summaries of what's currently on offer from the major Online Services. Be warned, though, that they are all in a state of flux, shifting material from their private networks to the Web proper, and integrating their own browsers with Internet Explorer.

CHOOSING AN ONLINE SERVICE

Online Services make a gentle introduction to the online
world. They're easy to set up, simple to find your way
around and, since they're major commercial operations
with moderated forums, they may have better quality or
at least more consistent material than the Web. But,
many users end up spending most of their time on the
Internet, paying extra for exclusive content, chat rooms,
and forums they never use. You can only work out
what's best for you by having a look around first.

So, try them out – the lot, if you have time. It won't
cost you anything, because they're all mad on free trials.
Between ten hours and a month is typical. Use them to
do your Net research on where to go next and appraise
them as we outlined in "Getting Connected" (see p.32). If
you enjoy one, then sign up. But if you're serious about
using the Net you should try at least one dedicated ISP,
too, so you can compare speed and service.

AOL (America Online)

With well over eight
million account hold-
ers, **America Online
(AOL)** is currently the
world's largest Online
Service. In fact its
number of users could
potentially be up to five
times that number,
because each member is allowed five "screen names".
That means five people – your friends and family, say –
can each have a sub-account at no extra cost. They can
then log in and do everything you can with a full
account. With one exception. As account holder, you

control how much they can access. So if you don't want your kids near binary newsgroups (mostly porn and pirate software), you can bar them, or ban decoding and downloading.

These **screen names** are actually email addresses. So if you choose the screen name Shelley, your email address would be Shelley@aol.com Unfortunately, with potentially forty million screen names, it's hard to get one quite that simple. Especially as once you've taken one, and changed it, it can't be re-used.

AOL has been aggressively pushing its software to the point where any computer magazine buyer in the US or UK should have several copies of its access program. Still, **signing up** couldn't be easier. You just pop in the disk, type in your personal details, click "yes" a few times, and within seconds you're asked to choose a screen name. And then you get a month's free access to not only all AOL's content but the full Internet as well.

Despite its name, AOL is not all American. UK members, for example, are greeted by Joanna Lumley's voice and UK news, travel, and entertainment guides. In addition to its range of **online encyclopedias, magazines, and databases**, AOL's greatest strength lies in its sense of community. AOLers do tend to mix online with other AOLers, aided by an Instant Messaging system which lets them know when their "buddies" are online. This eager AOLer personality really shines through in AOL's **chat forums**, where lucky members gather to grill popstar bigwigs like Michael Jackson, Paul McCartney, and the Spice Girls.

Although it now ships **Internet Explorer** integrated into its software bundle, of all Online Services AOL seems the most reticent to switch over to a Web/POP3 base. Consequently, you'll need the AOL program to access its mail and much of its exclusive content.

For a free trial and local pricing call: ☎800 827 6364 (North America); ☎0800 279 1234 (UK).

CompuServe

CompuServe started Online Services in the late 1970s and now has Points Of Presence in over 142 countries, more than five million members, and a content range second to none. It has support forums for just about everything supportable, company searches, online shopping, news, magazines, professional forums, chat, software registrations, program archives, flight reservations, and more services than you could look at in a lifetime. CompuServe is also a truly **international** access provider. So no matter where you join, you can dial in to any of its international numbers to browse the Internet or pick up your email. It's simple to register and provides all the necessary software, which now includes Microsoft's **Internet Explorer**, for free.

If all goes to plan, CompuServe will soon become two things, the world's most valuable Web site and the world's most expansive Internet provider. Once its content has moved onto the Web, it should be almost entirely navigable with any Web browser. This means non-members should soon be able to access it from the Net on some sort of pay per view basis. In addition, CompuServe has at last addressed its members' (and all their email partners') greatest bugbear, offering "real" email names (MilesAlmo@Compuserve.com) as an alternative to its old number system (12345.678@Compuserve.com). They are soon to add POP3 compatibility, too, so members can access their email with any mail program.

Although CompuServe, like AOL, delivers its share of home info-tainment, like online grocery shopping and entertainment guides, that's just floss on the cake. It's intent on pitching at the business market and offers more serious **data and services** than AOL.

CompuServe's charges can be complex, with premiums for some services, and different payment structures for different countries. Internet-only access is offered in some areas at a discount.

For a free trial and local pricing call: ☎1300 555 520 (Australia), ☎800 848 8990 (North America), ☎0800 442 374 (NZ), ☎0800 289 378 (UK).

LineOne (UK Only)

LineOne was launched in 1997 by the combined forces of Rupert Murdoch and British Telecom. At present it is marketed exclusively in the UK. Apart from Internet access and POP3 email, its main selling proposition is its traditional British family values content enhanced by the online debuts of *The Sun* and *News of the World* (Murdoch's *Times* and *Sunday Times* are available on LineOne, too, but already have established Web editions). So you can start your day with Uri Geller, Mystic Meg, Betty Shrine, a bit of footy, a page 3 stunner, and a randomly selected lotto number. Get the picture?

Well, thankfully it's not all like that. For instance, as with AOL, you can set up five **sub-accounts** and restrict their access, say, to strictly educational matter. And as well as the tabloid fluff, there's up-to-the-minute news and sport, Sky video feeds, Harper's reference titles, financial data and portfolio management, Kiss FM and Classic FM in Real Audio, online gaming and entertainment listings. It's all entirely Web-based, squats neatly inside **Internet Explorer**, doesn't meddle with your system, and hence isn't a bad introduction to the Net. After all, if it's not your style, you already have the Web software, so signing up with another ISP is as simple as switching your dial-up settings. And then again, maybe you'll become a *Sun* convert.

There are three LineOne **charging** options. Unlimited access costs £15.00 per month. Alternatively, you can opt for ten free hours and pay £1.50 per subsequent hour. If you already have Internet access, or live outside the UK, a content-only subscription costs £7.00 per month. For details, call: ☎0345 777 464 (UK).

Microsoft Network

After a false start into a proprietary based network, **Microsoft Network (MSN)** has now established itself as a major online player. And like CompuServe, it's on its way to becoming a fully Web-based service – essentially, a pay-to-enter Web site.

Being new on the block, and hard-linked into every

version of **Windows 95**, has clearly given MSN an edge. As Bill Gates admits, Microsoft doesn't need to make money out of its Internet presence. However, conversely, the Internet will be integral to everything Microsoft does from now on. So MSN at its worst could become another Pathfinder (Time/Warner's colossal Web site). Or a place to get the latest product patches, plus a smattering of news and entertainment to keep you coming back. All it has to do is keep you exposed to its product range. So don't be surprised if it becomes free or drops its prices dramatically.

The dial-up side is a different issue. Unlike its Online Service rivals, Microsoft isn't in the access game. It has deals with other providers to supply access. This gives it the flexibility to pull out if need be, and switch providers, perhaps to cable or ADSL.

In 1997, MSN relaunched for the third time in two years, this time with a new "TV channel" look, bubbling with bright animations and pretty graphics. It certainly out-wows CompuServe and AOL, but sure doesn't make browsing any quicker. In addition, it's not altogether apparent why you need pay MSN rates when much of its best content – like Encarta, Investor, and CarPoint – is already freely aired on the Web at: http://www.msn.com And with notable exceptions like Disney Blast, much of what's in the channels looks like it in perpetual beta testing. Still, that could change.

Like too much of the software giant's recent efforts, MSN looks great on paper, but falls short at the task. For example, right now, it only works with Windows 95 and **Internet Explorer**, while its non-POP3 mail won't work with Microsoft's very own Internet Mail & News or Outlook Express (Internet Explorer's companion mail clients). That means you need to infest your system with Exchange and Internet messaging. So until whoever's steering Microsoft's Internet bulldozer stacks it up against a tree yet again and puts the pieces back into a coherent shape, it's not a wholly attractive option.

To **register with MSN**, you simply click on the icon in Windows 95, and follow the instructions. Or to save your phone bill, call and get the latest software updates on disk.

For details call: ☎1800 257 253 (Australia), ☎800 386 5550 (North America), ☎0345 002 000 (UK), and ask how much they'd like to charge you today.

Prodigy

Prodigy was the first Online Service to add full Internet access. That used to be its drawcard. These days it's more like an ISP with the bonus of a reasonable wad of prime proprietary content, like Study Web and Investor's Business Daily, plus an aggregation of material plucked from the Web into a form that might make more sense to a newcomer. To date it's been primarily focused in North America, but it has recently made inroads into East Africa, Latin America, and Asia, including China. If you want an ISP, with a little of the added comfort and community of an Online Service, but without the associated annoyances like non-POP3 mail and clunky software, Prodigy might do the trick.

For a free trial in North America, call: ☎800 776 3449.

Email

If you need one good reason to justify hooking up to the Internet, email should suffice. Once you gather enough email contacts and get used to conversing by email, don't be surprised if it becomes your preferred way to get in touch. You will write more letters and respond a lot faster – and that means you'll probably become more productive.

Why email will change your life

Email is such an improvement on the postal system it will revolutionize the way and the amount you communicate. You can send a message to anyone with an email address anywhere in the world, instantaneously. In fact it's so quick that it's possible they could receive your message sooner than you could print it. You just **key an address**, or choose it from your **email address book**, write a brief note, and **click "send"**. No letterheads, layout, printing, envelopes, stamps, or visiting the post office. And once you're online your mailer can automatically check for post at whatever interval you like. You don't have to wait for the postie to arrive.

Email is also better than faxing. It's always **a local call to anywhere, at any time**. No busy signals, paper jams, or failed attempts. Plus you receive the actual text and not a photocopy, or an actual image file and not a scan. So that means you can send **color and full resolution**.

It also beats the phone at times. You can send a message to a part of the world that's asleep and have a reply when you get up the next morning. No need to synchronize phone calls, be put on hold, speak to voicemail, or tell some busybody who's calling. With email, you take the red carpet route straight through to the top. And you don't have to make small talk, unless that's the purpose of the message.

Replacing the post and fax is not email's only strength. You can also **attach any computer file to a message**. So, you can forward things like advertising layout, scanned images, spreadsheets, assignments, sound clips, or even programs. And your accompanying message need only be as brief as a Post-it note or compliments slip.

What's more, with email everything you send and receive can be stored in a relatively small amount of disk space. No filing cabinets, no taped phone calls, and no yellowing fax paper. All in writing, and instantly searchable for later reference.

Challenging the establishment

Email is steadily overcoming formal business writing. Since email messages are (for the most part) simply text files, there's no need to worry about fonts, letterheads, logos, typesetting, justification, signatures, print resolution, or fancy paper. It distills correspondence down to its essence – words.

But email has gone farther than that – it has encouraged **brevity**. This could be the result of online costs, busy users, or just the practical mindset of the people who first embraced the technology. Whatever the reason, it's good discipline and it means you'll be able to deal with several times more people than ever before.

Conversely, email is also putting personal correspondence back into letters rather than phone calls. Almost all new users remark on this – and the fact that email often seems to spark off a surprising intimacy.

What you'll need

To get started, you'll need a **connection to the Net, an email program, and an email address**. You don't need a full Internet connection to use email. You just need access to a gateway that leads on to the Net.

You will automatically get an **email address** when you sign up with an access provider or an Online Service. If you access through work or someone else's account, you could shop around your local providers for a mailbox only account or try one of the free services on the Net (see p.68).

You should routinely be given an **email program** with your Internet access account; if you're using AOL or CompuServe you may have no choice but to use their own (reasonably good and user-friendly) programs. However if you have a regular ISP account, and your email program is not up to scratch, it's easy to scrap it for another.

Choosing an email program

As your mailer will become the workhorse of your Net toolkit, you should choose it carefully. Until recently, the top popular mailer choice for both PC and Mac was **Eudora**. However, this has been supplanted by the mail programs built into the **Netscape** and **Microsoft Internet Explorer** Web browsers, which are reliable and easy to use, although Netscape can be heavy on memory.

The memory problems with Netscape are caused when its mail program launches its browser – a glitch built into versions 3 and 4, which proved frustrating for anyone with a computer short on RAM. Still, the program is evolving with every release and future versions of **Netscape Messenger** promise to address this, as well as adding pretty much every option you might want.

Internet Explorer 4.0's **Outlook Express**, successor to the basic and elegant Internet Mail & News, is top notch, free, and very simple to use. It lacks some of Messenger's advanced features, but loads quicker and fits better as a stand alone client. It is certainly light years ahead of Microsoft's **Exchange** (built into Windows 95) or Office 97's **Outlook** which wraps around Exchange in a unnecessarily confusing way. However if you've been lumped with these at work, they'll do and will no doubt evolve in future incarnations.

If you want a custom-built email program, **Eudora** remains the choice option. It maintains two versions: Light, which is free, and Pro, which is free for thirty days and then you have to pay. If you're presently using Light, check through the features at: http://www.eudora.com and decide if it's worth the upgrade.

Where to get an email program

For addresses of where to **download email programs and add-ons**, see our "Software Roundup" (p.375). If you're using any type of Microsoft mail, including Outlook 97, grab all the latest Internet upgrade patches from the appropriate sections under: http://www.microsoft.com/products/

Setting up

To get airborne, you'll need to fill in a few **configuration details** for whoever supplied your email account (usually your provider). This process is often automated by a wizard or your access provider's software. Whatever, it's worth taking some time to understand your email profile so you can enter it on other machines.

Open up your **account settings** and here's what you'll strike. Let's say you're Garret Keogh and your email address is garret@lard.com

Name: Garrett Keogh

(Who or what will appear as the sender of your mail.)

Email Address: garret@lard.com

(Where mail you send will look like it came from.)

Return Address: garret@lard.com

(Where replies to your mail will go. Most users opt for their regular email address but you could divert it to a work account, for example.)

Outgoing Mail (SMTP): mail.lard.com

(The server to handle your outgoing mail – usually your own provider. If you're on someone else's machine, and don't know what to put, try compuserve.com or mail.geocities.com as a temporary measure.)

Incoming Mail (POP3): mail.lard.com

(Where your mail is stored. This should be the same as the last part of your email address, though often with pop. or mail. added at the start.)

Account Name: garret.

(The first part of your email address.)

Password: ******

(Careful, don't let anyone see you enter this one.)

Note that the above only applies to **POP3 based mail systems** (see p.178), which at present doesn't include AOL. CompuServe is in the process of introducing POP3; see http://mail.csi.com/mail/

Sending and receiving email

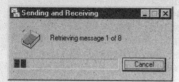

When you're ready to send your message, you'll need to **go online**. Sending is usually tied in with receiving (read on for more detail on both operations). Normally you do both at the same time, although it's possible if necessary to separate the two.

Microsoft and Netscape both store **queued mail** in the **outbox**. Once it's dispatched, it moves into the **sent mail box**. Other mailers may do it differently. Eudora marks unsent mail with a Q which changes to an S after it's sent. Incoming mail arrives in the inbox or wherever your filters dump it.

You can choose to be **alerted of new mail** by a sound, message or taskbar icon; configure whatever you prefer in your settings. Mailers also have ways of telling whether you've read your message, commonly by means of envelope icons or bold text. Netscape and Microsoft both let you **read mail as it arrives**, as well as preview messages in an adjacent pane. Eudora presently won't let you do anything while it's accessing your mail server. Plus you have to open every message individually. You'll tire of that.

Your first mail

The best way to get started is to **send yourself some email**. That way you'll get to both send and receive something. If you're dialing in, start this exercise offline.

Presuming you've completed your server details, the first thing to do is put yourself into your address book.

Next open up a new message, choose yourself from the address book, give the message a subject, enter something in the body and click "send" in the "new message" window.

Depending on your configuration, that will either place your message in a queue to be sent once you go online, or it will call up your dialer if it's trying to send it immediately. If it's gone to a queue, now attempt to retrieve/send your mail. That should bring up your dialer. If not, and you can't see how to make it happen automatically, call up your dialer manually, log in, and try again. Most mailers pop up a progress window to tell you what's going on.

Once you've sent yourself the message keep checking every 30 seconds until you receive it. It shouldn't take more than a few minutes. Now repeat this exercise until you're confident to face the rest of the wired world.

START YOUR SESSION ON THE NET WITH EMAIL

If you're running a dial up account, the first thing you'll want to do once you go online is check your mail and send your queued email. So you might as well use the mail page as your springboard on to the Net. You might need to investigate your mailer's connection settings to work this out but it should be straightforward, particularly under Windows 95. Most of the time, it's the default setting.

Otherwise you might have to specify to connect to the Net as required or that you're connecting via a modem. Anyway just try it first and see what happens. Make sure everything's connected and select the option to retrieve mail. If that doesn't start up your dialer, you'll need to fiddle. Refer to your help file for instructions.

Managing email

If your provider or phone company charges you by the minute to stay connected, it's best to **compose and read your mail offline** (i.e. when you are not connected by phone). That way, while connected you're actually busy transferring data, and getting your money's worth. Most mailers give you the option to send your messages immediately or place them in a queue, as well as to collect mail at regular intervals or on request.

Unless you're connected for long periods, you should use **queuing and manual checking**, otherwise your email program will try to send and collect when you're offline. It's best to go online, collect your mail, upload your queued mail, reply to anything urgent, log off, deal with the rest, and send your new bag of letters next time you go online.

Netscape Messenger detects whether you're online and should sort it out automatically. Well, it should, but you might have to choose "Go Offline" to get it to work. Then "Get Mail" to send it. Try it and see.

Filing

Just like you keep your work desk tidy, and deal with paper as it arrives, you should also keep your email neat. Most mailers can organize your correspondence into **mailboxes** or **folders** of some sort. It's good discipline to use several for filing. And choose to **keep a copy of all mail sent**.

Filtering

Most mailers offer **automatic and manual filtering abilities** to allow you to transfer incoming mail into designated mailboxes, either as it arrives or on selection. It looks for a common phrase in the incoming header, such as the address or subject, and transfers it directly somewhere other than the default inbox. This is indispensable if you subscribe to a lot of mailing lists (see the following chapter) or get a ton of junk office email.

Eudora Pro has a manual option. It's superior as you can leave messages in the Inbox until they've been handled. Then transfer them into archives for later reference.

Etiquette and tracking replies

It's common courtesy – and netiquette – to **reply to email promptly**, even if just to verify you got it. After all, it only need be a couple of lines. Leave email in your Inbox until it's dealt with so you can instantly see what's current. Do the same with your Sent box. Just leave the mail that's awaiting reply.

As email is quick, and people tend to deal with it immediately, if you don't get a reply within a few days you'll know what to follow up. Once you've received your reply, you can either archive or delete your original outgoing message.

Addressing email

Open up a new mail message window, and you'll see a line starting with "To:". That's where you type in your **recipient's address**. Internet email addresses should be along the lines of: user@host User is the sender's account name. Host identifies the server where they collect their mail.

If you submit a wrongly constructed or a non-existent address, your message should bounce back to you with an error message saying what went wrong. This tends to happen within a matter of minutes. Sometimes, however, mail bounces back after a few days. This usually indicates a physical problem in delivering the mail rather than an addressing error. When it occurs, just send it again. If it's your end that's caused the problem, you might have a whole batch of mail to resend.

Sending mail to Online Services

To make life a little harder, not all mail addresses start out in the standard user@host format

To **send email to CompuServe subscribers**, for example, you generally have to use the host name compuserve.com and replace the comma in the user name with a period. Thus to send mail to CompuServe member 12345,678 you need to address it to 12345.678@compuserve.com That is, unless your CompuServe e-mates have taken up "nickname" addresses – an option introduced to subscribers in 1997 and which operates in parallel with the old number system. Thus your old mate 12345.678@compuserve.com might just have changed his name to milesahead@compuserve.com

Most other Online Services maintain a regular Internet form for their subscribers' addresses. For example, to send to Keith Flint at Prodigy you might address it to keithf@prodigy.com while Ryan Giggs at America Online, might be giggsy@aol.com These Online Service subscribers get to choose their **"nickname" address**, as do regular ISP Internet users.

The address book

Despite first appearances, Internet email addresses aren't so hard to recall. CompuServe numbers apart, their name-based components are stacks easier to remember than telephone numbers and street addresses. However, there's no real need to memorize them, nor do you have to type in the whole address every time.

Investigate your mail program's **address book**. You should be able to enter and import addresses from messages without much fuss. You can generally summon the address book from the new message window by double-clicking beside "To:" or clicking an icon on the taskbar, though you may need to maintain it from a different menu selection.

Address book features vary markedly between mailers but most have some way of entering a short form of the address such as a **nickname**. For example, you might only have to enter a few letters and it will search the address book for the closest matches. Start off by entering every email address you know, and click on all the options until you've figured it all out. With most email programs you can either **click** or **double click** on addresses in your address book to create new mail, or with Netscape **drag and drop addresses** into the "To:" or "CC" fields of an email message.

Understanding your address book's capabilities will save you loads of time and tedium in the long run. But the simplest way to address a message is by replying to one previous. Here's how.

Replying to mail

Yet another great thing about email is how you can quote received mail. To reply to a message, simply select it and choose "reply". This will automatically **copy the original message and address it back to the sender**.

Depending how you set this up in your options or preferences menu (check your help file or experiment), this new message will commonly appear with **quote tags** (>) prior to each line. You can include parts or all of the original message, including the subject – or delete the lot. So when someone asks you a question or raises a point, you can include that section and answer it directly underneath or above. This saves you having to type it in, or them having to refer back to the message they sent. It also saves keying their address.

Don't fall into the habit of including the entire contents of the original letter in your reply. It wastes time for the receiver and its logical outcome (letters comprising the whole history of your correspondence) hardly bear thinking about.

Note that the **"reply all"** option addresses your message not only to the sender but to all recipients of the original. That's not something you'll always want to do.

Forwarding

You can also **forward** or (with Eudora only) **redirect a message** to somebody else. Forwarded messages may be quoted and edited like replies. Redirecting means sending it without the > tags. All mailers handle this differently. If you choose to use the quote tags in Microsoft mailers you'll have to temporarily change this option to omit them.

Carbon copies (cc) and blind carbon copies (bcc)

If you want to send two or more people the same message, you have two options.

When you don't mind if recipients know who else is receiving it, one address will have to go in the "To:" field, and the other addresses can also go in this field or in the **"CC" (carbon copy)** field.

Any recipients put into the **"BCC" (blind carbon copy)** field are masked from all others. However everyone, including those in "BCC", can see who's in the "To" and "CC". To send a bulk mailer without disclosing the list, put yourself in the "To:" field and everyone else in "BCC."

The subject

Let your email recipients know what your message is about. Put something meaningful in the **"Subject:"** heading. It's not so important when your correspondents first receive the message – they'll probably open it even if it's blank. However, if you send someone your résumé and you title it "Hi," two months down the track when they're looking for talent, they're going to have a hard time weeding you out of the pile.

Filling in the subject is optional when replying. If you don't enter anything, most mailers will retain the original subject and insert **"Re:"** before the original subject title to indicate it's a reply. Netscape's Messenger can also thread these replies together so you can scan through the entire dialogue. Pretty clever, huh?

Signatures

```
 /////\       //////\\      //\//\\       //////\\    All mailers let you add
/`0-0'     ` @ @\      //o o//      a a    your personal touch at
 ]            >          ) | (          _)     the end of your compo-
 -            -          ~              ~      sition in the form of a
John      Paul      George     Ringo
```

signature file. This appears automatically on the bottom of your email, like headed notepaper. It's common practice to put your address, phone number, title, and perhaps round off with a witticism. There's nothing to stop you adding a monstrous picture, frame, or your initials in ASCII art. Except you have more taste than that.

Attaching non-text files to your email

Suppose you want to send something other than just a text message – such as a **word processor document, spreadsheet, or an image** – via email. It's quite feasible, and no longer requires technical expertise. To send a file, look in your mail menu for something along the lines of

"Send Attachments" or "Attach File." Either that or try dragging and dropping the file into the new message window. It will normally work without a second thought from you.

How it does it is like this. Internet mail messages are transmitted in plain ASCII text and must be no larger than 64 kb. That means to send anything larger than 64 kb and anything other than text it has to be processed first. This includes all binary files such as images, spreadsheets, word-processor documents, and programs. Thankfully, these days, your mailer can handle this for you. It converts the binary coding into 7-bit ASCII and chops the message into units less than 64 kb. Then when the message arrives, it's automatically decoded, then lobbed into a designated download directory or can be accessed from an icon in the message.

Well, it's almost that simple. A residual problem, while people are using a variety of mail programs, is that both parties' mailreaders need to support a common encoding standard, otherwise it will appear in gibberish. The most used methods are **MIME**, **UUencode**, and **Binhex**. It doesn't really matter which you use as long as it works every time, so try a practice run first.

If you have problems getting a file to someone, refer to your Help file on how to specify an encoding method, as it varies between packages. MIME is gaining acceptance across all platforms (it's all that Netscape's older mailers recognize), so if you have the option, set it as the default. On Macs it might be called Apple Single or Apple Double. Always choose Apple Double.

If your mailer doesn't automatically decode attachments, ditch it for one that does. Old office systems like early Microsoft Mail are notoriously fussy. If you're not allowed to use one that handles attachments with grace, consider a new job.

HTML and rich text mail

Not long ago, email was a strictly plain text affair. The odd mailer such as Microsoft Exchange allowed formatting, but it didn't really make an impact until Netscape introduced HTML mail as a new standard. Today, if your mailer lacks HTML support you'll feel a bit backward.

HTML mail blurs the distinction between email and the World Wide Web, bringing Web pages right into your mailreader. This means Web publishers, particularly magazines and news broadcasters, can send you regular bulletins formatted as Web pages complete with links to further information. It also means you can **drag and drop Web pages into your messages** to send to someone else. However, your recipient must also have an HTML compliant mailer to appreciate all the features, otherwise they'll get all the formatting as a useless and time-wasting attachment.

Additionally, although the concept of fancying up your email by adding color, logos, and signatures might seem appealing, it's unlikely to increase your productivity and actually detracts from one of email's strongest features – simplicity. So don't spend too much time worrying about the appearance of your email. Just get the words right.

For a quick lesson in Internet Explorer 4.0's HTML mail see Outlook Expressions: http://www.barkers.org/ie/oe/

GET YOUR FREE EMAIL ADDRESS HERE

You already have an Internet connection and an email address – but you don't like sending email to your friends as angus@fishpaste.com No problem. You can get hold of an extra email address and it needn't cost you a thing. You just have to suffer a little advertising.

There are three main types: POP3 mail, Web mail, and mail redirection.

The best free deal going is **Geocities**: http://www. geocities.com This provides a full **POP3 address** that works with any mailreader, plus a free homepage in a sort of Web theme village. It might strike you as a bit corny, but it's exceptionally well organized.

Pick of the **Web mail** is probably **Hot Mail**: just log into: http://www.hotmail.com give a few details and you'll have a mail account in seconds. It's not like normal mail. It's all stored on and sent via the Web. That makes it handy for collecting and sending on the road, especially as you can use the same page to pick up your POP3 mail, but a bit inconvenient for everyday use. As you can give any details you like, and recipients can't pick the header apart to tell where it's from, it's a perfect anonymous mailer – though abusers can still be traced.

Other Web mail deals include Rocket Mail(http://www.rocketmail.com), Magicia (http://www. magicia.com), which also provides free Web space, and NetAddress: http://www.netaddress.com which provides both Web and POP3 mail addresses ending in @usa.net

If you already have an email address and simply want a **funkier address**, you can get one ending in anything from @struth.com to @flippingheck.com What's sent to this address gets redirected to wherever you choose. You're then free to switch providers while retaining a fixed address. See: iName: http://www.iname.com StarMail: http://www.star-mail.com and NetForward: http://www.netforward.com

Staying anonymous

Occasionally when sending mail or posting to a news-group, you might prefer to **conceal your identity** – for example, to save embarrassment in health discussions. There are three main ways to send mail anonymously. As mentioned in the box above, **Web Mail** is one.

The second is less ethical. You can **change your configuration** so that it looks like it's coming from somebody else, either real or fictitious. However, if anyone tries to reply, their mail will attempt to go to that alias, not you. But, be warned, it's possible to trace the header details back to your server, if someone's really keen – and your local law enforcement agency might be.

The third way is to register with a server dedicated to **redirecting anonymous mail**. These generally act as go-betweens. When someone receives such mail, it's plainly masked, as it comes from an obviously coded email address. When they reply, the anonymous server handles the redirection. That's as good as it gets, but if you break the law in the process, they can still find you by demanding your details from the server's administrator. For more information see: http://www.stack.nl/~galactus/remailers/

Privacy

Although there's been a lot of fuss about hacking and Net security, in reality email is way more secure than the telephone or postal system. Most new generation email programs (including Netscape and Internet Explorer) have some kind of **encryption** built in.

If you're really serious about privacy, you may want to investigate **PGP (Pretty Good Privacy)**, a powerful method of encryption which generates a set of public and private "keys" from a passphrase. You distribute the public key and keep the private key secure. When someone wants to send you a private message, they scramble it using your public key. You then use the private key, or your secret passphrase, to decode it. For more on this, see http://www.prairienet.org/~jalicqui/pgpfaq.txt

Digital Signing and Encryption

Internet Explorer 4.0, Netscape Communicator 4.0, and their associated mailers already support emerging **encryption** and **digital signing** standards but it's yet to be seen how they'll be received.

Digital signing proves your identity via a third party certificate. Here's how to get yours.

First up, fetch a personal certificate from Verisign: http://www.verisign.com You can't go wrong there if you follow the instructions. Once it's installed, open your mail security settings and see that certificate is activated. You may choose to digitally sign all your messages by default, or individually. Then send a secure message to all your regular email partners, telling them to install your certificate. Those with secure mailers can add your certificate against your entry in their address books. From then on, they'll be able to verify that mail that says it's from you is indeed from you.

Encryption works similarly, though you'll also need email partners' certificates to encrypt messages to them. Also, as each certificate only works on one installation, you'll need a different one for work and home. This makes it a bit cumbersome if you're collecting mail on the road. It also means anyone with access to your machine could pretend they're you.

Yes, it's all a bit flaky at this stage. So spend a few minutes in your help file figuring out the finer details, try it with your friends, and decide amongst yourselves whether it's worth the bother.

Finding someone's email address

See our chapter on "Finding It" – p.134.

The Net by email

If your Internet access is restricted to email only, you can still get to a fair bit of the Net via automatically responding mail  servers (see the section following). It's hardly on a par with full Internet access, but you're not shut out altogether. For example, if you can't use FTP, you could try using an FTP mail server to supervise the transfer. It's even possible to retrieve Web page text. To find out how, mail: mailbase@mailbase.ac.uk with this line only in the message body: send lis-iis e-access-inet.txt

Help

If you're frustrated by Microsoft's **Internet Mail & News** or **Outlook Express** try Ed Miller's IMN tips: http://home.sprynet.com/sprynet/edm/ or resort to the newsgroups: microsoft.public.inetexplorer.ie4.outlookexpress or microsoft.public.internet.mail

For **Eudora**, try: comp.mail.eudora.ms-windows or comp.mail.eudora.mac

For **Netscape**, try: comp.infosystems.www.browsers.ms-windows or comp.infosystems.www.browsers.mac or their respective home pages: http://www.eudora.com and http://www.netscape.com

Mailing Lists

If you want email by the bucketload, join a mailing list. This will mean giving your email address to someone and receiving whatever they send until you tell them to stop. There are thousands of lists and they fall into two categories: closed (one way) or open. Closed lists are set up by some sort of authority or publisher to keep you informed of news or changes. That could be anything from hourly Antarctic weather updates to product release announcements. They're one way only: you don't contribute. What comes through an open list is sent by its members – and yes, that could be you.

The purpose of most lists is to broadcast news or encourage discussion about a specific topic – anything from progressive rock to bike maintenance. In some cases, the list itself forms a group, like a social club, so don't be surprised if discussion drifts way off topic or into personal and indulgent rants. You'll see. But you'll also find lists are an easy way to keep up with news and to meet a few peers, maybe in person, too. The only drawback is you have to browse a load of mail.

Climbing aboard

Joining is never hard. In most cases, you **"subscribe"** by sending a single email message. Or maybe fill out a form on a Web page. It depends on who's running the list. But it's never complicated. Once you're on an open list, you'll receive all the messages sent to the list's address, just as everyone else on the list will receive whatever you send. Unsubscribing is equally simple. Your first message should be a confirmation that you've joined and it nearly always tells you how to jump off again. Keep this handy, as chances are you will.

Mailing list basics

Each list has two addresses: the **mailing address** used to contact its members; and the **administrative address** used to send commands to the server or maintainer of the list. Don't get them mixed up or everyone else on the list will see you're a bozo.

Most lists are **unmoderated**, meaning they rebroadcast messages immediately. Messages on **moderated** lists get screened first. Moderation can be used as a form of censorship but most often it's a welcome bonus, improving the quality of discussion and keeping it on topic by pruning out irrelevant and repetitive messages. It all depends on the moderator, who is rarely paid for the service. Certain other lists are moderated because they carry messages from one source, such as the US Travel Warnings. Such lists often have a parallel open list for discussion.

If you'd rather receive your mail in large batches than have it trickle through, request a **digest** where available. These are normally sent daily or weekly, depending on the traffic.

Most lists are maintained by a "robot" these days, but some are still manual. For those, the administrative address is the same as the list's address with -request appended. For example, the administrative address of the list dragster-bikes@sissybar.net would be dragster-bikes-request@sissybar.net To subscribe or unsubscribe to such a list, you just send a one-line message (see below) to the administrator.

Listserv

LISTSERV, the most popular automated list system, uses listserv as the administrative address. So to join the list muck@rake.com you'd send a subscription message to: listserv@rake.com

Requests are interpreted by a program which usually reads only the message body. Messages may contain several requests as long as they're on separate lines, but you shouldn't include a signature/address at the end as it will confuse the program. Since all LISTSERV systems are hooked together, you can send your request to any LISTSERV host and your request will be redirected. If you're not sure which host to use, send your request to listserv@bitnic.bit.net (in North America) or listserv.net (in Europe).

To join a LISTSERV list, send the following message:
    SUB listname your name
To take yourself off, send:
    SIGNOFF listname
To find all options, send:
    HELP
To find out all the lists on a LISTSERV system, send:
    LIST
To find lists throughout all LISTSERV systems, send:
    LIST GLOBAL (It's over 500 Kb, so brace yourself!)
To hear of new lists as soon as they appear, join:
    new-list at listserv@vml.nodak.edu

Note that many LISTSERV lists are mirrored in Usenet newsgroups under the bit.listserv hierarchy.

MajorDomo

MajorDomo is another list manager similar to LIST-SERV. It uses the address majordomo@host

To join a MajorDomo list, send:
    subscribe listname address
To get off, send:
    unsubscribe listname address

In both cases adding your email address is optional but useful if you want to subscribe someone else.

To find out which lists you're on at any MajorDomo host, send:
    which

As MajorDomo hosts are independent, you can't request an overall list – you have to request it from each host individually. To receive a list of all hosts, send:
    list

In Box Direct

You'll find the most organized collection of high quality closed (or one way) lists rounded up by Netscape and loosely known as **In Box Direct**. These range from fashion probes like *Elle Direct* to techie bulletins like *PC Week*. But they all have one thing in common: they're all sent as Web pages, less the images. This means you need a mail program – like those built into Netscape or Internet Explorer – that reads HTML mail.

You don't actually need to use Netscape Mail for this but the whole process may work smoother if you sign up using a Netscape browser. The initial signup is fairly convoluted and requires you go off and fetch a digital certificate. Nonetheless, it's worth it. Just look for a link from Netscape's home page at: http://home.netscape.com and follow the instructions. It takes weeks to get on some lists but persevere, it does eventually work. Or bypass this and go directly to the home site and sign up there.

In the same way, keep your eye out for interesting lists as you browse the Web. Almost all the best sites have them.

Finding a list to join

See our chapter on "Finding It" (p.138).

Starting your own list

To find out how to start your own list, mail:
  listserv@bitnic.educom.edu and listserv@uottawa.bitnet
see The List Owners Survival Guide at:
  http://www.lsoft.com/manuals/owner/owner.html
and ask your access provider.

Privacy

Consider anything sent to a mailing list to be in the public domain. That means discussions could end up archived on the World Wide Web. This isn't usually the case, and may not even be legal, but it's safer not to test it. So take care not say anything you wouldn't like to see next to your name on the front page of your local paper.

Vacation alert!

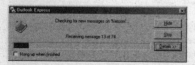

If you're going on vacation or away from your mail for a while, consider unsubscribing to lists for a while. Otherwise you might face a serious mailjam when you return.

File Transfer (FTP)

Before you can crack open the Internet's treasure chest, you'll probably need to stock up on software. Even if you have the best access provider's connection kit going, it won't be long before you'll want to try out alternative components, upgrade, or add the latest multimedia toys.

The good news is you can download almost all the Internet software you'll ever need for free, from the Net itself. And, surprisingly, many of these freely distributed programs are actually superior to those bundled into commercial packages. In fact, they're almost always better. So don't be afraid to turf out components that you've acquired in a starter kit. As Internet software must comply with TCP/IP specifications, units should be seamlessly replaceable, and the only (minor) drawback in add-ons is that you might have to launch them by clicking on their icons and not from the menu in your all-in-one package. That's no big deal.

(Incidentally, any bundle that won't let you mix and match components isn't worth keeping. That goes, in particular, for running Windows 3.xx connection software under Windows 95: don't, replace it with Dial-up Networking so you can run 32-bit software.)

Before you can download anything, however, you'll need an **FTP (File Transfer Protocol) program**. You can use a stand-alone dedicated program or do it all from your World Wide Web browser. Netscape and Microsoft's browsers are continually improving for FTP, though if you're short on memory, dedicated programs still have the edge. They certainly have more features and if you're uploading or accessing password protected sites, you might find them necessary.

We've dedicated a whole chapter of this book to a roundup of Net software (see p.369), giving the FTP or Web addresses to contact. You may want to refer to it in conjunction with this section.

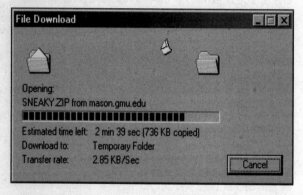

Free software programs from the Net

While the Internet might be a veritable clearing house of freely available software, it's not all genuinely free. There are three types of programs you're allowed to use, at least for a while, without paying. They are called **freeware**, **shareware**, and **beta programs**.

Freeware

Freeware is provided by its author(s) without any expectation of payment. It could be a complete program, a demonstration sample with crippled features, a patch to enhance another program, or an interim upgrade. In some cases, a donation, or even an email postcard, is appreciated.

Shareware

Shareware usually has certain conditions attached, which you accept when you install or run the program. Commonly, these may include the condition that you must pay to continue to use it after an initial free trial period, or that you pay if you intend to use it commercially. Sometimes a shareware program, while adequate, is a short form of a more solid or better-featured registered version. You might upgrade to this if you like the shareware, usually by paying a registration fee, in return for which the author or software distributor will mail you a code to unlock the program or its upgrade.

Beta programs

Betas (and Platform Previews) are distributed as part of the testing process in commercial software development. You shouldn't pay for them as they're not finished products. But they're often good enough for the task, and usually right at the cutting edge of technology. Take Netscape's interim releases of their Web browsers for example, which vast numbers of people have been using, as their main programs, for years.

With all beta programs, expect to encounter bugs and quirks now and again and don't be too upset by having to restart the program (or your computer) occasionally – it's all part of the development process. But do report recurring faults to the developers; after all that's why they let you have it free. If you notice a pattern, email the distributors and ask for a fix. If it's just too buggy, get an alternative.

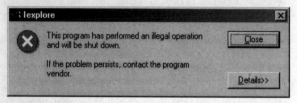

How to use FTP

Of the several techniques for transferring files across the Internet, by far the most popular is FTP. **Obtaining files by FTP** is straightforward if you have an FTP client with a graphical interface. They're much alike – any of them will do to get started. And if you don't like one, you can use it to download another.

Unless you've been granted special permission to log into a server and transfer files, you'll have to use one that permits **"anonymous FTP."** Such sites follow a standard log-in procedure. Once you're in, you can look through the contents of a limited number of directories and transfer files to your computer.

Many Net servers have areas set aside for anonymous FTP. Some even carry massive specialist file archives. And most software houses provide updates, patches, and interim releases on their own anonymous FTP sites. No single server will have everything you need, but you'll soon find favorites for each type of file. Your access provider should have an FTP area, where you can transfer files for updating Web pages, download access software, and exchange files with colleagues.

FTP domains are often prefixed by ftp. but that's not a rule. When you're supplied a file location it could be in the form ftp.fish.com/pub/dir/jane.zip That tells you that the file jane.zip is located in the directory pub/dir on the ftp.fish.com server

Logging in and downloading a file

Before you can download anything, you have to **log on to the server**. FTP programs use different terminologies, so it won't hurt to read its help or "read me" file. It should tell you what to key in where. Basically, though, the procedure is fairly routine and goes like this:

To retrieve ftp.fish.com/pub/dir/jane.zip enter the server's address ftp.fish.com as **host name**, anonymous as **user name**, and your Internet email address (in the form user@host) as a **password**.

Next, enter the **directory** you wish to start looking in, in this case, /pub/dir Make sure the path and file details are entered in the correct (upper/lower) case. If you enter Dir instead of dir on a UNIX host, it will return an error because UNIX is case sensitive. If you have the file's full location, try entering that as the initial directory. However, don't be surprised if a file isn't where it's supposed to be – system managers are forever shuffling directories. And it's not necessary to get the location exactly right: once you're in, you can always browse around until you find it.

Having entered the details above, you're ready to **log in**. If it's busy, you may not be admitted the first time. Don't let that discourage you. If you can't get in within ten attempts, try again later, perhaps outside the local peak hours. If you're accessing a US site from Europe or vice versa, try when that continent is asleep. You're also likely to get a better transfer rate.

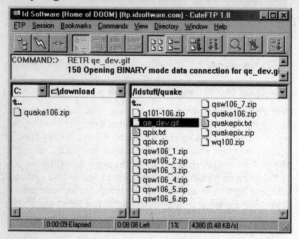

Once you're accepted, you'll see a listing of the initial **directory's contents**. Look for a contents file called readme, index, or the like. Read it if you're unsure of the contents, and read, too, any accompanying **text files** before downloading a program. You can usually do that by either clicking on them or selecting "view" or "read" from the menu.

Most FTP programs work in a similar way to Windows' file manager or the Macintosh folder system. That means when you click, something happens. Look at the top of the directory contents. **Clicking on ".."** will send you up a directory level. **Clicking on "."** will take you back to the root directory. Directories should stand out from files by having a different color, typeface, folder icon, or at least not having extensions. **Clicking on a** directory will open it, clicking on a file will start the download.

Make sure you select **"binary transfer"** before downloading any files other than plain text. If you're unsure of the file type, always choose binary. It will transfer text files as well. Although it may be slightly slower, text files aren't usually that large, so it's not really an issue. But if you download a graphic, sound, or program as "text" it will be useless. Everyone makes that mistake at least once.

Your FTP client should give you a **transfer progress report** to tell you how long it's going to take. You can either sit and watch the bits zip into your hard drive or relegate it to the background while you do something else, like explore the Web.

Unfortunately, if the **transfer fails or is canceled**, or your line drops out, you won't be able to pick up where you left off unless your FTP program supports **"resume transfers."** Both Microsoft and Netscape are rumored to be introducing this **"resume"** feature into future browsers, but at the time of writing programs that support it are the exception rather than the rule. Bear this in mind when shopping for an FTP program.

Uploading files

FTP isn't just for scoring files, you can **upload** as well. It might be more practical to submit stories, documents, graphics, and applications this way, rather than burden the email system with bulky attachments. For example, suppose you want to submit artwork to a magazine. You could FTP the scans to an area set aside for downloads (often a directory called incoming), and then notify your editor by email. The editor could then instruct staff to upload them for approval. If they're okay they could then be processed and moved to an outgoing directory for print house access.

In some cases an area is set aside where files can be uploaded and downloaded to the same directory. Useful maybe if you want to transfer files to a colleague who's having problems with handling mailed attachments (it happens!). It's frustrating waiting for several megabytes of mail attachments to download and decode before you can read your mail. Especially if it has to be re-sent.

FTP through the World Wide Web

It's approaching the point where you can do almost everything on the Internet from the helm of your **Web browser** (see our Web chapter, p.121). You can certainly download files through FTP with your browser. And that's indispensable as Web pages often have links to FTP addresses. In fact, this is where you'll encounter most of your archive leads.

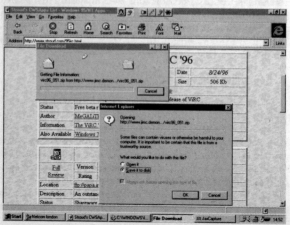

To **follow an Web FTP link on a Web page**, just click and wait to be logged in (it will take longer than loading a Web page). Depending on the link, you'll either see a page of the directory's contents, a prompt asking where you'd like to store the file, or it will be on its way to your hard drive. As with any FTP transfer, if the file has moved, you'll either be defaulted back to a higher directory or face an error message. If the file isn't where it should be, or you want to enter an unlinked location, just enter it as a Web address.

Instead of http: use ftp: in the first part of the address. So, to look for a file at: ftp.chook.com in the path: /pub enter: ftp://ftp.chook.com/pub

Once connected, just click on what you want in the usual fashion.

Netscape and **Microsoft Internet Explorer** browsers are superb FTP clients. You can kick off multiple transfers and surf the Web while you wait for downloads to finish. Most other Web browsers are FTP-ready too, but very few automatically send the session to background and let you do something else while you wait. If your browser isn't this flexible, get another.

FTP by email

Several services offer **FTP by email**. They can take up to a few days, but may save access charges over slow networks – it's usually quicker to download your mail from a local server than to transfer files from a distant busy server. If you're in more of a hurry to get offline than get the file, give it a shot. To find out how, mail: mailbase@mailbase.ac.uk this line only in the message body: send lis-iis e-access-inet.txt

File types and compression

There are two reasons why archived binary files are compressed. One is to decrease their storage demands, the other to reduce transfer times. After you download a compressed file, you must decompress it to get it to work. Before you can decompress it you need the right program to do the job.

	Name	Date	Time	Size	Ratio	Packed	Path
	dos32.exe	15-08-96	23:54	9,008	24%	6,830	
	license.txt	26-02-97	12:24	3,474	52%	1,653	
	order.frm	24-03-97	01:24	856	61%	330	
	readme.txt	24-03-97	01:23	3,279	51%	1,593	
	xevious.exe	24-03-97	12:05	33,771	39%	20,752	
	xevious.txt	19-04-97	09:36	7,120	57%	3,061	

Menu bar: File Actions Options Help
Toolbar: New Open Favorites Add Extract View CheckOut Wizard

It's usually easy to tell which technique has been used just by looking at the file name or where it's located. Unless the site is specifically targeted at one platform, you're usually offered a **directory choice** between DOS, PC/Windows, Mac, and UNIX. Once you've taken that choice everything contained in that directory and its subdirectories will be for that platform only. If not, you can usually tell by the file extensions. The following table shows common file extensions and the programs needed to decompress or view them.

Extension	Filetype	Program to decompress or view
.arc	PC Compressed archive	PKARC, ARC, ArcMac
.arj	PC Compressed archive	UNARJ
.bin	MacBinary	MacBinary, usually automatic in Macs
.bmp	Bitmap	Graphics viewer, MS Paintbrush

.cpt	Mac Compact Pro archive	Compact Pro, Stuffit Expander
.doc	MS Word document	Word processor such as MS Word or Wordpad
.exe	PC executable	Self executing from DOS or Windows
.gif	Graphic Interchange Format	Graphics viewer
.gz	UNIX Compressed archive	GNU Zip
.hqx	Mac BinHex	BinHex, Stuffit Expander
.jpg	Compressed graphic	Graphics viewer
.lha, .lzh	Compressed archive	LHA
.mpg	Compressed video	Video viewer
.pict	Mac picture	Graphics viewer
.pit	Mac PackIt	PackIt
.ps	PostScript	PostScript printer or GhostScript
.sea	Mac Self-extracting archive	Click on icon to extract
.sit	Mac Stuffit compressed archive	Stuffit Expander
.tif	Tagged image format	Graphic viewer
.txt	Plain ASCII text	MS Notepad, text editor, word processor
.uu, .uue	UNIX UU-encoded	UUDECODE, Stuffit Expander
.z	UNIX Gnu GZip archive	GZip
.Z	UNIX compressed archive	UNCOMPRESS
.zip	PC PKZip compressed archive	PKZip, WinZip, Stuffit Expander
.zoo	Compressed archive	ZOO

PC archives mostly end in .exe, .zip, .lzh, or .arj. The .exe files are usually **self-extracting archives**, which means they contain a program to decompress themselves. All you have to do is execute them. Just transfer them to a temporary directory and double-click on them in File Manager or Explorer. Or run them from DOS by changing into the temporary directory and typing what comes before the .exe.

If you're on a PC, get the latest copy of **WinZip**, which lodges itself within File Manager, and the latest **Stuffit Expander** for Windows and place it on your desktop. The great thing about this combination is that it will handle just about everything, including files compressed on Macs. And it's easily configurable to automatically extract archived files just by double-clicking them in File Manager or Explorer, or by dropping them onto the Stuffit or WinZip icons.

Compressed **Macintosh files** usually end .cpt, .sit, .sea, or .hqx. The .sea files **self-extract** by clicking on them, the rest by dropping on, or opening with, Stuffit Expander. All recent Web browsers add support above your standard multimedia software to cope with the most common **audio and video** formats. Anything else is likely to need a browser plug-in or specialist program. This includes compressed **multimedia files** like Fractal Image Format, Lightning Strike, and MP3. Most of the time there'll be a link to download the player on the Web site where you found the file. See our **Software Roundup** (p.369) for details of how to obtain the above programs.

How to set up your directory structure

Before you start installing every Internet program you can find, first sort out your **directory structure**. Otherwise, you'll turn your hard drive into a tangled jungle.

Hard drives are organized into tree-like structures. In DOS and Windows 3.x, each level is called a **Directory**. In Windows 95 and Macs it's called a **Folder**. Both mean the same thing, they're just represented different graphically. For simplicity's sake we'll call them directories. The top level of a drive is called the Root Directory. It's for system start-up files only, so don't lob anything in there. No matter what system you're running, you should create the following first-level directories:

Programs: Install all programs into their own separate subdirectories under a first-level directory called Program Files, Apps, or similar. It's wise to have a second level separating the types of programs such as

Net, Graphics, Office, and such. Thus, you'd install Netscape and Eudora into their own subdirectories under Net, Word and Excel under Office, ACDSee and PaintShop under Graphics, and so forth.

Download: Configure your Net clients to download to a common Download directory and create a shortcut (alias) on your desktop to open it. Think of it as an in-tray and clear it accordingly.

Temporary: Once you've downloaded an application, extract it to an empty Temporary directory and then install it under the Programs hierarchy. Once done, delete the contents of the Temporary directory. If you have space, keep the original installation file in case you need to reinstall it. Put it in your Archive directory.

Archive: Rather than clog up your Download folder, dedicate an Archive directory with enough subdirectories to make it easy to find things again. As you download new versions of programs, delete the old. You could also open it to your peers through a Windows 95 Dial-Up, or FTP server. It should be the first place to delete files to make space.

Data: Put irreplaceable files, such as those you create, into a Data directory tree and regularly back it up onto another medium such as a floppy disk, Zip drive, or even an FTP site. Use WinZip or Stuffit to compress it all into manageable chunks.

Where to find an FTP client

See our "Software Roundup" chapter (p.372).

Finding Files

See our chapter on "Finding It" (p.125).

Usenet Newsgroups

The Internet is not a bad place to catch up on the latest bulletins, health warnings, celebrity gossip, sports results, TV listings, film reviews, and all that stuff commonly known in the popular media as news. It can even be delivered by email, like a virtual newspaper run. But, don't be confused – that's not what's called "news" on the Internet. In Net-speak, if you're "downloading news," you're retrieving messages posted to Usenet discussion groups. And these can make regular news look positively tame, outdated, and filtered in comparison.

Usenet messages – or **articles** as they're called – are similar to email messages but are transmitted in a separate system. Articles are grouped by topic into **Newsgroups**. Each Newsgroup has a single theme with hardly a subject imaginable left uncovered. Whether you're interested in baseball, be-bop, Buddhism, or brewing beer, there's sure to be a Newsgroup deliberating over the issues closest to your heart.

With a growing total of over 25,000 Newsgroups accessible to more than 40 million users, you'll have access to the world's experts (and okay, a few loonies) in every field. Want to know the recipe for Lard Surprise, whether it's safe to go to Kashmir, Quake's secrets, or where to sell that unexploded land mine in your garden?

Fine, just find the right Newsgroup, post your query, and wait for the results. It's the Net as virtual community in action: fun, heart-warming, contentious, unpredictable, and ultimately useful – and, after email, the Internet's most valuable resource.

We've listed a selection of popular and interesting Newsgroups in our "Guide to Newsgroups" (see p.342). This chapter covers the basics of how to jump in and join their discussions.

Accessing Usenet

You can access Usenet in several ways. With **full Internet access** you can read and post articles online, switching between Newsgroups as you please. It's possible to read any article, in any group, as long as it remains on your news provider's system. If you just have a **BBS (Bulletin Board) or a "shell" account**, you usually have to subscribe to groups and then wait for articles to arrive. A third route is **via satellite**. A few companies provide read-only access through a decoder that sits between the dish and your computer. They transmit the entire Usenet database overnight. You can subscribe to what you want and scan through it over breakfast. But, as it's a one-way feed, you still have to post conventionally.

Even a full Internet connection does not guarantee **access to all groups**. Sometimes Newsgroups are cut, due to logistics or because of a policy to exclude certain types. That decision lies with whoever supplies your **newsfeed**. Although most Newsgroups cater to above-board hobbies, there's a share of pornographic, incendiary, provocative, and plain moronic material. So it's not surprising that many government, educative, corporate, and conservative bodies want to filter them.

How it works

Your Usenet provider (usually your ISP) keeps a **data-base of articles** which it updates in periodic exchanges with its neighboring news servers. It receives articles anything from once a day to instantly, and dispatches locally created articles as well as the articles it receives from neighbors. Due to this pass-the-ball procedure, articles may appear immediately on your screen as you post them, but propagate around the world at the mercy of whoever's in between. Exactly how much newsfeed you get, and what you see, depends on your provider's neighbors and how often they update their articles. Most of the time, these days, it's almost as fast as email.

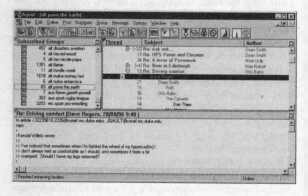

No provider, however, can keep articles forever as it needs the space for new ones, so it **expires postings** after a certain holding period. It's usual to delete articles after about four days and even sooner for large groups and binaries (articles containing encoded programs, images, or formatted text). Each provider has a different policy.

In addition, some Newsgroups are **"moderated"** – which means that postings are screened before they appear. Officially moderated groups are screened by whoever started the group or an appointee, but it's possible, though uncommon, that articles could be censored anywhere between you and the person who posted.

How to read addresses

Newsgroups are divided into specific topics using a simple **address system**. You can usually tell what a group's about just by looking at its address. The first part is the broad category, or **hierarchy**, it falls under. Here are some of the top-level and most popular hierarchies (with the most popular areas asterisked):

Hierarchy	Content
alt.	Alternative, anarchic, and freewheeling discussion*
aus.	Of interest to Australians
ba.	San Francisco Bay Area topics
bionet.	Biological topics
bit.	Topics from Bitnet LISTSERV mailing lists*
biz.	Accepted place for commercial postings
clari.	ClariNet subscription news service
comp.	Computing discussion*
ddn.	The Defense Data Network
de.	German groups
k12.	Education from kindergarten through grade 12
microsoft.	Microsoft product support
misc.	Miscellaneous discussions that don't fit anywhere else*
news.	Discussions on Usenet itself*
rec.	Hobbies and recreational activities*
sci.	All strands of science*
soc.	Social, cultural, and religious groups*
talk.	Discussion of controversial issues*
uk.	British topics

Note that Newsgroup addresses contain periods/full stops, like domain names. But they're interpreted differently. Each part of the address distinguishes its focus, rather than its location. The top of the hierarchy is at the far left. As you move right, you go down the tree and it becomes more specific. For instance rec.sport.cricket.info is devoted to the compelling recreation that is cricket. Also, though several groups may discuss similar subjects, each will have its own angle. Thus while alt.games.gravy might have light and anarchic postings, biz.market.gravy would get down to business.

To find which Newsgroups discuss your area of interest, think laterally and use your Newsreader's filtering capabilities to **search its Newsgroup list** for key words. Or easier still, search **DejaNews** (http://www.dejanews.com), the biggest Newsgroup directory on the Web.

Getting access to more groups

Your newsfeed might not carry every hierarchy, nor every group within that hierarchy. Many local-interest categories, for example, will only be available within their own localities. Your newsfeed provider selects the groups it wants to maintain and that's all you get to see.

This is not entirely a bad thing as it takes less bandwidth to keep the Usenet file up to date and thus reduces the general level of Net traffic. And most providers are flexible. If, say, your provider has arbitrarily decided to exclude all foreign-language and minor regional groups, and you're interested in Icelandic botany and Indian plumbing, you should be able to get the **groups added to the feed** simply by asking. However, sometimes omissions are due to **censorship**. Many providers remove groups on moral grounds, or to avoid controversy. The usual ones to get the chop are the alt.binaries.pictures.erotica (pornography), alt.sex and alt.warez (software hacking and piracy) hierarchies.

If you can't get the groups you want from your provider, either take your business to another provider, or, if that's not convenient, try a publicly accessible news server with a better selection. There's a list maintained on the Web at: http://www.jammed.com/~newzbot/

Frequently Asked Questions (FAQs)

Every Newsgroup has at least one **FAQ (Frequently Asked Questions)** document. This will describe the Newsgroup's charter, give guidelines for posting, and compile common answers to questions. Many News-groups carry several FAQs on various topics. They should always be your first source of information. FAQs are periodically posted, usually every couple of weeks. To view a huge selection on the Web, see **FAQ Finder**: http://ps.superb.net/FAQ/ or http://www.lib.ox.ac.uk/internet/news/

Choosing a Newsreader

Of all Internet appliances, **Newsreaders** – the programs you use for viewing Newsgroups – are less consistent. You can become proficient with one yet bewildered when faced with another. That particularly goes for the set of various mutations bundled throughout the history of Microsoft's and Netscape's Web browsers.

If you are running **Netscape Communicator 4.0** or **Internet Explorer 4.0** you shouldn't need to look for another Newsreader unless you have high demands. (Earlier versions, Netscape Navigator 3.0 and Internet Mail & News are satisfactory though not cutting edge.) However if you want more power and value from your session, you might consider a dedicated client. If you're a PC user the one to go for is **Agent** from Forté. It has two versions: Free Agent which is free, and Agent, the registered full featured Swiss army knife edition. For Macs, a reasonable choice for Macs is **NewsWatcher**.

As ever, for download addresses, see our "Software Roundup" (see p.375).

Getting started

Before you can get your news you'll need to tweak a few knobs on your **Newsreader**. It's hard to give definitive instructions because the features differ so markedly between programs. However, here's what to look for.

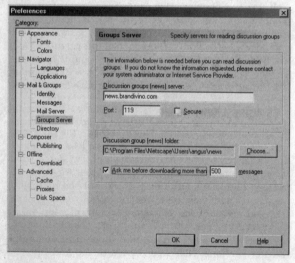

Configuring the Newsreader

You'll need to specify your **news server**, your **identity**, and your **email address**, to start off with. That shouldn't be hard – look under "Options" or "Preferences." Most Newsreaders then offer a whole bunch of options for how long you want to keep articles after you've read them, how much to retrieve, and so forth. Leave those in the default settings and go back when you understand your demands. Right now, it's not so important.

Going online

When you first go online, you'll need to **compile a list of Newsgroups** available on your server. Your Newsreader should do this automatically when you first connect – be warned, it could take several minutes. When the Newsgroups arrive on your list, they either appear in a window titled New Groups or go straight into the main list (commonly called All Groups).

The list of Newsgroups comprises just the names of the groups, not the actual articles. You have to **retrieve articles** in a separate two-part process. This generally involves selecting the Newsgroup (usually by clicking on it) to download the headers. The **headers** contain the article subject, posting date, and name of poster, and can be threaded by subject, or sorted by date or poster. When you see an interesting article, you can usually just click on it to bring it down.

Again, that's not a rule: some readers use a combination of menu choices to go through the same motions. The latest versions of Netscape and Internet Explorer download article bodies as you select them, displaying them in the line below (or adjacent). To get this right, you'll need to either read the "Help File" or randomly click everything the first time. Yes, really: it's the only way. As long as you understand the process, it'll all come together, whatever the terms and instructions.

For example, you might be confused by the term **"subscribe."** Don't think of it like subscribing to a magazine, although it can work that way. It really means putting a Newsgroup into a special folder so that it's away from the main list. You might be able to give it special priorities, like automatically updating headers or retrieving all article bodies on connection, or it might just make it easier to locate.

Participating in Newsgroups

When a Newsgroup article raises a new topic, it's called **starting a thread**. Follow-ups to that initial article add to this thread. You can configure your Usenet reader to sort threads together to follow the progress of a discussion. But if you follow a group regularly you might find it more convenient to sort by date, to see what's new.

Posting

Posting is like sending email – and equally simple. You can start a new thread, follow up an existing one, and/or respond privately by email.

How you go about it varies slightly according to your Newsreader software. Most programs automatically insert the Newsgroup you're reading in the "Newsgroups:" line. When starting a thread, pick a **subject entry** to summarize your query or statement. That way people scanning through the postings will know whether it's interesting. The subject line will also be used to identify the thread.

To **crosspost** (post an article to more than one group), just add those groups after the first group, separated by a comma, and then a space. Replies to crosspostings are displayed in all the crossposted groups. If you want replies to go to a different group, insert it after "Follow up – To:"

So, for example, if you want to stir up trouble in alt.shenanigans and rec.humor and have the responses go to alt.flame, the header would look like this:

Newsgroups: alt.shenanigans, rec.humor
Follow-up – To: alt.flame

Replying

Replying (or responding) is even easier than posting. Most Newsreaders give you the option of **following up** and/or **replying** when you read each message. This means you can send your contribution to the relevant Newsgroups and/or email the poster directly.

It's usually good practice to **reply as well as post**, because the original poster will get it instantly. It's also more personal and will save them having to scan through the group for replies. It's quite acceptable to continue communicating outside Usenet as long as it serves a purpose. Before long you'll have a circle of new virtual friends.

Like email, you also have the option of **including part or all of the original message**. This can be quite a tricky choice. If you cut too much, the context could be lost when the original post is deleted. If everyone includes everything, it creates a lot of text to scan. Just try to leave the main points intact.

Sending a test post

As soon as anyone gets Usenet access, they're always itching to see if it works. With that in mind, there are a few **Newsgroups dedicated to experimenting**. Post whatever you like to alt.test, gnu.gnusenet.test or misc.test You'll get several automatic (and maybe even humanly) generated replies appearing in your mailbox within a few days, just to let you know you're in good hands.

Kill files

If you don't like a certain person on Usenet, then kill
their mail. Just add their email address to your Newsreader's **"kill" file**. Then you'll never have to download
articles they've posted again. The same goes for any subject or topic: simply include the recurring string in your
kill file. But don't make it too broad or you might filter
out interesting stuff as well.

Image and sound files – and decoding

As with email, Usenet can carry more than just text.
Consequently there are entire groups dedicated to the
posting of **binary files** such as images, sounds, patches,
and even full working programs. Such groups usually
have .binaries in their address.

Again like email, binary files must be processed, most
commonly in UUencoding, before they can be posted or
read. You can use a separate program to handle the
encoding/decoding, but it's far more convenient to leave it
up to your Newsreader. As postings are restricted to 64
kb, the file could need to be chopped into several messages. Each part will have the same subject heading
followed by its number. Depending on your Newsreader,
to retrieve this file, you might need to highlight all the
parts and decode them in one go. Agent/Free Agent rec-
ognizes a set, just by clicking on one part. Netscape's
Collabra and Microsoft's Outlook Express both decode
automatically within the window, but at the time of writing neither could cope with parts. Hopefully that will be
sorted out by the time you read this. With many Newsreaders, you need to retrieve the article body and decode
in two stages. Best to read your help file to get it straight.

To **post a binary**, just attach it as in email and your
Newsreader will look after the rest.

One **important warning**: be wary of downloading any program that's posted to a Newsgroup. It's the surest way to contract a virus.

Starting your own group

With more than 25,000 Newsgroups already, you'll need fairly specialized tastes to get the urge to start your own group – plus a fair bit of technical knowhow and a monk's patience. It's one of the more convoluted and arcane procedures on the Net.

Before you can create a new group – in anywhere but the alt. hierarchy – you need to drum up support. It's a good idea to start a **mailing list** first. To get numbers, discuss the proposal in the Newsgroups related to your topic and then announce your list.

Once you have a case, and support, you have to put it before the pedantic news.groups for a savaging. Then through a long process that culminates in an election where the number of "yes" votes must be at least 100 more than, and twice the number of "no" votes.

Starting alt. **Newsgroups** is much easier. You just have to post a special control message. The hard part is getting people to frequent the group.

For more see:

So you want to create an alt. Newsgroup
http://www.math.psu.edu/barr/alt-creation-guide.html

How to write a good new group message
http://www.cs.ubc.ca/spider/edmonds/usenet/good-newgroup.html

Newsgroup netiquette

Apart from your provider's contract, the Net itself is largely devoid of formal rules. Instead, there are certain established, or developing, codes of conduct known as **netiquette** (Net-etiquette). These apply principally to Usenet Newsgroups.

If you breach netiquette, you could be ignored, lectured by a self-appointed Net-cop, or flamed. A **flame** is personalized abuse. You don't have to breach netiquette to get flamed – just expressing a contrary or naive opinion may do the trick. When it degenerates into name calling, it's called a flame war. There's not much you can do to avoid compulsive flame merchants, but if you follow these tips, you should be welcome to stand your ground.

Read and locate

Most importantly, before posting to any Newsgroup, **read a range of its existing postings** first. If it's a big group you might get a good enough idea of what's going on within one session, but more likely you'll need at least a few. Download all the **relevant FAQs** first, to make sure your article isn't old hat. Some Newsgroupies are not too tolerant of repeats.

Next, make an effort to **post in the most relevant group**. If you were to ask for advice on fertilizing roses in rec.gardening you might find yourself politely directed to rec.gardening.roses but if you want to tell everyone in talk.serious.socialism about your favorite Chow Yun Fat film, don't expect such a warm response.

Type and language

Less obviously, **never post in upper case** (CAPITALS) unless you're **"shouting"** (emphasizing a point in a big way). It's regarded as rude and ignorant. And keep your **signature file** short and subtle. Some people believe massive three-page dinosaurs and skyscrapers sculpted from ASCII characters tacked to every Usenet posting gives them cred. That's unlikely.

In similar fashion, express yourself in plain English (or the language of the group). Don't use **acronyms** or **abbreviations** unless they reduce jargon rather than create it, or use affected misspellings. And avoid over-using **smileys and other emoticons** (see "Net Language" – p.409). Some might find them cute, but to others they're the online equivalent of fuzzy dice hanging from a car's rear view mirror.

In addition, don't post **email you've received from someone else** without their consent.

Get in there

These warnings aside – and they're pretty obvious – don't hold back. If you can forward a discussion in any way, contribute. That's what it's all about. **Post positively** and invite discussion rather than making abrasive remarks. For example, posting "All programmers are social retards" is sure to get you flamed. But: "Do programmers lead healthy social lives?" will get the same point across and invite debate, yet allow you to sidestep the line of fire.

Overall it's a matter of courtesy and knowing when to contribute. In Usenet, no-one knows anything about you until you post. They'll get to know you through your words, and how well you construct your arguments. So if you want to make a good impression, think before you post, and don't be a loudmouth.

If you're a real stickler for rules you should read: http://www.idot.aol.com/netiquette/ Or if all this seems a tad twee, you might appreciate 101 ways to be obnoxious on Usenet at: http://www.indirect.com/user/steiners/usenet.html

Posting commercial messages

Having such a massive captive audience pre-qualified by interests is beyond the dreams of many marketeers.

Consequently you will frequently come across flagrant **product advertisements and endorsements** within Usenet. There have been cases where many – and even all – Newsgroups were unselectively crossposted by a single advertiser.

This process, known as **spamming**, is a guaranteed way to incur the wrath of a high percentage of Usenetsters. It usually incites mass mailbombing (loads of unsolicited email) and heavy flaming, not to mention bad publicity. Use the hierarchy .biz for commercial announcements, or tread very subtly if you must plug your new book, CD, or whatever, in a regular Newsgroup. It's entirely legitimate, for example, to **put a Web address in your signature**, so anyone can explore material you've posted on your own or your company's Web page. No-one objects to that.

Searching Usenet

See "Finding It" (p.133).

Surfing the
World Wide Web

When you see something that looks like
http://www.come/and/get/me.html taunting you in adverts
or news articles, on TV shows, or business cards, don't
get shy. These cryptic addresses are simply invitations
to the World Wide Web (the Web), the world's most
exciting, fastest-growing, communications medium.
Unlike other more arcane areas of the Internet, it's
remarkably simple to find your way around – just by
the click of a mouse – and after a while you should
even be able to find what you're after.

The Web's popularity is deserved as it has made the
Internet genuinely user-friendly, with point-and-click
graphics, and has sparked off more publishing, both
professional and DIY, than at any time in history. But its
popularity and size mean you'll need a little help to get
started. This chapter explains how to fit yourself out;
we've devoted a separate chapter to how to find things
once you're there (see p.125), and most of Part Two
(pp.193–341) to reviews of interesting and useful sites.

What to expect

The Web is the glossy, glamorous, user-friendly face of
the Internet: a media-rich potpourri of shopping, music,

magazines, art, books, museums, games, job agencies, movie previews, self-promotions, and plenty more. And for the most part, it's all free. Its coverage includes everything from Disneyland to Wall Street, everywhere from Iceland to Antarctica, and upwards of half a million companies, all from the keyboard of your computer. If you can't find a reference to an event on the World Wide Web, chances are it's not happening.

Requirements

Make no mistakes. The Web is one hungry beast. It will lap up every bit of computer power and connection speed you throw at it, and still want more. While you can get away with yesterday's computers in the rest of the Net, the World Wide Web is far more demanding.

That means you'll need a **PC with at the very least a 486 DX33 processor with 8 Mb RAM**, or a **Macintosh 68030 with 8 Mb RAM**, or the **equivalent Atari or Amiga** machine. But ideally, you'll have the latest state of the art PC or Mac, revved to the max with RAM (memory). That's what the latest Web browser programs expect. As to your **Net connection**, you will need to be hooked up at a **modem speed** of at least 14.4 kbps, preferably 56.6 kbps, or better still via an ISDN, cable, or ADSL link. Sure, you can get away with less, but it will groan. You will too as you wait for graphic intensive pages and background sound to load.

Once equipped and connected, you'll need a **browsing program** to provide the graphical interface. The most popular are **Netscape Navigator** and **Microsoft Internet Explorer** – in fact these are the only two really worth considering. To keep it simple, we'll refer to Netscape's browser as "Netscape" although strictly speaking the browser itself is called Navigator and comes in a suite of

Internet tools called Communicator. Despite that everyone still calls the browser, Netscape. We discuss browsers in depth, later in this chapter.

Home pages

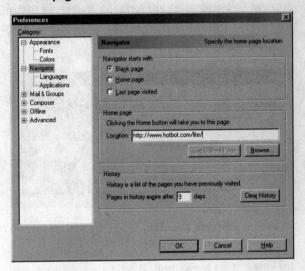

On the World Wide Web, **home page** has two meanings. One refers to the document that appears when you start your browser and acts as your "home base" for exploring the Web. Whenever you get lost or want to return to somewhere familiar, you can just click on the "Home" button and back you go. The other usage refers to a person or company "first base" Web document.

For instance, Rough Guides' own home page – found at: http://www.roughguides.com – is the top page in its set of

Web documents. Its Web site includes this home page, as well as numerous interconnected pages, published as a set. Each page can be accessed simply by keying its unique Web address into your browser or by following a link from another page.

These Web addresses are formally known as **URLs** (Uniform Resource Locators).

Keying URLs

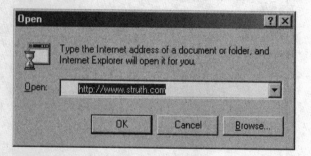

To visit a Web site, you simply **key its URL** (address) into the box on your Web browser where it says "URL," "Go To," "Address," "Open Location," or similar and then **hit enter**. If all works well, your browser will retrieve the page and display it on your screen.

It's crucial to know that URLs are **case sensitive**. So you need to key them carefully, taking note of capitals as well as their sometimes bizarre punctuation.

Web (http) addresses

URLs can look insanely complex at first glance, but they soon make sense. An address has three parts. Reading from left to right they are: the **protocol**, such as http://ftp://news: or gopher:// the **host name** (everything before the first single forward slash); and the **file path** (everything after and including the first single forward slash).

Consider the address:
http://www.star.com.hk/~chow/Yun/fat.html The http:// tells us it's a HyperText file located on the World Wide Web, the domain www.star.com.hk tells us it's in Hong Kong, and the file path indicates that the file fat.html is located in the directory /~chow/Yun/

Although the majority of URLs include the file's path, the trend is moving toward **shorter addresses**, especially for the home page, which for companies tends to be just their name followed by .com (for the US), or .co.uk (for Britain), and so on. For example, if you key in: http://www.apple.com you'll reach Apple's home page. If you have a recent browser you needn't key the http:// part as it's an automatic default. And the latest browsers can cope if you just key in a company name, filling in the rest of the address automatically. Try it and see.

Other addresses

As discussed in earlier chapters, you can also access **FTP**, **Gopher**, **Telnet**, and **Usenet** from the helm of your Web browser.

To **use FTP**, you just add ftp:// to the file's location. So, to retrieve duck.txt located in the directory /yellow/fluffy from the anonymous FTP site ftp.quack.com you should enter: ftp://ftp.quack.com/yellow/fluffy/duck.txt (In fact, with recent browsers you can omit the ftp:// part as they know that any domain starting with ftp. is an FTP site.)

Gopher and **Telnet** work in exactly the same way. So does **Usenet**, except that it omits the // part. Thus, to access the newsgroup alt.ducks key: news: alt.ducks

Hypertext

Web pages are written in **HTML (HyperText Markup Language)**, which means links to other documents can be imbedded within the text. This creates a sort of third dimension. If you've used Windows Help or Macintosh Hypercard, you'll be familiar with the concept.

Depending on how you've configured your browser, **text which contains links** to other documents (or to another part of the same document) is usually highlighted in another color and/or underlined. To pursue the link, simply **click on the highlighted text or object**. When the new document appears, it will be entirely independent of the one where you found the link. The previous document is now history. And as the new document needs no connection with it, there mightn't be a reciprocal link. However, there is an easier way to return, as you'll soon see.

GOPHER

Before the Web's explosion, **Gopher** was the smartest way to archive data on the Internet. As the name suggests, Gopher is used to "go for" information. Although it stores data in an entirely different architecture, it looks and acts similar to the Web. In many ways, the Web is its natural successor and what was once stored in Gopher is now on the Web – and for most purposes you need not read on. However, certain old battlers like government bodies and

---

universities still use it to archive stuff, so we feel obliged to mention it.

Gopherspace is a separate entity from the Web, although when you link out of the Web and into a Gopher site you may not recognize the difference. Its clickable directory listings work just like hyperlinks, however these Gopher burrows are dead-ended. You can surf from page to page following links all day on the Web, but with Gopher, once you find your text file, you have to tunnel back out again.

To **get to a Gopher from the Web**, key in gopher:// before the address in your Web browser. For example, to access the "Mother of all Gophers" at Minnesota University, key:

gopher://gopher.tc.umn.edu:70/ It has all you need to know about Gophers, including how to search by subject or geographic region.

For more on searching Gophers, see "Finding It" (p.135).

Browser basics

Web browsers are a dynamic technology. By the time you read this, they will likely have moved forward at least one generation. **Netscape** – the industry leader, for now – has been releasing updated browsers every few weeks since early 1995. There are now over thirty other browsers on offer, though with the notable exception of **Microsoft Internet Explorer**, none come anywhere near close to Netscape's in terms of features or performance.

Despite the various quirks that distinguish different

browsers, they achieve the same end through similar means. The following intrinsic **functions** are described for Netscape and Microsoft Internet Explorer but should be common to all latest generation brands (with only menu wording changing between platforms, brands, and releases).

At time of writing, these are the main features you'll find when you set a browser running:

A dialog box where you enter URLs

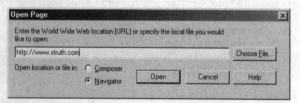

This box runs horizontally above the browser panel. In Netscape, when it's blank, it says **"Go to"** beside it, and when it retrieves a URL the wording changes to **"Location"** or **"Netsite"** (for sites housed on Netscape servers). In Internet Explorer it says **"Address."**

Key the address you're looking for in the box. After you've typed it in, hit your enter (or return) key, and wait. It rarely takes more than a minute or two to locate and load Web pages, or if you've a fast connection, it can be a matter of seconds.

Push buttons to go back, forward, or home

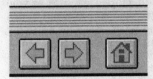

These **navigation buttons** are located on the toolbar above the main browser panel. Displaying them is usually optional, but they're hard to live without. To **go back to a previous page**, just click the "Back" button until you find it. To **return to where you were**, keep pressing "Forward." And to go back to your startup page hit **"Home."**

You can go back and forward through pages pretty much instantly once you've visited them during a session, as your computer stores the document in its memory. How much material you can click through in this fashion, however, depends on the amount of storage space that's been allocated to **cache** in your settings. We explain cache later under "Offline Browsing" (see p.117).

Identifying links and a History file

An **"active" link** is like a signpost to a new page. You click on the link to go there. After you've been, nothing changes on the page, but your browser records your visit by storing the URL in a **history file**. It's then called a **"followed" link**.

You can customize links by displaying them as **underlined** and/or a **special color**. The default is usually underlined blue for active links and red for followed links. See how this works for yourself. Look at any page. Links you haven't followed should appear blue and underlined. Just click one and load the page. Now, click "Back" and return to the previous page. The link should now be red.

What's more, these **customized links** will appear red wherever they crop up, even on a completely different page that you are visiting for the first time. This can be useful if you're viewing directories and lists, as you can instantly see which sites you have previously visited. Customized links, however, have an optional expiry period, after which they revert to the normal color. If you choose "Never," visited sites will stay red forever and remain in your history file. But it's wiser to keep the expiry short. A big History file will slow things down.

You'll find the **History file** under the Communicator or Window menu in Netscape, or on a toolbar button or under the File menu in Internet Explorer. Think of it as as a collection of signposts. You can use it to return to a visited page, rather than clicking the "Forward" and "Back" buttons. We'll discuss another use for the History file ahead in "Offline Browsing and Cache."

A button to stop transfers

To **cancel a transfer** (a "Go to" site request), because it's taking too long, or you've made a mistake, just hit the **"Stop"** button. In the middle of a transfer, you might have to hit "Stop" before "Back" will work.

Another button to refresh

Sometimes a page doesn't load properly the first time, so hitting **"Refresh"** or **"Reload"** will load it again. It's also useful if a page changes regularly, and you want to load a new version rather than one that's stored in your session "cache."

An option to withhold images

The drawback of the Web's graphic richness is the time it takes to download images. To speed things up, you have the option of **not showing images**. You'll find this either in your Preferences or Options settings, or in a menu choice.

It can be worth declining images when you're browsing specific information, and know what you're after. Casual Web surfing, however, demands graphics, as some pages are nothing but images with links behind them. If you're browsing with images off, however, you can always choose **"Show Images"** or change your settings and refresh the page.

Netscape is more attuned to surfing without images than Internet Explorer. However, Internet Explorer tends to be better at loading text before images, so you can read the page while waiting for the graphics to arrive.

An option to choose your initial home page

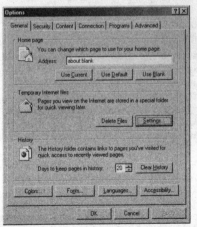

Browsers come preconfigured with a **default home page** – their own, or that of whoever supplied it to you. This will come up every time you start your browser, or when you hit "Home." If you'd prefer to see an alternative page, you can specify your choice in the Preferences (or Options). You may find it most convenient to specify "none" or a blank page.

Bookmarks or Favorites to store useful addresses

Whenever you find a page that's worth another visit, you should file its location. In Netscape that's called adding it to your **"Bookmarks."** Internet Explorer calls the same thing **"Favorites."**

Both file addresses into folders for later retrieval, but they approach the task from very different angles. That's most apparent if you want to send the addresses to someone else. **Netscape** stores them in an **HTML file** – that's actually a Web page in itself. That means you can put it on the Web, specify it as your home page, or send it to a friend as a single file. **Internet Explorer** stores each address as an individual **"Internet Shortcut"** in the same way it makes shortcuts to programs in Windows 95. You can mail individual links, or folders, to a friend but only if they're using the same setup.

The ability to send mail

Browsers generally run "straight out of the pack," and need no configuration to run. However, there are several dialog boxes hidden away in your settings that should be completed if you want to get the most from a session. For example, before you can **send email** and post to newsgroups directly from a browser, you'll have to **complete your email and news server details**. Your provider will supply this information. If you're not sure what to put, just ask.

Web pages offer various email opportunities. You'll often see a contact name inviting email. When you click on it, you'll either get a form, a dialog box, or a mail client will open – either your browser's or your main mailer, depending on your configuration. Just type your message and send it. Replies arrive through the normal email channels.

The ability to read newsgroups

Both Internet Explorer and Netscape come with companion **newsreaders**, which is handy as newsgroups are often entwined into the Web experience. And unless you're fussy both will probably do you as your main newsreader. If not, you can specify another in your settings to have it summoned as required. Either way you can follow links to newsgroups on the Web.

To **access a newsgroup** directly as a URL, type news: followed by the newsgroup name. But remember to configure your news server settings first.

The option to browse offline

If time online is costing you money, consider spending it gathering pages rather than reading. And then running back through your session after you hang up. You can do this by choosing **"Go Offline"** or **"Work Offline"** under the File menu in Netscape Navigator and Internet Explorer, versions 4.0 or later.

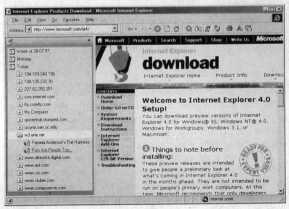

Once in this mode, you can **call up sites** either by typing in their addresses or following links as if you were online, or by clicking on sites in your History file. This works by retrieving files stored temporarily in a folder called **"cache"** in Netscape and **"temporary Internet files"** in Internet Explorer. Their primary purpose is to speed up browsing. When you return to a page, your browser will check the cache first rather than download its components again from the Net.

These pages won't sit on your hard drive forever – they're governed by your **Cache or Temporary Internet Files settings** and they'll also be overwritten next time you visit that same address. However, if you want to **archive a page**, you can choose "Save as" from the File menu. The only problem is it won't save the images as well. You'll need to save those all separately.

You'll find your Cache (Temporary Internet Files) settings in your Preferences (Options). While you're there, it's best to select the **option to check for newer versions** just once per session. Then if you suspect the document's changed during a session revisit, just hit Refresh/Reload. Unless you plan to read offline, it's wise to delete these files regularly as, like the History file, if it gets too big, it can slow things down.

Plug-ins and ActiveX

Although your browser can recognize a mind-boggling array of multimedia and other file formats, every so often you'll come across something it can't deal with. Generally, there'll be an icon nearby suggesting you grab a **"plug-in"** or an **"ActiveX control."**

A plug-in is an auxiliary program that works alongside your browser. You download this program, install it, and your browser will call on it when need be. ActiveX controls work similarly, although their scope is

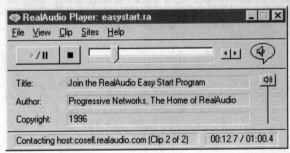

	Do you have a link to Plug-In Plaza on your web site? If so, you can now use the cool new GIF if you like!
The Full List	This is the whole list, but I gotta warn ya its getting big
Just MultiMedia	Multi-Media Plug-Ins, AVI, QuickTime, ShockWave...
Just Graphics	Graphic Plug-Ins, PNG, CMX, DWG...
Just Sound	Sound & MIDI Plug-Ins, MIDI, ReadAudio, TrueSpeech...
Just Document	Document Viewer Plug-Ins, Acrobat, Envoy, MS Word...
Just Productivity	Productivity Plug-Ins, Map Viewers, Spell Checkers...
Just VRML	VRML & QD3D Plug-Ins
By popular demand! We now have pages for each platform!!	
Macintosh	Macintosh Plug-Ins
Unix	Unix Plug-Ins
Windows	Windows Plug-Ins

far greater. When you arrive at a site that relies on an ActiveX control, it checks to see if you already have it, and if not, installs it automatically. At this stage, ActiveX only works under Windows 95 versions of Internet Explorer, or Windows 95 versions of Netscape when aided by the NCompass ScriptActive plug-in (http://www.ncompasslabs.com). Both Netscape and Microsoft plan to eventually introduce ActiveX as a standard across all platforms.

There are two plug-in/ActiveX controls you'll definitely need: the **RealPlayer** (which includes RealAudio) for live music and Internet radio, and **Shockwave** for multimedia effects. Both are becoming ubiquitous standards so chances are you might find they're already incorporated into your browser, or your ISP kit. But drop in and grab the latest versions anyway at: http://www.real.com and http://www.macromedia.com/Tools/Shockwave/

See our "Software Roundup" (p.376) for a selection of more useful plug-ins.

Copying and Pasting

To **copy text from Web pages**, highlight the section, choose "Copy" from the Edit menu (or use the usual shortcut keys), then switch to your word processor, text editor, or mail program and choose "Paste."

Mouse menus

Recent browsers enable or activate useful commands like "Back" and "Forward" from your **mouse button** (the right button on PCs). Just hold it down and try them out. "Save this link as" or "Save target as," for example, can come in handy to save time loading a large page or image. The saving process goes into the background while you continue in the foreground.

Saving an image

Web pages often display reduced images. In Web art galleries especially, such images often have links to another with higher resolution. To **save an image**, you can select it and choose "Save as" or "Save image as" from the File, or mouse button, menu. Or, you can save the link ahead as explained above. Windows 95 browsers can also save images as desktop wallpaper.

Uncovering the source

The smartest way to **learn Web design** is to peek at the raw HTML coding on pages you like. Choose "Source" from the View or mouse button menu. (See p.145).

Downloading files

Almost, if not all, your **file downloads** and **software upgrades** can be initiated by a link from a Web page. When you click on that link both Netscape and Internet Explorer will start an **FTP operation** in the background, and let you carry on surfing. Depending on your settings, once the file is found, you'll be asked where you'd like to save it. If it can log in but can't find the file, or you'd like to browse the FTP site, copy the address using the mouse button menu, paste it to the URL window, and delete the file name from the address. Then you can log into the FTP server and browse it like a Web site.

Juggling jobs

Since things don't always happen instantly on the Net, it's usually practical to do two or more things at once. You might as well download news, mail, and the latest software releases while you surf. If your browser supports **multitasking**, and most do, you can also have multiple Web sessions running. So if a page takes ages to load, just open a **"New Window"** or **"New Browser,"** and look at something else while you wait. You should also be able to set up multiple file downloads.

Bear in mind, however, that each process is competing for computer resources and bandwidth, so the more you attempt, the higher the likelihood that each will take longer – or that your machine will crash.

Choosing a browser: Netscape Navigator v. Internet Explorer

The only browsers you should consider are the range from **Netscape (Navigator)** and **Microsoft (Internet Explorer)**; all other browsers are history. The ideal, if your computer can handle it, is to have access to the latest

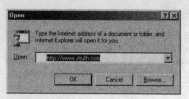

versions of either along with all the associated chat, mail, and editing add-ons. But if your computer's a mite undernourished, you might need to consider one of the earlier versions of Netscape (which use less memory). If it's downright feeble, say a 286 PC, consult BrowserWatch (http://www.browserwatch.com) for an alternative – or bite the bullet and get a new PC.

Separating Netscape and Microsoft's browsers is a bit like comparing Ford and General Motors. Don't buy the Microsoft = evil, Netscape = heroic underdog guff. They're both in it to make money for their shareholders, and neither produce flawless merchandise. As far as money goes, there's little difference. Internet Explorer, technically, is free. Netscape has various qualifications: its beta versions are free but full versions involve license payments, which means almost every ISP and Online Service now bundles Explorer and not Netscape. So, while Netscape is presently the market leader, it's unlikely to remain that way. Plus the general consensus is that Microsoft will eventually render the browser concept meaningless as it integrates the Web into its Windows and Office products.

As to which is the better browser, right now, well that's a close call as each tries to outdo the other every other week with new releases and features. To a large extent you'll prefer the one you become most familiar with, so try them both out before you get stuck into a groove. Or if you're into reading product comparisons, check the comments at http://www.browsers.com

You can **download the latest versions** of Internet Explorer at: http://www.microsoft.com/ie/ and Netscape Communicator, the suite which includes Navigator, at: http://home.netscape.com

Java

When Java – Sun Microsystems' vision of a platform independent programming language – arrived, it was instantly pounced upon by the Web community. What once was a static environment quickly sprung to life with all sorts of "animated" applications thanks to its simple HTML adjunct, **Java Script**.

Java applications are the most common reasons for your computer crashing while you're browsing the Web.

Script that works fine with Netscape can cause Internet Explorer to crash, and vice versa. If you have a lot of problems, open your settings and disable Java.

To find out more about Java and its latest applications, see Gamelan at: http://www.gamelan.com

Push and shove

There's been enormous hype about **"push technology"** on the Net in recent months. The Web used to be a "pull" kind of thing: you click on a link to make something happen. Push is often described as being like a TV or radio channel, though it's really more like subscribing to a one-way mailing list. With push, you configure some preferences, and leave a series of requests. Your browser then retrieves (or a third party sends) you items relating to your request at certain intervals. These could vary from world and sports news to stock prices or new CD releases. They can be (kind of) useful.

With various push offerings you can specify all sorts of rules, like how and when you want stuff delivered, and what to include or exclude. At the time of writing both Netscape and Microsoft are still teething their technologies, and drumming up deals with content providers. Be careful how much you subscribe to or you might only end up cluttering your connection with the Web equivalent of junk mail.

Censoring Web material for kids

If you wish to do so, it's possible to **bar access to certain sites** which might be on the wrong side of educational. Internet Explorer is most advanced on this front, as it employs the **PICS** (Platform for Internet Content Selection) system. You can set ratings for language, nudity, sex and violence under the Content settings in Options.

Most Online Services employ similar schemes, and there are also several third party programs like **SurfWatch**, **ImageCensor**, and **NetNanny** that allow you to impose all sorts of restrictions. None, however, are foolproof, and many exclude content that's worthy. If you're really that concerned about your kids, maybe you should surf the Web with them.

Finding It

Once you've selected an access provider, installed your software, and the whole thing's purring along, you'll be faced with yet another dilemma. How on earth do you find anything? Relax, it's easier than it looks, once you've learned a few tricks. How you find something depends on what it is, how new it is, where it's likely to be stored, and who's likely to know about it. In this chapter, we show you the first places to look, and as you gain experience the rest will fall into place. We also show you how to fix addresses that won't work. Assuming you have Web access, the only program you'll definitely need is a Web browser.

What's out there

Anything you can link to through the Web, you can find using a **Web search tool**. Plus you can find anything that's been archived into an online Web database, such as email addresses, phone numbers, program locations, newsgroup articles, and news clippings. Of course, first it has to be put online, and granted public access. Just because you can access US government servers doesn't mean you'll find a file on DEA Operative Presley's whereabouts.

First we'll examine the range of search tools. You'll find all the addresses detailed in the **Search Tools and Directories** section of our Web guide (see p.125).

The main search tools

There are basically three types of Web search tools: search engines, intelligent agents, and hand-built directories. All have their specific uses.

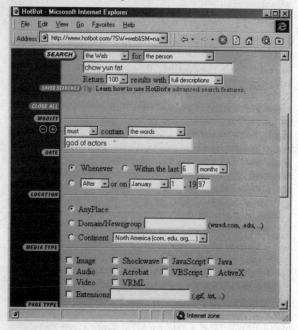

Search engines – the best of which are **Altavista**, **Hot-Bot**, and **InfoSeek** – run a program called a trawler, crawler, spider, robot, wanderer, worm, or some such unsavory term, that scouts around the Web and comes back with its findings. These pickings, such as each page's location, title, and an amount of text that varies between crawlers, are then stored in an online database. You can search for something specific by submitting **keywords**, or **search terms**, to these databases through a simple Web page form. The results, which usually come back within seconds, are clickable like hot links on any other Web page.

Intelligent agents search the Net, or certain sites, live. There aren't too many on the Web yet, other than **Bargain Finder Agent**, which attempts to find the cheapest CDs for sale on the Net. But there are a few other dedicated clients like **WebFerret**, **NetAttaché**, and **WebCompass**, which query multiple engines and scan sites. However, they're a bit specialized and questionably useful, so we won't discuss them here. And, for now at least, there's little to be gained from supposed wonder sites that search several search engines simultaneously. You'll get more, and better quality, results by going directly to the engines.

The **hand-built directories**, such as **Yahoo**, **Magellan**, **What's New**, and **Cool Tools**, usually sort sites into categories and sometimes include reviews or comments. Sites are sorted by subject, date, platform, or even their level of "coolness." In the pages following, we call these **directories** or **guides** when they cover a broad range of subjects (like Yahoo), **specialist sites** when they are more focused in one area (like Cool Tools), or **lists** when they mainly rank sites (like Cool Site of the Day).

Finally, there are a few hybrids that might fit into a combination of these categories. If in doubt we'll call them **directories**.

As with just about everything on the Net, the easiest way to learn is to dive straight in. But before you do, pause to read the instructions first. Every search engine or directory has a page of **"Read Me"** tips on how to use them to their full potential. A few minutes study will make your searching more effective.

Search engines

Generally the quickest way to find specific reference to something on the Web is to use a **search engine**. These look like normal Web pages, with a form to enter the search terms of what you're looking for. It in turn feeds these terms into a database and returns a list of results or **"hits"**.

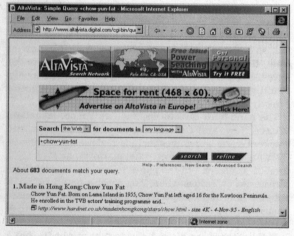

Depending on the engine, the results should include enough information to judge whether the found pages will be useful. However, each engine can return only its crawler's most recent findings, which may be just a small proportion of what's actually there – and can potentially be months old.

The various engines source, store, and retrieve their data differently. Always start with the best. Look for the biggest, freshest database and the ability to fine tune your search with extra commands and return the most relevant hits first. Currently, HotBot is the top candidate, followed by Altavista and InfoSeek. Excite and Lycos are useful when the others fail, but you often have to wade through a lot of poor-quality results as their search mechanisms are relatively crude. That hopefully will change. **Search Engine Watch** (http://www. searchenginewatch.com) will tell you exactly how they rank plus things like whether they index the entire text, and not just extracts, of Web pages.

Getting the most out of a search engine

Call up a search engine and study its instructions. The most important sections are how you state whether **terms should be included or excluded** (or more precisely, preferably included/must be included/must be excluded), and how to state that multiple terms are part of a set. HotBot is the simplest: you just choose the category from a pull-down menu.

For example, if you're looking for something about Lotus software, and not Lotus cars, you'd want to **include** Lotus and **exclude** cars. Since there's only one term to include, it automatically must be included. Now if you'd prefer something on spreadsheet programs, but don't want to exclude other software, you could state that Lotus **must be included**, spreadsheet should **preferably be included**, and that cars **must be excluded**. In both Altavista and InfoSeek you'd enter: +lotus spread-sheet –car The **+** sign says that it must be included, the **– sign** that it must be excluded. In HotBot, you'll need to open the "modify" option twice to get two boxes with pull-down menus. Then it's straightforward.

Now let's say you're specifically looking for something about the band Stereolab, preferably a review of their album *Mars Audiac Quintet*. The album name is an unusual phrase, and unlikely to result in false hits, so it would be a good term to specifically include. However, specifically including it would exclude any pages about Stereolab that don't mention that particular album. Thus it would be wiser to state that it should, rather than must, appear. And you'll need to instruct the engine to treat the **three words as one phrase**, or you'll get hits on Mars, Audiac, and Quintet – and lots of links to NASA and chocolate bars. So to refine it further, you could state that "Stereolab" **must appear**, the phrase "Mars Audiac Quintet" **should appear**, and "review" **should appear**. That way it's most likely that a page with all the terms will appear near the top of the results and the next most relevant under that.

Altavista and InfoSeek have their own intricacies in grouping adjacent keywords into phrases, but **joining words by dashes** (mars-audiac-quintet) works on both. The dashes state that a single space, not a letter, must appear between the words. You should read both help files for instructions on more complex searches – and observe how they interpret capitals. In HotBot and Excite, you need to **enclose the phrase within quotes**.

Search engines are not the final word of what's on the Web. Just because they can't find something, doesn't mean it isn't there. It just means their trawlers haven't visited that site yet. Which means you'll have to turn to another, maybe fresher source. For instance:

Directories and lists

To browse the **range of sites within a subject category**, turn to one of the **directories**. There's no shortage of them, and they all seem to offer something unique. Indeed, they're so diverse that lumping them together is somewhat ambitious. What they all have in common is that humans, rather than automatons, collate the sites, and usually add a comment. The sites are then cataloged in some kind of logical fashion.

You usually have the choice of browsing directories by **subject group** and sometimes by other criteria like **entry date or rating**. Most directories also allow you to search their own sites through a form, rather like a search engine. Unlike search engines, directories don't keep the contents of Web pages but instead record titles, categories, and sometimes comments or reviews. So adjust your searching strategy accordingly. Start with broad terms and work down until you hit the reviews.

Good all-purpose directories include: **Yahoo, Magellan, Lycos 5%, The Internet Directory, World Wide Web Virtual Library**, the **InfoSeek Guide**, the **Argus Clearinghouse**, and our own **Rough Guide** (we post online the Web sites and reviews in Section Two of this book). All these directories are useful for finding specialist sites, which in turn can point you to the obscure cauldrons of your obsessions.

Specialist sites

Whatever your interest, you can bet your favorite finger it will have several dedicated Web pages. And there's probably a page somewhere that keeps track of them all. Such **mini-directories** are a boon for finding new and esoteric pages – ones that the major directories overlook.

In addition, these specialist directories sometimes run **mailing lists** to keep you posted with news. If you have similar interests, you can email the Webmaster and introduce yourself. That's how the Web community works. You'll find hundreds of specialist sites all through our Web Guide, including the most popular in the **Internet Search Tools** category.

Lists

If you're not looking for anything in particular, just something new, entertaining, or innovative, maybe you'll find it in a **list**. In fact, it can be worth checking into a few lists like **Cool Site of the Day**, **Geek Site of the Day**, **Stroud's What's New**, **Gamelan**, and the **Internet Chart Show** regularly to keep up to date. And to see what's popular, try **100 Hot Websites**. Again, addresses for all these are featured in our Web Guide section.

Finding stuff

If you start your search with the search engines and guides they'll invariably lead you to other sites, which in turn point you closer toward what you're after. As you get more familiar with the run of the Net, you'll gravitate toward specialist sites and directories that index more than just Web pages, contain their own unique content, and shine in specific areas. What's best depends largely on what you're looking for. When you find a useful site, **store it in your bookmarks, hotlist, or favorites**, so you can return. Here are a few examples, using a mixture of techniques to:

Find new and interesting sites

Search engines aren't good at finding the very latest sites. Nor do they give subjective advice, so you won't know what a site's like until you visit. Directories like **Pointcom** and **Magellan** are better because they review. But to find brand new sites, try: **What's New**, Internet Chart show, and sites that showcase latest technology, like **Gamelan**.

Also scan **newspaper technology sections** and **magazines** like *Wired*, *Internet World*, *Internet*, *.Net*, and *PC Magazine*. And as mentioned above, **lists** like Cool Site of the Day, Web100, and Geek Site of the Day are all great value for finding the cream.

Find something from Usenet

Usenet's newsgroups are by far the best place to find opinions and personal experiences but they carry a daunting amount of text to scan. Although it's sorted into subject bundles, if you had to find every instance of discussion about something, it could take you days. And if it was tossed around more than a couple of weeks ago, the thread might have expired. But, with **archives** like **DejaNews**, **HotBot**, and **Altavista**, you can scan close to the entirety of Usenet, for up to a year in retrospect, depending on the archive.

DejaNews keeps articles the longest, bundles threads, and profiles contributors. This makes it easier to follow

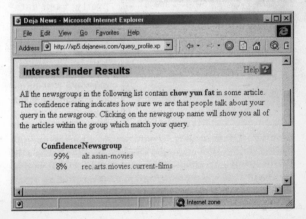

a whole discussion, as well as check out whose advice you're taking and how well they're usually received. Plus the longer the history, the more chance you have of finding something obscure. DejaNews will also identify which groups are mostly likely to discuss a subject. Hot-Bot and Altavista, on the other hand, can be better for crunching recent articles and weeding out the noise.

Like all search engines, these tools are pretty self-explanatory, but as ever it pays to read their help file.

Find someone's email address

You can often find personal and business email addresses by consulting **mail directories** like **Four11**, **Bigfoot**, and **WhoWhere**. These get most of their data

from Usenet postings and visitors, so they're not in any way comprehensive, but they're pretty vast databases – and, of course, growing by the day.

If these fail, try using the sought person's full name as a **people search term** in HotBot's Web or Usenet archive. Alternatively, if you know where someone works, search that company's Web pages – or better still (obvious but effective!) **ring up and ask**. And if you're fanatically keen see the definitive **FAQ on finding email addresses**: http://www.qucis.queensu.ca/FAQs/email/finding.html

Find games, hints, and cheats

Try one of the big games sites like the **Games Domain**, **PCME**, or **Happy Puppy**, or search through **Usenet** as explained above. Stuck on a level? Look for a walk-through, or ask in Usenet.

Find something in Gopherspace

Gopherspace is just like the Web, but more navigable. Individual Gophers are internally searchable from a menu entry. To search the menu titles in "all Gopher-space" use **Veronica**, the Gopher search engine. Veronica's database is compiled by trawling Gopher-space every couple of weeks, and retrieving the menu titles. All Veronicas contain the same data although some might be slightly fresher. Veronica searches produce a menu of Gopher items, which in turn point to Gopher data sources. It's on the "Other Gophers" menu on Minnesota's Gopher server, or at: gopher://futique.scs.unr.edu/11/veronica

Some of the **Web's search engines and guides**, particularly Lycos and Yahoo, cover Gopher as well as the Web. So you'll often find Gopher addresses interspersed among their Web addresses. Lycos, in fact, may actually be more useful than Veronica, since it retrieves sample text, not just menu titles.

The Gopher of all Gophers has to be **Gopher Jewels** at: http://galaxy.net/GJ/index.html or gopher://cwis.usc.edu/11/other_gophers_information_resources/gophers_by_subject/gopher_jewels

This provides a catalog of Gopher resources and contains over 2000 pointers by category.

Find the latest news, weather, finance, sport, etc.

Apart from hundreds of newspapers and magazines, the Net carries several large **news clipping archives** assembled from all sorts of sources. Naturally, there's an overwhelming amount of technology news, but there's also an increasing amount of services dedicated to what you would normally find in the newsstands – and it's often fresher on the Net. Occasionally there's a charge. For pointers, check our Web Guide under News, Fashion, Finance, Weather, and so forth.

Find out about a film or TV show

See the Film and TV section of our Web Guide or try the entertainment section of any major directory for leads to specialist sites. The **Internet Movie Database**, for example, is exceptionally comprehensive.

Find commercial support and services

Apart from being user-friendly, the major justification for joining an **Online Service** has traditionally been the quality of the content and the user support forums. **AOL** and **CompuServe** once had the market cornered in things like travel booking services, online banking, financial data, and product support. They're still leading players but the Net is reaching out, and often surpassing their standards. And now as the Online Services are moving their content onto the Web on a pay-to-view basis, even if you only have regular Net access you can still get the best of both worlds.

Use the guides like Magellan, Yahoo, and the Internet Directory to point you toward **specialist databases, services, and companies** in your area of interest. Or try one of the **business directories** from our Web Guide. The most professional outfits also buy banner advertising on popular sites like search engines. So you probably won't have to find them. They'll find you.

Some companies offer **product support** channels through their Web sites, but if you want advice from other users, go to Usenet.

Find the latest software

Most people start software searches using an **Archie program** to query one of the Archie databases that accumulate FTP listings in the same way as search engines trawl the Web. We don't. Nor do we use the Web version, which you'll find in the Internet Search Tools section of the Web Guide. It's too hard. For one, you have to know the program's exact file name, or at least part of it. Half the time you're not even sure of the program's name. Imagine you've heard about a beta program called Net Drill, Netdriller, Nedrilla, or something, that caches DNS queries locally. How are you going to find that with Archie when its program name's nedrrlb3.exe?

A much easier route is to try one of the **specialist file directories** like **Stroud's** or **TUCOWS**, and look under an appropriate category. Failing that, try coining **search terms** like "caches DNS" or "Netd*" and feeding them into the search engines, Usenet archives, and technical news clipping services like InfoMarket. As a bonus you'll likely find a description or review to tell you whether it's worth getting.

Once you've found a file, if it's proving slow to download, feed the file name into one of the **FTP engines** like **Snoopie**, **FTP Search**, or even **Archie**, to find an alternative FTP site from which to download it.

Find a mailing list

Tracking down a **mailing list** is a cinch. Subject search any of the directories in the Mailing List section of our Web Guide's **Internet Search Tools**. If that's not satisfactory, try the same search in a **Usenet archive** and check the FAQs from groups with hits.

Find help

If all else fails – and that's pretty unlikely – you can always turn to someone else for help. Just post a query in an appropriate **Usenet** group. Summarize your quest in the subject heading, keep it concise, and you usually get an answer or three within a few days.

How to fix broken Web addresses

It won't take long to encounter a **Web link** or **address that won't work**. Don't get too perturbed – it's common and usually not too hard to get around. We already know that many of the URLs in our Web Guide will be wrong by the time you try them. Not because we're careless. They just change. For example, in the five months between the last edition of this book's first and fifth printings, almost 100 sites needed addresses updating. That's the way of the Net. The most useful thing we can do is show you how to find the new addresses.

Error codes

When something goes wrong, your browser will pop up a little box with a message and **error code**. Either that or nothing will happen, no matter what you try. To identify the source of the problem, get familiar with the types of errors. Different browsers and servers will return different error messages, but they'll indicate the same things.

As an exercise, identify the following errors:

Incorrect host name
When the address points to a **nonexistent host**, your browser should return an error saying "Host not found." Test this by keying: http://www.rufgide.com

Illegal domain name
If you specify an **illegal host name** or **protocol**, your browser will tell you. Try this out by keying http://wwwrufguide and then http:/www.ibm.com noting the single slash.

File not found
If the **file has moved**, **changed name**, or you've over-looked **capitalization**, you'll get a message within the page from the server telling you the file doesn't exist on the host. Test this by keying a familiar URL and slightly changing the path.

Busy host or Host refuses entry
Occasionally you won't gain access because the host is either **overloaded with traffic**, or it's temporarily or per-manently **off-limits**. This sometimes happens with busy FTP servers, like Netscape's. It's a bit hard to test, but you'll come across it sooner or later. You might also make a habit of accessing foreign sites when locals are sleeping – it's usually quicker.

When no URLs work

Now that you're on speaking terms with your browser, you're set to troubleshoot that problem URL. The first thing to verify is that you have a **working connection** to the Web yourself. Try another site. If it works, you know the problem's with that URL.

If you can't connect to any Web site, try **closing your browser and reopening** it. It could be a software bug. If that doesn't fix it, it might be your connection to the Net. First, **check your mail**. If that looks dodgy, log off and then back on again. Check it again. If it still doesn't work, **ring your provider** and see if there's a problem at their end.

If your mailer connects and reports your mail status normally, you know that the connection between you and your provider is okay. But there still could be a problem between it and the Net. Try **Pinging** (see p.41) a known host – say www.ibm.com – or logging in to an FTP site. If this fails, either your provider's connection to the Net is down, or there's a problem with your Domain Name Server. Get on the phone and sort it out.

If you've verified that all connections are open but your browser won't find any URLs, the problem lies with your **browser set-up**. Check its configurations and reinstall it if necessary. Ensure there are no winsock.dll conflicts. And finally, check you have the right browser for your operating system. For example, 32-bit browsers won't work properly with Windows 3.1.

When one URL doesn't work

If it's only an individual URL that doesn't work, you know that either its address is wrong or the host at the other end has problems. Now that you're familiar with error messages you can deduce the source and fix that address. **Web addresses disappear and change** all the time and there's nothing you can do about it. It's often because the address has been simplified, for example from http://www.netflux.co.uk/~test/New_Book/ComPlex.html/ to http://www.roughguides.com

If you're lucky, someone will have had the sense to leave a **link to the new page** but sometimes even that pointer gets out of date. Since the Web is in a constant state of construction, just about everything is a test site in transit to something bigger. Consequently, when a site gets serious, it might relocate to an entirely new host and forget the old address. Who said the life of a professional surfer was easy?

Finding that elusive URL

The most obvious clues in **tracking elusive URLs** are to use what you've deduced from the error messages. If the problem comes from the host name, try **adding** or **removing the www part**. For example, instead of typing http://roughguides.com try http://www.roughguides.com On current generation browsers this shouldn't make any difference, but it can be worth trying all the same. Other than that you can only guess. Host names are not case sensitive, so changing that won't help. If the host is busy, refusing entry, or not connecting, try again later.

If you **connect to the host but the file isn't there**, there are a few further tricks to try. Check **capitalization**, for instance: WorldWideMusic instead of worldwidemusic. Or try changing the **file name extension** from .htm to .html or vice versa, if applicable. Then try **removing the file name** and then each subsequent directory up the path until finally you're left with just the host name. In each case, if you succeed in connecting, try to locate your page from the links presented or by browsing through directories and hotlists.

If you haven't succeeded, there's still hope. Try submitting the main **key words** from the URL's address or title to **HotBot** or **Altavista**. Failing that, try searching on related subjects, or scanning through one of the subject guides like **Yahoo** or Magellan.

By now, even if you haven't found your original target URL, you've probably discovered half a dozen similar, if not more interesting pages, and in the process figured out how to navigate the Net.

Creating Your Own Web Page

It won't take much time on the Web before you'll get the itch to have a go yourself, and publish your own Web page. You don't need to be anyone particularly important, or a company with something to sell. You just need three things: something to say, some way to convert it into HTML, and somewhere to put it. Finding a location isn't too hard, or expensive. The logical place would be on your access provider's server. Better providers usually include at least 1 Mb storage as part of a subscriber account. Alternatively, you could try one of the Web space and site development specialists.

Once you have the space, you can publish anything you like from the way you feel about your hamster to your Mad Cow conspiracy thesis. Or you can use it to publicize yourself, push causes, provide information, sell your products, or entertain. But before you leap out of the closet and air your obsessions or money-making schemes, do check you're not breaking any laws of decency or trade. Your Web space provider will know.

Putting your thoughts into HTML

Dozens of programs claim to simplify the procedure of **converting text into HTML**. These days most attempt to make it a **WYSIWYG** (What You See Is What You Get) desktop-publishing affair. However well they succeed, you'd still be advised to spend a couple of hours **getting to grips with how HTML works**. The good news is that, unlike computer programming in general, it's dead easy. But, it is rather tedious. It basically boils down to writing the page in plain text, adding formatting tags, inserting instructions on how to place images, and embedding links to other pages.

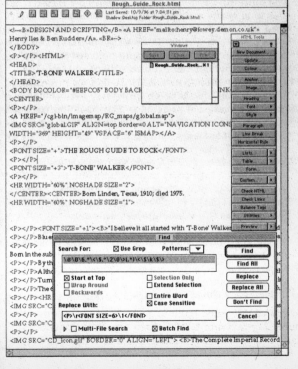

There's a small catch in that, like all Net protocols, HTML is under constant review – particularly by Netscape and Microsoft. As such, although a drawn-up standard exists, certain new **HTML enhancements** only work on some browsers. Yes, as ever with the Net, the whole affair is quite a muddle.

Editing packages

The quickest way to get familiar with how HTML operates is to **create a simple page from scratch**. You won't need any complex compiling software – a text editor, or word processor, will do. However, a specific **HTML edit program** can help by automating much of the mark-up process so you don't have to learn all the tag codes.

The competition between HTML editing programs is as intense as that between browsers, with the choice down to a matter of preference. They can approach the task from various angles, such as converting word-processed documents, applying the tags from toolbar and menu choices, using step-by-step wizards, or by hiding the code altogether. A good way to start would be to use one of the free, fairly basic, editors bundled with the full editions of either **Netscape** or **Microsoft's browsers**. Or you could get by (just) with desktop publishing afterthoughts like Office 97's Internet assistants.

For professional WYSIWYG site building though, have a look at **GoLive CyberStudio**: http://www.golive.com (Mac only), **Microsoft FrontPage**: http://www.microsoft.com, **NetObjects Fusion**: http://www.netobjects.com or **Drumbeat**: http://www.elementalsw.com

Despite WYSIWYG's apparent advantages, even the least techie Web builders end up getting into raw code. So even if it looks pretty barbaric right now, just bear with it. It pays off in the long run.

Plundering code

Once you're comfortable with mark-up logic, you can glean advanced techniques by **analysing other Web pages**. Just find a page you like and choose **"View Source"** from your browser menu to see the raw code. You can even cut and paste selections into your own page. If you save the file and view it with a text editor or word processor, you'll also see the code. However, it disappears when viewed with a browser. The same applies to your own work. To **see how it would look on the Web**, open it up as a **local file** in your browser. Look under the File menu for "Open" or "Open page." Alternatively, drag and drop it into your browser window. And then to **see changes while editing**, hit "Refresh."

Tags

Next time you're online, view the source of any Web page (see above). The first thing you'll notice is that the text is surrounded with comments enclosed between less-than and greater-than symbols like this: <TITLE> My Home Page </TITLE>

These comments are known as **tags** or **styles**. Most, but not all, tags come in pairs and apply to their enclosed text. The first tag typically looks like: <TAG> and the closing tag like: </TAG>

THE CODE

It's good practice, but not mandatory, to **enclose HTML documents** within the following structure:

    <HTML>(identifies the document as HTML)
    <HEAD><TITLE>(the title goes in here)</TITLE></HEAD>
    <BODY>(everything else goes in here)</BODY>
    </HTML>(end of document)

A Web document has two parts: a **head** and a **body**. The head contains the title, which is displayed on the top bar of your browser window. The body appears within the window.

Backgrounds and colors

It's possible to apply formatting to the entire body of a document by placing extensions within the <BODY> tag. For example, <BODY BGCOLOR="#00E4FF"> changes the **background color** to #00E4FF, the RGB code for aqua. Luckily, most HTML editors automate the color to RGB conversion, so you won't have to know these numbers. Recent model browsers also recognize literal words such as blue, red, and purple (but don't rely on it).

To **change the color** of the document text, standard link, visited link, and active link, insert any or all of TEXT="a", LINK="b", VLINK="c", or ALINK="d" respectively within the <BODY> tag, where a, b, c, and d are your chosen RGB color codes. To **display a background graphic**, insert BACKGROUND="(image file location here)". You can apply all sorts of fancy effects. However, until you're confident, don't go overboard, as loud backgrounds almost always make the text hard to read.

Headings

In a word processor, when you want to emphasize something using larger or smaller text, you change its point size. In HTML you use a **heading** of the appropriate proportion. Headings are enclosed within <Hn></Hn> tags, where n is from 1 to 6 with <H1> being the largest and <H6> the smallest. The actual size it appears when read depends on the viewer's browser and the way that they've configured the browser settings.

Playing with text

Standard HTML ignores multiple spaces, tabs, and carriage returns. To get around that you can **enclose text** within the <PRE></PRE> (preformatted text) tag pair. Otherwise, any consecutive spaces, tabs, carriage returns, or combinations will produce a single space.

However, it's more conventional to **end paragraphs** with <P>, which creates a **single line break**. To create **multiple line breaks** use <BR>. One <BR> will start the text on a new line, two will create a line break, three will create two line breaks, and so on.

Browsers automatically **wrap text** so there's no need to worry about page widths. To **center text** use:

<CENTER>(text here)</CENTER> and to **indent** from both margins use: <BLOCKQUOTE>(text here)</BLOCKQUOTE>

Three simple, but effective, ways to **emphasize text** are to use bold, italic (though beware this can be hard to read on the Web), or colored or enlarged type. To **bold** text, enclose within <B></B> or <STRONG></STRONG>

To **italicize**, use: <I></I> or <EM></EM> To **change color or size**, use <FONT COLOR="RGB" SIZE=n>(insert text here)</FONT>, where RGB is the RGB color code and n (-7 to +7) is the increment above or below your regular font size.

Images

Placing **Web graphics** is an art form. The smaller they are in bytes and the fewer you use, the quicker your page will load. So it's wise to reduce them first using an **image editor**. With practice, you can **reduce byte size** considerably without overly sacrificing quality.

The simplest way to display an image is to place it within the <IMG> tag, like this: <IMG SRC="(image location

here)"> This will display it full size and bottom-aligned with adjacent text. You can also insert extra specifications between IMG and SRC.

For example,

`<IMG HEIGHT=300 WIDTH=400 ALIGN=TOP VSPACE=60 HSPACE=70 BORDER=100 SRC="image.gif">` would set the dimensions of your image.gif to 300 high by 400 wide, align its top with the tallest item in the line, give it a border of 100 and separate it from the text by 60 vertically and 70 horizontally. All measurements are in pixels.

You can specify all manner of **alignments** including:

ALIGN=right

Aligns image with left margin. Text wraps on right.

ALIGN=left

Aligns image with right margin. Text wraps on left.

ALIGN=texttop

Aligns top of image with tallest text in line.

ALIGN=middle

Aligns the baseline of text with middle of image.

ALIGN=absmiddle

Aligns the middle of text with middle of image.

ALIGN=baseline

Aligns the bottom of image with the baseline of the current line.

ALIGN=bottom

Aligns the bottom of image with the bottom of the current line.

It is generally accepted as good practice to include an **alternative text version** for browsers with images switched off. To do this, insert ALT="description of image" anywhere between IMG and SRC. This is especially important if the image describes a self-contained link.

Lines

A **horizontal rule** can be created using <HR> or, in more detail, <HR WIDTH=X% ALIGN=Y SIZE=Z>, where X is the percentage proportion of page width, Y is its positioning (CENTER, LEFT, or RIGHT) and Z is its thickness. The default is 100 percent, CENTER and 1. Or you could insert an image of a line or bar.

Lists

HTML offers three principal types of **lists: ordered, unnumbered**, and **definition**.

Ordered lists

Ordered lists are enclosed with the <OL></OL> pair. Each item preceded by <LI> is **assigned a sequential number**. For example:

<OL> On the command, "brace! brace!":
On the command, "brace! brace!":
<LI> Extinguish cigarette
   1. Extinguish cigarette
<LI> Assume crash position
   2. Assume crash position
<LI> Remain calm
   3. Remain calm
   </OL>

Unnumbered lists

Unnumbered lists work similarly within the <UL></UL> pair, except that <LI> **produces a bullet**:

   <UL>Suspected carcinogens
   Suspected carcinogens
   <LI>Television
   • Television

    <LI>Red gummy bears
    • Red gummy bears
    <LI>Toast
    • Toast
    </UL>

Definition lists

Definition lists are enclosed within the <DL></DL> pair.
The <DT><DD> pair **splits the list into levels**:
    <DL>
    <DT>Best screenplay
    Best screenplay
    <dd>Eraserhead II, Son of Henry
        Eraserhead II, Son of Henry
    <DT>Best lead actor
    Best lead actor
    <dd>Chow Yun Fat, Duke Nukem
        Chow Yun Fat, Duke Nukem
    <DT>Best lead actress
    Best lead actress
    <dd>Diana Spencer, Queen of Hearts
        Diana Spencer, Queen of Hearts
    </DL>

Links

The whole idea of HTML is to add a third dimension to
documents by **linking them to other pages**. This is
achieved by embedding **clickable hot-spots** to redirect
browsers to other addresses. A hot-spot can be attached
to text, icons, buttons, lines, or even images. Items containing hot-spots usually give an indication of where the
link goes, but the address itself is normally concealed.
Most browsers reveal this address when you pass your
mouse over the link.

You can embed hot links to anywhere on the Net. Here's how to:

Create a link to another Web page

<A HREF="http://www.roughguides.com">Rough Guides</A>
Clicking on "Rough Guides" would load the Web page at:
http://www.roughguides.com

Create a link to a local page

<A HREF="trap.html">Step this way</A>
If the file trap.html is in the same directory or is mapped as a local file, clicking on "Step this way" will launch it.

Embed links in images

<A HREF="fish.html"><IMG SRC="fish.gif"></A>
<A HREF="bigfish.gif"><IMG SRC="fish.gif"></A>
In both cases, the locally stored image fish.gif contains the hot-spot. The first case launches the local Web page fish.html while the second would display bigfish.gif, which could be a different image – for example a more detailed version of fish.gif

Invite mail

<A HREF="mailto:bigflint@texas.net">GPF Browne</A>
On most browsers, clicking on "GPF Browne" would bring up the send mail dialog box, already addressed to bigflint@texas.net

Route to a newsgroup

<A HREF="news:alt.elvis.sighting">Find Elvis</A>
Clicking on "Find Elvis" would bring up articles in the alt.elvis.sighting newsgroup.

Commence a Telnet session

`<A HREF="telnet://pctravel.com">PCTravel</A>`

If the browser is configured to launch a Telnet client, clicking on "PCTravel" would initiate a Telnet session with pctravel.com

Burrow through to a Gopher

`<A HREF="gopher://gopher.scs.unr.edu>Veronica</A>`

Clicking on "Veronica" would transfer you to the Gopher at gopher.scs.unr.edu

Log in to an anonymous FTP server

`<AHREF="ftp://ftp.bennett.com/paul/packet.exe">Packet Plus</A>`
`<A HREF="ftp://ftp.microsoft.com/">Microsoft</A>`

Clicking on "Packet Plus" would commence the download of packet.exe while clicking on "Microsoft" would bring up a listing of the root directory of ftp.microsoft.com

But wait, there's more

That's about all you'll need to know in about 99% of cases, but if you're adventurous there are no bounds to the things you can do with a Web page. At the first level there are dozens more fairly straightforward tags to create **tables, frames, forms, blinking text**, and assorted tricks. Then there are multimedia options like **audio, video, animation, and virtual reality**. And at the top level there's **form processing** and **interactive pages**.

As you move up the levels of sophistication, you'll start to move out of the standard HTML domain, into complex **scripting and programming languages** like **ActiveX, Java Script, Java, PERL, CGI**, and **Visual Basic**.

You may also need access to the special class of storage space reserved for Web programs, known as the **CGI bin**.

To be going on with, though, if you see a feature you like, just look at the page source to see if you can work out how it's done – or ask the site's Webmaster, or search the Web for a good DIY document. There are plenty of books on the subject, but beware: the technology's moving so fast that they date instantly.

Java and Java Script

Amongst the most over-hyped things to hit the Web in the past couple of years is **Java**, a programming language which can be interpreted by any computer, and will soon to be built into all operating systems. Netscape and Internet Explorer already feature in-built Java interpreters, so you won't need any extra software to view it. As for writing it yourself, you'll need to be keen: it's a hard core language, like C++. Still, like all other aspects of Web DIY design, you mightn't find it so hard to copy and adapt Java Script from pages created by Java eggheads. And if you master that, you may just decide to start learning the script yourself.

Your own Web or FTP server

Once your computer's connected to the Net, it can act as a **Web** or **FTP server**, just by running the right software. You can even run your own server on a regular dial-up account, though of course your pages or files will only be accessible while you're online. And if you're using PPP, you'll have a different IP address each time you log in, so you won't be able to pass it on until you're online. This is functional enough if you just want to show a couple of Web pages to a colleague or friend. However, if you want a serious Web presence, you'll need a permanent connection to run your own server.

Servers are remarkably simple to install – read the help file and you'll be up within half an hour. But take the time to set up your **security options** to allow only appropriate access to the appropriate directories. That means things like making your Web pages read-only and your FTP incoming write-only. Otherwise you might get hacked. You'll find server software detailed in the Software Roundup (see p.379).

How to publicize your site

Once you've published your page and transferred it to your server (which for most of us means lodging it with your ISP), the real problems begin. You'll need to **get people to visit it**.

Before you crank up the publicity campaign, consider how you'd find such a site yourself and whether, if you stumbled across it, you'd bother stopping or returning. Most of all, decide whether publicity now would be good, or if you want to keep the site under construction awhile before you take out the full-page adverts in *The New York Times*.

On a basic level, most people will arrive at your site by taking a **link from another site** or by **typing in the URL**. That means if other pages link to yours, or people can find your address written somewhere, you'll stand a chance of getting traffic. Look around the Web for sites of parallel interest to your own and send them email suggesting **reciprocal links**. Most will oblige.

The best publicity machines of all are the **search engines and directories**. Before you submit your URL to them (and you should), find out how they work. This means, for example, establishing whether they'll accept a brief review, scan your page for key words, or index it in full. You might find tricks like stringing repeated key words outside the HTML body, which can trick engines into prioritizing your page for that subject. See Search Engine Watch (http://www.searchenginewatch.com) for how they all tick.

To save time tracking down all the various engines, several sites such as Submit-it (http://www.submit-it.com) and Broadcaster (http://www.broadcaster.co.uk) will **send your details to multiple engines and directories** at once. And if what you're doing is **new**, ask Yahoo to create you a new category, and try Emap's what's new pages (http://www.emap.com/whatsnew/). Once you've done all that, Web Position Agent (http://www.webposition.com) can tell you how you're ranked.

Next, generate some off-Web interest. Announce your site in appropriate **newsgroups and mailing lists**. You can get away with posting the same message periodically in Usenet, and as many times as you like if it's part of a signature file, but don't post to a mailing list unless you have something new to say.

Don't forget about the old world, either. **Include the URL** on your stationery, business cards, and in all your regular advertising. And flash it in front of everyone you can. Finally, if it's really newsworthy, send a press release to whatever media might be interested. And just quietly, it mightn't hurt to throw a party, invite some journos, and wave some free merchandise about.

But before you tell anyone, install a hit counter and statistics service (see: http://www.digits.com and http://www.dbasics.com/counter/). Then sit back and watch them roll in.

Where to next?

For more about HTML, Web programming, and publicity try the Web Developer's Virtual Library (http://www.stars.com) and CNET's Builder.com (http://www.builder.com) You'll should find everything you need either on or linked to these sites. And for HTML editors see our "Software Roundup" (see p.373).

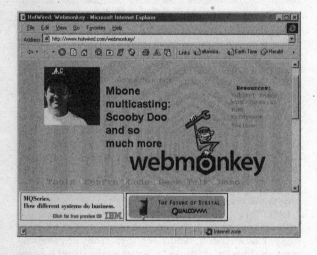

Internet
Relay Chat

There's a side to the Net that's often described as the online equivalent of CB radio. Where you can hold live keyboard, and more recently voice and video, conversations with people all over the world. Part of that mechanism is called Internet Relay Chat (IRC) and with other live Net chat techniques it's developing into a cheap alternative to long-distance telephone calls. It is hosted on a multitude of channels, mostly on the wider Internet, though Online Services – and in particular AOL and CompuServe – also have live chat forums, often featuring celebrity guest interviews. The latter are easy to master. IRC on the Net is more complex – and it's this which we address in the following pages.

IRC, since starting in Finland in 1988, has played a worthy part in transmitting timely eye-witness accounts of every major world event – including the Gulf War, LA riots, Kobe earthquake, Oklahoma bombing, and the Olympics. During the Gulf War, for example, IRC channels formed to dissect the latest news as it came in from the wire services. But, as you'll soon discover, politics, crises, and sport are not the only things discussed.

Unlike Usenet, on IRC your conversations are live. What you key into your computer is instantly broadcast to everybody else on your channel, even if they're logged into a server on the other side of the world. Some channels are obviously dedicated to **particular topics**, for example, #cricket, #quake, and #worldcup, but most are just **informal chat lines**. Who knows, your perfect match could be waiting for you in an online chat channel like #hottub. Okay, so maybe not, but IRC has brought the odd couple together. A few have even held their wedding ceremonies online. If you ever get to attend one, be sure to throw some rice, like this: "ⁿⁿⁿⁿⁿⁿ". So, if you want to find out where the real pointy-heads play, read on.

What's IRC? A veritable online Love Boat, say Mr. and Mrs. A. Hunt at:
http://www.andyhunt.demon.co.uk

Requirements

What you enter into an IRC channel is sent immediately to everyone else in that channel, wherever they are. The only way that can happen is through **full Internet access**, or through a **local chat server**. However, you don't need a particularly fast connection nor a powerful computer. Ideally, you don't want to be paying **timed online charges** either, because it's another medium where, once you're hooked, you'll end up spending hours online.

Many chatsters have free direct connections through university or work, so they can afford to leave their line open all day. That's one of the reasons why you'll often find idle occupied channels. When you enter a channel and "beep" an occupant, if they're in the vicinity of the terminal, they should answer. It's also possible they could be chatting or lurking in other channels, reading email, on the Web, or playing an online game, so give them time to respond.

A caution

Of all the Internet's features, IRC is the one most likely to trip up newbies. Mainly because you can't hide your presence. For example, on Usenet, unless you jump in and post, no-one will know you've visited. However, the second you arrive in an IRC channel **you'll be announced** to all and your nickname will remain in the names list for as long as you stay.

Sleuthful chatsters may be able to find out who you are behind your nickname and possibly tell whether you're a newbie from your settings. And the odd devious joker might try to persuade you to enter commands which could hand over control of your computer. **Never enter an unfamiliar command at the request of another user**. If someone is bothering you privately, protest publicly. If no-one defends you, change channels. If they persist, get them kicked out by an operator. Think we're exaggerating? Then try a Web search on "hacking IRC."

Getting started

Net software bundles don't always include an IRC program. If that's your case, fire up FTP and grab the latest **GUI client** (see our "Software Roundup" on p.370). Once it's installed, read the instructions and work through any tutorials.

Reading the instructions first might sound a bit boring but in this case it's necessary. GUI IRC clients have an array of cryptic buttons and windows that are less intuitive than most Internet programs. And before you start randomly clicking on things to see what they do, remember people are watching.

Additionally, before you can start, you have to **configure your client** to connect to a specific IRC server's address, and enter your nickname, real name, and email address. If you're worried about embarrassing yourself, try an alias. Some servers, however, refuse entry if their reverse lookups detect discrepancies.

The servers

To ease the strain on network traffic, start with a **nearby host**. There are hundreds of open IRC hosts worldwide. The best place to get a fresh list, or indeed any information about IRC, is from the alt.irc newsgroup. But the quickest would be from: http://www.irchelp.org/irchelp/networks/

For starters, just choose a host from your client's menu or try: undernet.org on port 6667.

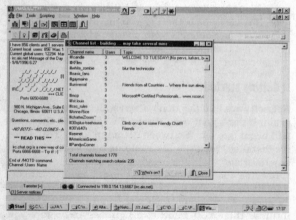

IRC commands

IRC has **over 100 commands**. Unless you're really keen, you'll only need to know a few. However, the more you learn, the more you can strengthen your position. You can almost get away without learning any commands at all with GUI clients, but it won't hurt to know the script behind the buttons, and you may even prefer it. Your client won't automate everything, so each time you're online test a few more. Its "Help" file should contain a full list. If not, try: http://shoga.wwa.com/~edge/irc.html or: http//www.undernet.org

There are far too many commands to list here, but those below will get you started. **Anything after a forward slash (/) is interpreted as a command**. If you leave off the slash, it will be transmitted to your active channel as a message and you'll look a right clot.

Commands are NOT case sensitive

/AWAY \<message\>	Leave message saying you're not available
/BYE	Exit IRC session
/HELP	List available commands
/HELP \<command\>	Return help on this command
/IGNORE \<nickname\>\<*\>\<all\>	Ignore this nickname
/IGNORE \<*\>\<email address\>\<all\>	Ignore this email address
/IGNORE \<*\>\<*\>\<none\>	Delete ignorance list
/JOIN \<#channel\>	Join this channel
/KICK \<nickname\>	Boot this nickname off channel
/LEAVE \<#channel\>	Exit this channel
/LIST \<-MIN n\>	List channels with minimum of n users
/MOP	Promote all to operator status
/MSG \<nickname\>\<message\>	Send private message to this nickname
/NICK \<nickname\>	Change your nickname
/OP \<nickname\>	Promote this nickname to operator
/QUERY \<nickname\>	Start a private conversation with this nickname
/TOPIC \<new topic\>	Change channel topic
/WHO*	List users in current channel
/WHOIS \<nickname\>	Display nickname's identity
/WHOWAS \<nickname\>	Display identity of exited nickname

Step by step through your first session

By now, you've configured your client, chosen a nickname you'll never use again, and are raring to go. The aim of your first session is to connect to a server, have a look around, get a list of channels, join one, see who's on, say something public, then something private, leave the channel, start a new channel, make yourself operator, change the topic, and then exit IRC. The whole process should take no more than about ten minutes. Let's go.

+ Log on to a server and wait to be accepted. If you're not, keep trying others until you succeed. Once aboard, you'll be greeted with the MOTD (message of the day) in the server window. Read the message and see if it tells you anything interesting.

+ You should have at least two windows available. One for input, the other to display server output. Generally, the two windows form part of a larger window, with the input box below the output box. Even though your client's point and click interface will replace most of the basic commands, since you probably haven't read its manual yet, you won't know how to use it. So instead just use the commands.

+ To see what channels are available, type: **/LIST** You'll have to wait a minute and then a window will pop up, or fill up, with hundreds of channels, their topics, and the number of users on them. To narrow down the list to those channels with six or more users, type: **/LIST - MIN 6** Now you'll see the busiest channels.

+ Pick a channel at random and join it. Channel names are always preceded by #, so to join the lard channel, type: **/JOIN #lard** and then wait for the channel window to appear. Once the channel window opens, you should get a list of the channel's occupants, in yet another window. If not, type: **/WHO*** for a full list including nicknames and email addresses.

+ Now say something clever. Type: **Hi everyone, it's great to be back!** This should appear not only on the screen in your channel window, but on the screen in every other person's channel window. Wait for replies and answer any questions as you see fit.

+ Now it's time to send something personal. Choose someone in the channel and find out what you can about them first, by typing: /WHO followed by their nickname. Your client might let you do this by just double clicking on their nickname in the names window. Let's say their nickname is Tamster. To send a private message, just type: /MSG Hey Tamster, I'm a clueless newbie, let me know if you get this so I won't feel so stupid. If Tamster doesn't reply, keep trying until someone does. Once you're satisfied you know how that works, leave the channel by typing: /LEAVE Don't worry, next time you go into a channel, you'll feel more comfortable.

+ Now to start your own channel. Pick any name that doesn't already exist. As soon as you leave, it will disappear. To start a channel called lancelink, just type: /JOIN #lancelink Once the window pops up, you'll find you're the only person on it. Now promote yourself to operator by typing: /OP followed by your nickname. Others can tell you have channel operator status because your nickname will appear with an @ in front of it. Now you're an operator – you have the power to kick people off the channel, change the topic, and all sorts of other things that you can find out by reading the manual as recommended. To change the topic, type: /TOPIC followed by whatever you want to change the topic to. Wait for it to change on the top of your window and then type: /BYE to exit IRC.

That's it really, a whirlwind tour but enough to learn most things you'll need. Now before you can chat with other chatsters, you'll need to speak their lingo.

The language of IRC

Just like CB radio, IRC has its own dialect. Chat is a snappy medium, messages are short, and responses are fast. Unlike CB, people won't ask your "20" to see where you're from, or type "breaker" when they enter a discussion, but they will use **short-forms**, **acronyms**, **and smileys** (:-). Acronyms are mixed in with normal speech and range from the innocuous (BTW = by the way) to a whole panoply of blue phrases. Don't be too shocked. It's not meant to be taken seriously. And don't be ashamed to use plain English either. You'll stand a better chance of being understood.

For just a taste of what you might strike, see our "Glossary of Net language" on p.407.

IRC netiquette

IRC attracts a diverse bunch. You're as likely to encounter a channel full of Indian expats following a ball-by-ball cricket commentary as a couple of college kids flirting. So long as no-one rocks the boat too much, everyone can coexist in harmony. Of course, there's bound to be a little mayhem now and then, but that usually just adds to the fun of the whole event.

However, some actions are generally frowned upon and may get you kicked from channels, or even banned from a server. These include dumping large files or amounts of text to a channel, harassment, vulgarity, beeping channels constantly to get attention, and inviting people into inappropriate channels. Finally, if you make a big enough nuisance of yourself, someone might be vindictive enough to track you down and make you regret it.

What and Who's on

Although most of what goes on in IRC is spontaneous, it also hosts loads of organized events, like **celebrity interviews and topical debates**. The big ones tend to hide within the confines of the Online Services but the Net still attracts its share. For a calendar of what's planned across all forms of Internet chat, including the

structured Web-based alternatives, like Talk City:
(http://www.talkcity.com), see Today's Chat Schedule:
http://www.yack.com

And if you'd like to know when your friends are online, get them to grab **ICQ** from: http://www.mirabilis.com

IRC games

Many IRC channels are dedicated to **games**. You can sometimes play against other people, although more commonly you're up against programs called **"bots."** Such programs are written to respond to requests in a particular way, and even learn from the experience.

To find out more about IRC games, send:
info irc-games to listserv@netcom.com or see:
http://phobos.cs.ucdavis.edu:8001/~mock/irc.html
and http://www.yahoo.com/Recreation/Games/Internet_Games/

Internet telephony

The concept of using the Internet as an alternative to the telephone network is getting some quarters quite excited – mainly because it can **cut the cost of calling long distance** to that of a local call. But it's an area that's well and truly in its teething phase. Although it works, don't expect the same fidelity as your local regular phone network.

To make a Net call, you need a **soundcard, speakers**, and a **microphone** – standard multimedia fare. If your soundcard permits duplex transmission, you can hold a regular conversation,

like an ordinary telephone, otherwise it's more like a walkie-talkie where you take turns to speak. As for your modem, generally 14.4kbps is ample to the task but the higher the bandwidth at each end, the better your chance of decent sound quality.

There are plenty of **Net phone programs**. There's even one built into Netscape's browsers. Some, like **Internet Phone**, work very similarly to IRC – you log into a server and join a channel. Others, such as **WebPhone**, are more like an ordinary phone and start a point-to-point connection when you choose a name from a directory. It's worth trying a few to see what works best for your setup. **Microsoft NetMeeting** is as good as any. It has real-time voice and video conferencing, plus things like collaborative application sharing, document editing, background file transfer, and a whiteboard to draw and paste on. Plus it's free.

You'll find a variety of these clients in our "Software Roundup" (see p.370).

Video conferencing

You might like the idea of being able to see who you're talking to, but even with ISDN connections and snazzy graphics hardware, **Internet video conferencing** is more like a slide show than real-time video. But if it means seeing live footage of a loved one across the world, perhaps it's worth it, even at 14.4 kbps.

Again, see our "Software Roundup" (p.370) for a selection of video-conferencing programs.

Chat worlds

There's no doubt Virtual Reality can look quite cute, but there's not much call for it. The best applications so far seem to be among the plethora of **chat worlds**, **virtual cities**, and **avatars**. These tend to work like IRC, but with an extra dimension or two. So rather than channels, you get rooms, playgrounds, swimming pools, and so forth. To switch channels, you might walk into another building or fly up into the clouds. You might be represented by an animated character rather than a text nickname and be able to do all sorts of multimedia things like build 3D objects and play music.

This all sounds pretty futuristic and it's certainly impressive at first, but whether you'll want to become a

regular is another matter. Some interesting ones include **World's Chat**, **The Palace**, and **VizScape**. Microsoft's **Comic Chat** is also worth a quick look. You take on a cartoon character persona, and the chat creates a comic strip; it should keep you amused for several minutes. Once again, you'll find these programs detailed in our "Software Roundup" (p.370).

If it's action and hi-tech graphics you're after, however, ditch chat, and head straight to the world of Online Gaming. Read on . . .

Online Gaming

Playing games against a computer is dull: you'll win only if it lets you. Fire up Quake, Duke Nukem, or Command & Conquer on a lone PC, and you may become adept with virtual cutlery like chainsaws, flame tanks, and rocket-propelled grenades – but you'll only take on a level of computer generated menace you feel safe against. But over the Internet, playing against real people – people you may never have met – such games take on a whole new dimension. Things can get a whole lot more serious.

Back in the 1980s, as computers invaded homes, a few games let players compete against each other through joysticks or a shared a keyboard, while other battles could be waged on game-dedicated consoles. Today, multi-player racing and martial arts games dominate the arcade, while at home players compete on the same games by **connecting two personal computers** together. These machines needn't be in the same room. Or even in the same country. So, serious gamers no longer loiter in arcades. Not when they can have more fun in their bedrooms playing online.

Multi-player gaming is becoming a standard feature in most new games and it's not all shoot-em-up and knock-em-down, either. Any computer game that can be played by two or more people can be played online – from Snakes and Ladders up. Current hot numbers include: Command & Conquer, Warcraft, Doom, Marathon, Chessmaster 5000, Hornet FA-18, Descent,

Mech Warrior, CivNet, Panzer General, Caesar's Palace Virtual Casino, Monopoly, You Don't Know Jack, Diablo, Commanche 3, and SimCity 2000.

Come on in – we won't hurt you

To bring in another player to a computer game, you'll need to connect to their machine. The simplest way is via a **serial link**. Just run a null modem cable between your serial ports. It's a fast connection, and quick to set up, but restricts it to two players at cable's length apart. The same can be done over a **telephone line**, using modems or ISDN terminal adapters. Again it only links two players and is limited by the speed of the modem.

To conscript more victims, you need a proper network. A **local area network (LAN)** is best. That's where you connect all the machines via network cards and cables. It doesn't cost much to set up at home, though everyone will have to bring their machines round. Easier still is to use a LAN at work. Just be sure to invite your boss to take the flak if things go wobbly.

Online gaming

A far easier way to find new opponents, or someone who'll play you at 4 am, is to chime into a public network – such as the **Internet**.

This can be done from a few different angles. **Commercial services** such as **Mplayer** (http://www.mplayer. com), Engage (http://www.engagegames.net) and **Dwango** (http://www.dwango.com) provide Internet accessible game servers. You log in via your ISP or Online Service, sometimes paying a premium above your regular Internet access charges. In turn your ISP may give priority to your gaming traffic to help smooth play.

Then there are **dial-up networks** set aside solely for gaming, sometimes with Internet access thrown on top. For example, **E-On** (http://www.e-on.com), **Wireplay** (http://www.wireplay.co.uk), **Thrustworld** (http://www.thrust.co.uk), **Internet Gaming Zone** (http://www.zone.com) and **Ten** (http://www.ten.net). Almost all **Online Services**, and many **ISPs**, also have local gaming servers set aside for exclusive customer use.

Another recent trend is for game software houses to set up their own **game servers** as part of the product package, like **Battle.net** (http://www.battle.net) for Diablo, and **Bezerk** (http://www.bezerk.com) for You Don't Know

Jack. It's also possible, though trickier, to play **across the Net** directly without logging into a special server by configuring the game to find all the players' Internet (IP) addresses.

The problem with Internet Gaming

Although it's undoubtedly the easiest way to meet other players, the Net has its drawbacks for games that require split second reactions. **Latency** is the biggest issue. That's the length of time it takes data to reach its destination. If it takes too long on a fast game like Quake, it becomes unplayable. Then there's **packet loss**. That's where segments of data fail to reach the other end and must be retransmitted. This has the same effect as high latency.

Game designers are now writing latency correction algorithms which attempt to predict likely moves. The first, built into QuakeWorld (see below), works better than you might imagine. However players with lower latency times, usually those close to the server, will always be at a distinct advantage, making the game unfair. On the plus side, those who play on their ISP's server or on a non-Internet dial-in server, are hardly affected by latency.

IPX and Kali

Network games which use the Internet's TCP/IP protocol are virtually plug and play on the Internet. However, older games such as Warcraft 2, Descent, Command & Conquer, Doom 2, and Duke Nukem 3D rely on the Local Area Network protocol, **IPX**.

The most popular way around this is to use an IPX to IP emulating program like **Kali** to sit between the game and the Internet. This way almost any network game

can be used over the Internet by logging into a Kali server or even directly between two PCs. More about Kali, the world's largest Internet gaming network with over 350 servers in 54 countries, can be found at: http://www.kali.net

QuakeWorld

id Software's **Quake** was the first major game designed primarily for online play. Over a network, it's usual to switch off the 'monsters' and fight with or against other players. You can compete independently or in teams, in some cases with a mission to capture the enemy's flag. Serious Quakers form clans, complete with their own custom designed outfits, called skins. Clan members compete side by side against other clans or individuals.

QuakeWorld is a special version of online Quake with several enhancements such as enabling players to compensate for latency lags. It's fun, but with up to 32 players, can get crowded at times. That's where **QuakeSpy** comes in handy. It's a program which works with Quake to find the closest server with the lowest latency and the ideal number of opponents. For more see http://www.blues-news.com and http://www.stomped.com

Where to find the real twist tops

Remember those ancient **text-based games** where you'd stumble around imaginary kingdoms looking for hidden objects, uttering magic words, and slaying unicorns? Believe it or not, they're still going strong on the Net. Admittedly, they've come a long way, and blended with the whole Dungeons and Dragons caper, but they're still mostly text. That's "mostly," because a few are starting to appear with **graphical interfaces**.

What sets them apart from conventional arcade games is the community spirit. Within each game, participants develop **complex alter egos** enabling them to live out their fantasies and have them accepted within the group. But it can also become an obsession where the distinction between an alter ego and the self becomes blurred, and players retreat into the reassurance of the game. If they're dialing in from a home account, it can also become an expensive one. In other words, it's about as geeky as it gets. If that sounds your bag, see http:www.cis.upenn.edu/~lwl/mudinfo.html and the newsgroup hierarchies: alt.mud and rec.games.mud

Somewhat up the evolutionary ladder graphically, but along similar lines, **Ultima Online**, the latest in the Ultima fantasy series, promises a continuous, evolving virtual world, complete with day and night. The idea being to create not only a battleground, but a social community for thousands of players. Again, unlike strictly competitive games, the object is to play a role, and belong, rather than win. See http://www.owo.com

For more information

Magazines, like *Netgamer* (http://www.netgamer.net), *Computer & Netplayer* (http://www.ogr.com) and *Computer Gaming World* (http://www.zdnet.com/cgwuk/) are often the best place to find out what's hot in online gaming. Not just because gaming companies send them software evaluations early, but because they invariably come with a free CD ROM full of games. Although you can generally get game programs off the Net sooner, with some games weighing in at over 20 Mbs, it's a worthy save in download time. Especially when you'll flick most of them out after a few minutes.

On the Net, the best source of news and downloads are the main **games Web sites** (see p.258).

On the Road

Wherever you travel, if you can get to a phone line, you can get to your email. Unlike a phone number, fax number, or postal address, you can take your email address anywhere, picking up and sending your mail as if you were home. Read on and we'll show how the Internet can liberate you from your desk.

Going Portable

Anyone who's serious about work mobility has a **laptop (notebook) computer**, often as a desktop replacement. After all, almost anything you can do on a desktop you can do on a portable. And although at present, they're still more expensive than their bulkier equivalents – and lag slightly in chip, video, and sound technology – that margin is rapidly closing. When shopping around, here are a few things to look out for:

Weight: No matter how small a laptop might seem in the shop, it's a different experience carrying it over your shoulder for a few hours. Get one that's light.

Power: If you plan to use it on a plane, in your car, or anywhere away from a power socket, go for long battery life and consider a spare. Also ensure your power adapter supports dual voltage (100-240 V and 50/60 HZ). It's becoming standard on notebooks, but still double check before you buy. A built-in transformer is an added bonus, as it cuts space and weight.

Modem: Another space saver is a built-in modem, or failing that, one that plugs into the PCMCIA slot. Neither need an external power source so that cuts down on leads as well. If you can, get one that is flash-upgradable to higher speeds. There's also a new breed of PC cards that combine a **mobile phone and modem**. For details, see: http://www.option.com/fifo.htm

Network card: Modems are convenient but nowhere near as fast or as cheap as hooking into a corporate network. If you're on business, visiting a branch office, ask the IT manager to fill in your network settings. Now, that's luxury. But only practical if you plan to spend extended time there. Otherwise it's the back to the phone jack.

Warranty: Having a notebook go down with all your mail and data onboard is one of life's least rewarding experiences. If you can have a replacement shipped to you anywhere in the world the minute you have problems you'll never regret having paid a bit extra.

Scaling down

If the risk of having your $5,000 technological triumph shorted by tropical rain, or filched from your backpack, makes your skin creep, look at taking something smaller and/or cheaper. Exactly what, depends on how small or cheap you want to go, and why you need it.

If reducing size and weight without losing features is the issue, then look towards **sub-notebooks** and **palmtops** that can run Windows 95 programs. But they'll cost as much as, if not more than, their larger equivalents. If price is the key, or you just need a powerful organizer, consider something like the **Psion Organiser**, **US Robotics Pilot**, or **Apple MessagePad**, that combine basic office programs with Net connectivity, and can upload later to your main machine.

Scaling down further, you can collect your email, and surf the Web (just), with a **Nokia 9000 mobile phone**. Or, if you only need to receive mail, see what your local paging services have to offer. These, however, only work within one country.

An address that moves with you

Once you have a reliable fixed email address, no matter where you roam, people can reach you. Put it on your business card and say, "If you want a swift reply, email me." You might shift house, business, city, or country, but your email address need never change. So,

Road Trip '97

take care when choosing your address as it might become your virtual home for years to come. For more on email addresses, see p.67. Here's how to use the various types on the move:

POP3 and IMAP

Almost all ISP mail accounts these days are **POP3** (ask your provider if you're unsure), and so long as you can get full Internet access, accessing your POP3 account is a doddle.

If you're taking **your computer** with you, it's doubly easy. You don't even have to change your mail settings – only your dial-up configuration. On **another computer**, to collect mail you need to enter your user name, your incoming mail server address, and your password, when prompted. To send email you also need to enter your identity (who you want your mail to appear it's come from), and your return address (your email address). Although you can use your regular outgoing mailserver address, you'll get a faster response if you use the one maintained by the ISP through whom you're dialing. So if the machine you're using has one set, leave it be.

If your connection's slow or difficult, you can configure your mail program to download the first 1 kb or so of each message and then select which you want to read. Alternatively, if your mailserver supports **IMAP** (a superior form of POP mail which allows you to manage mail on the server – again, ask your provider), you can download just the headers. So when you're up in a plane paying 14¢ per second to download at 2400 bps you can leave all those massive mail list digests for later.

Another way to be efficient on the move is to maintain a particular address for **priority mail**.

Web-based mail

With Web-based mail accounts like **Hotmail** and **Rocket-Mail**, you can send and collect email on any machine with access to the **Web**. If you don't already have an account, visit their home pages on the Web (see p.68) and you'll be granted one, free, right away. When you access mail, you don't need to change any settings on the computer you're using; you just log into your account using a Web browser. The accounts have another plus in that you can scan through your headers first and retrieve only what interests you. HotMail also provides a way to read your POP3 mail on the Web.

A few ISPs – for example **UUNet Pipex** in the UK – also provide a Web interface for their email accounts. So you can just dial into their Web page, from any machine, enter your email address and password, and read your mail.

The disadvantage to all these accounts is that you need Web access, which can make things slow or impossible over low bandwidth connections.

CompuServe's global connection

Probably the biggest advantage of CompuServe is its truly global range of dial-up points of presence. You can dial indirect to a CompuServe number in pretty much any country in the world (see p.48).

Hats off to CompuServe, too, for providing an extra and bizarre way to collect your mail. You can call a toll-free number, punch in your account number and PIN, and have your **mail selectively read back to you over the phone**. This service also doubles as an international phone calling card. In CompuServe, GO Globalconnect.

AOL mail

Like CompuServe, AOL has heaps of international points of presence. Its drawback is that to collect mail you have to use **AOL's own software**. However, you **don't have to dial AOL** itself. If you go to Setup and change the Network setting under the Location from AOLnet to TCP/IP, you'll be able to access AOL over any full Internet connection. That's easy enough if you have your own machine, or you can get to one that has AOL. However if you're traveling outside the US, it would be wise to carry a CD ROM with AOL on it, just in case.

Telnet

Many universities and workplaces don't maintain POP3 mail accounts. If that applies to you, you might have to use **Telnet** to log in. Once you get over the indignity of not being able to point and click, it's not so bad.

Telenet involves logging into your mail server over the Net, supplying identification, then **typing commands** into a UNIX mail program. You can also read your POP3 email by Telnetting to your mailserver on port 110, entering user then your user name, pass then your password, and list to list your messages. To read messages selectively, type retr followed by the message's number. This can be handy when you're operating over a very low bandwidth or limited by software, for example with a palmtop. Ask your ISP or systems manager for further instructions.

How to stay connected

Keeping in touch needn't mean expensive long-distance calls home to your provider. It's possible to travel the world on a single **ISP account**, dialing locally wherever you are. Depending on your deal and where you travel between, that should work out considerably cheaper – though if you only need to dial in every few days, then calling long distance with a discount calling card may be both practical and economical. Only you can tell what suits you best, but these are your most likely options:

Cybercafés and Net terminals

When you're traveling without hardware, you have to use someone else's machine. If you can't get to one through a friend or work, look for somewhere to rent Internet time. That's most commonly available through so-called **cybercafés**. These are basically coffee shops or bars, with a few Net-connected computers up for public use. You generally pay by the half hour.

Cybercafés appear and disappear overnight but they can be a traveler's best resource. If you're new to the Net, they can double as somewhere to test drive it under supervision. Or if you're after a temporary account on your travels they can point you to a provider. Most of all though, they're an easy access point to do your email.

Whether you're using a cybercafé or someone else's computer, the procedure is the same. Look for a **mail program**. There should be one attached to the Web browser. If not, chances are they use Eudora. Open the settings, and fill out your details as described above (under "POP 3" – see p.178). Then set it to "leave mail on server," and "CC" yourself everything you send. That way when you get back to your main machine, and download for the first time, you'll have a record of all your correspondence. Once you've finished, delete all your mail (don't forget the "sent" box), and change the settings back.

To **find a cybercafé** before you leave, try the following directories: Internet Café Guide (http://www.netcafeguide.com), Cybercafés of Europe: (http://www.xs4all.nl/~bertb/cybercaf.html), and Yahoo: (http://www.yahoo.com/Society_and_Culture/Cyberculture/Internet_Cafes/)

If that fails, look in the local computer press or ask at a computer store or library when you arrive. And keep your eye out for Netbooths in places like airports, major hotels, or shopping malls. They're like public phones, except with a computer screen instead of escort ads.

National ISPs

Most of the **ISPs in our directory** (see p.427) have national coverage or at least multiple dial-up points across a country. But this doesn't mean they'll have local call access everywhere – it may be restricted to major urban areas. Before you sign with a provider, ensure it covers your territory at local call rates. Many ISPs, particularly in the US and Australia, have a national number charged at a higher rate. Check that first and do your sums. All our listed UK providers have local call access throughout Britain.

International ISPs

Several **Online Services** and **ISPs** have international points of presence (POPs). These include:

AOL: Although AOL has POPs in more than 100 countries, many are serviced by third-party networks. Outside the UK, North America, and select European cities, you'll be hit with a surcharge. For full details, log onto AOL and type Global

APC: Set up mainly to link non-governmental organizations and social activists worldwide, APC is represented by GreenNet in the UK, IGC in the US, and Pegasus in Australia. APC members in more far-flung places like Ethiopia might not have full Internet access, but you could get your mail forwarded if you plan ahead. See: http://www.apc.org/dial.html

CompuServe: Nothing will get you up and running faster when you land in a new city than a CompuServe account. Like AOL, though, it relies on variety of networks once you stray a little. And once again, pricing varies between countries. It's never going to be as a cheap as a local ISP. But you can treat it like any ISP, forgo its software and dial through, say, Windows 95 Dial-up networking.

However at the time of writing not all countries offer full IP, and some require a different dial-up script. If you intend to visit any such countries you'd better keep a copy of CIM handy (easy enough on a CD Rom). Then its just a matter of picking the network from a drop-down menu. Of course, if it's not full IP you won't be able to browse the Web, or pick up your POP3 mail. But you will be able to use CompuServe mail. Best to do your research before you set out. You'll find all you need to know at: GO Phones

EUNet: The leading Europe-based ISP, EUNet maintains local POPs in most of Europe, the former USSR, North Africa, and North America. Charges are US$40.00 for the first 90 minutes than 12¢ per minute thereafter. See http://traveller.eu.net

IBM Internet Connection: Big Blue subscribers get full reciprocal Internet access in over 50 countries – though charges vary between regions. Outside the US, it's aimed more at the corporate user. See http://www.ibm.net

Microsoft Network: Just click on the icon in Windows 95 for details of MSN's full Internet access in worldwide centers including the US, UK, Australia, France, Germany, Canada, and Japan. Or see http://www.msn.com

Netcom: Local call access is offered throughout much of North America, and the entire UK, plus global roaming through GRIC. (see below). More details at http://www.netcom.com and http://www.netcom.net.uk

Prodigy: With ventures in China, Africa, and Latin America you'd expect reciprocal access from Prodigy, however as yet it hasn't been announced. At this stage, it's restricted to North America. If you're venturing into the regions above, though, it might be worth calling to see if you can secure a local account before you leave. See http://www.prodigy.com

UUNet: UUNet/Pipex Dial subscribers can pay extra for a month (or more) reciprocal international access – in the US or Europe. The network also offers free Web-based mail through their Web page. For more, see http://www.dial.pipex.com/services/roaming/

Global roamers

Another way of ensuring international access is to join an ISP that belongs to a **global roaming group**. This means you can dial into any ISP in the group. However you'll be billed by the minute for the convenience. That is fine for email but if you plan to surf the Web abroad, it might be better value signing up with a local. See GRIC (http://www.aimquest.com) and the i-Pass Alliance (http://www.ipass.com) for their lists of participating ISPs, or to access i-Pass members without a home account, see HomeGate (http://www.homegate.net).

Jacking in

No matter what your account, you'll get nowhere fast if you can't get your modem talking to the phone system. This is where it can get a bit technical, especially when you're abroad, so be prepared to roll up your sleeves. Here's what you should know:

Foreign plugs

If you think the variety of power plugs is crazy, wait until you travel Europe with a laptop and modem. There are six different varieties of phone jacks in Germany alone. Nevertheless, thanks to wired  travelers, the US **RJ11 plug** is becoming somewhat of a world standard.

Trouble is, some countries use this plug but connect the two wires to different pins. So, before you set out, get a **lead/adapter** that plugs into your modem at one end with a US-wired RJ11 plug/socket at the other. As long as you travel with this setup, you'll have no trouble finding an adapter at a local airport, electrical store, or market. Or if you'd like to prepare in advance, grab a plug bundle such as TeleAdapt's Laptop Lifeline. (http://www.teleadapt.com)

Dial tone detect

It's a rare modem that's smart enough to recognize every foreign dial tone, and if it's been instructed to **wait for a tone before dialing**, you mightn't get anywhere. If dial tone errors persist, or your modem refuses to dial, switch this setting off. It's usually as simple as checking a box in your dialer. If not, you'll need to insert the **Hayes command X1** into the modem's initialization string. Refer to your modem manual for more on initialization strings.

Then there is the question of **pulse or tone**? Pick up a phone and dial. If it sends beeps, set it to tone dialing. If it makes clicking sounds, set it to pulse.

Manual dialing

Sometimes you need to dial with a **phone in parallel**. For example, if you have to go through an operator or calling card company, or if the phone system won't recognize your modem's tones. If that's the case, **turn the dial detect off** and set it to dial a short number, say 123. Have it ready to dial with one key press or mouse click. Now, dial your provider with the phone. When the other modem answers, press, or click, to fire off your dialer. As soon as you hear the two modems handshaking, hang up the phone and you'll be away.

Public phones

In the US, Australia, and Asia (though rarely at present in Europe), an increasing number of phones at airports, convention centers, and hotel lobbies have modem ports – generally RJ11 sockets. Other public phones can be

used by means of an **acoustic coupler**, which you just strap over the handset. TeleAdapt sells a useful one that transfers as high as 24 kbps. Roadwarrior's (http://www.warrior.com) will do up to 28.8 kbps.

If the phone uses a carbon microphone, neither will get better than 2400 bps. However you connect, you'll need to dial manually (see above).

Planes

Don't set your hopes too high on surfing the Net at 35,000 feet. Yes, with the wide-scale introduction of **satellite telephony** in planes, it's possible. But, at present it's limited to a speed of 2400 bps, with 9600 bps some way on the horizon. At up to US$10.00 per minute, it's also more suited to urgent email.

Digital PBX

Most offices and hotels run their own **internal PBX phone systems**. What matters to you is whether the extensions are hooked to the exchange using **digital** or **analogue** techniques. If it's digital, your modem won't like it. At worst, it could cause damage. If you strike a digital system, look around for an alternative line. Try the fax line, for starters. Otherwise, you might need to use an acoustic coupler or a device like TeleAdapt's **TeleSwitch** or Road Warrior's **Modem Doubler** to tap you in between the handpiece and the phoneset.

Hard wiring

More often than not, hotel phones are wired directly into wall sockets. If you don't have an acoustic coupler, you'll have to tap in which means a couple of light accessories. Before you set out, pick up a **telephone line tester** and a **short patch cord** with an RJ11 female socket at one end

and a pair of alligator clips on the other. You can get both from TeleAdapt, Road Warrior, or any good computer store. If you can't get a patch cord it's easy enough to make – just find an extension lead, cut off the male end and crimp clips to the right two wires (usually the red and green, but use your line tester for confirmation). You'll find clips at any electronic store.

When you're ready to operate, fish around for something to unscrew that will expose wires. Inside the mouthpiece is sometimes a good bet. Once you've tapped in, check the polarity with the line tester. Keep trying wires until you get the green light. That's all there is to it. Just plug in to your new extension and dial.

Dropouts

If you keep losing your connection, it could be something simple. First check that **"call waiting"** is switched off. Those beeps that tell you someone's waiting will knock out your modem every time. Next, **unplug any phones that share the same line**. Some phones draw current from the line every few minutes to keep all those numbers stored in memory.

It could also be the **secret police** bugging your line. Don't laugh, it happens in certain countries. And after all, if your hotel cleaner spots you hunched on the floor tapping in messages, jacked in through a nest of clips and wires, you probably will look a bit suspicious.

Mostly, however, it's just a noisy line and there's nothing you can do.

Tax impulsing

A few countries – Austria, Belgium, Czech Republic, Germany, India, Spain, and Switzerland, among them – send metering pulses down the line to measure call times. Unless your modem is approved in these countries, the pulses will slow down or knock out your connection. A solution is to fit a filter, such as TeleAdapt's **TeleFilter**, between your modem and the line.

Faxes and voicemail

Although thanks to email, the fax's days are clearly numbered, many still cling to this antediluvian protocol. But what to do if your fax is in Phoenix, and you're in Foochow? **Jfax** (http://www.jfax.com) has the answer. It can allocate you a phone number in one of several cities worldwide. Any fax sent to this number is converted to an email attachment and redirected to your email address. It can also take voicemail messages, forwarding them on as highly-compressed audio files.

Most **Online Services** offer this, or a similar, service, as do several large ISPs such as **UUNet** (http://www.uu.net) and **PSInet** (http://www.psi.net).

Further info

As the world wakes up to this new era of computer mobility, you'll see loads of new products and new opportunities.

For **general news** read Mobilis (http://www.volksware.com/mobilis/) and On the Road (http://www.roadnews.com). For tips on how to **connect worldwide**, see Help for World Travelers (http://www.cris.com/~Kropla/). For **adapters, insurance, advice, and support** see: TeleAdapt (http://www.teleadapt.com) and Road Warrior (http://www.warrior.com). And for more on **portable computers** see Notebook Jungle (http://www.lynge-mark.com/jungle/) and LapLand (http://www.ccia.com/~wsw/lapland/).

PART TWO

The Guide

World Wide Web
Usenet Newsgroups
Software Roundup

A Guide to World Wide Web Sites

No-one knows exactly how many addresses are accessible from the World Wide Web. Hundreds of millions, probably. But that's not just Web pages. Its tentacles also reach into Usenet, Gopher, Telnet, and FTP, through links embedded into the pages. The Web itself, though, is the most popular part. It's a little like having your own library, chocked with magazines, music, business catalogs, academic journals, and fanzines from just about every obsessive, enthusiast, and wacko out there.

Technically, Web site addresses start with the prefix http: – anything else, although accessible from the Web, really belongs to another system. What sets the Web apart is its hypertextual navigation. Any Web page can link to any other Web page, whether it's on the same system or on the other side of the world.

Almost all Web sites contain links to similar sites as well as to some of general interest. It's entirely up to the whim of whoever owns the site. For example, at the Virtual Pub, you'll find original content as well as links to other beer-related sites. Take one of those links, and you'll most likely arrive at another site with links to even more related sites. So even though there are only about 800 sites reviewed in the following pages, they'll lead you to millions more.

Finding what you want

The keys to finding your way around the Web are the **Internet search tools and directories**. They're listed first. See "Finding It" (p.125), for how to use them.

How to get there

To reach a site, carefully enter its **address** (taking note of capitalization) into your browser's **URL, Location, or Address** window. Neither Netscape nor Internet Explorer, requires you type the http:// part of the address, so just type in whatever comes after the //.

How to find a site again

When you see something you like, save its address to your **bookmarks**, **favorites**, or **hotlist**. To find it later, just click on its name in the list. Or you could read it offline by saving the page to disk or retrieving it from cache. For instructions, see "Surfing the World Wide Web" (p.105).

When it's not there

Some of our listed sites will have disappeared or changed address. But don't let that deter you. Refer to "Finding It" (p.125) for advice on how to track them down. The easiest way is to enter the title, and/or related subjects, as keywords into one of the search engines such as HotBot, Altavista, or InfoSeek. Once you've mastered the Internet Search Tools and Directories, you'll be able to find anything. So, wax up and get out there!

Web Sites Directory

Most human life has found its way onto the World Wide Web, so it doesn't easily lend itself to **categorization**.

We've adopted the following headings to make our listings easier to navigate. However they do tend to blur into each other at the slightest opportunity. So, if you're into music, you might want to explore "Music," "Entertainment," "Ezines," "Shopping," and "News, Newspapers, and Magazines." If you're up for fun, check under "Comedy," "Entertainment," "Weird," "Ezines,"and "Games," and so on. To search the net by **subject or keyword**, try out some of the tools in our "Search Tools and Net Directories" section.

THE ROUGH GUIDE TO THE INTERNET – ON THE NET

We've posted the whole of this Web Guide section on the Net itself at the Rough Guides' home site. So rather than type each of these addresses individually, simply browse this chapter, get an idea of what you'd like to see, go online, then type: http://www.roughguides.com/net/ and follow the links from there.

PART ONE

SEARCH TOOLS AND DIRECTORIES

First, the sites you need to get you started and help you find your way around the Web.

THE SEARCH POWERHOUSES

These are the most comprehensive search engines and directories. They'll enable you to find just about anything you might want. Get to know them all in depth, compare their services, and come to your own conclusions about which is best for what. Save their addresses somewhere convenient as you're sure to return often.

Our search engine choice is Altavista when we're in a hurry and expect results in the first few hits, HotBot for serious searches, then Excite for extra depth.

For directories, Yahoo has the greatest breadth, Lycos 5% and Magellan are big but still subjective, and the Internet Directory is the freshest.

Most of the following have international versions, personal editions, and a host of other services tacked on. Although, in many cases such facilities are fed from other sites.

Altavista

http://www.altavista.digital.com

Web and Usenet searches. Huge, fast, multilingual, and discriminate.

DejaNews

http://www.dejanews.com

Largest archive of Usenet articles. Best for profiling users, reading old articles, and finding the right group to join, but you might find HotBot gives better relevancy for recent posts.

Excite

http://www.excite.com

Possibly the largest and freshest Web/Usenet database, but requires fine key word tweaking to get relevant results. Also maintains a reasonable site directory with some ratings. Comes in several international editions all padded out with a plethora of services like TV listings, news, weather, stock quotes, people finding, email lookup, flight booking, maps, and yellow pages.

HotBot

http://www.hotbot.com

First-class Web/Usenet database, sponsored by *HotWired*, with several useful search options. Particularly adept at finding instances of people's names on sites. Supremely discriminate and easy to tune, and gives 100 results per time.

InfoSeek

http://www.infoseek.com

Search the Web, Usenet, various newswires, and Web FAQs plus loads of other services similar to Excite. Easy to search, discriminatory, but with a smaller Web database than Altavista, and not always that fresh.

Lycos

http://www.lycos.com

Various services, like news, city guides, and maps. Differs
between countries. Its Web search, Lycos Pro, is highly
discriminate due to a fancy Java front end though flawed by
a small database. Still, you can weave through Web directory
hell to Point's Top 5% of the Web (whatever that means) and
see what it rates as the strongest sites in each genre.

Magellan

http://www.mckinley.com

Another massive directory, which reviews and rates sites.
But don't bother with its Web search.

Yahoo

http://www.yahoo.com

This is the closest the Net has to a central directory. Big and
easy to navigate by subject, though light on reviews. Loads
of specialist stuff like national and metropolitan directories,
weather reports, kids guides, yellow pages, sport scores, plus
outstanding news and financial services. Essential.

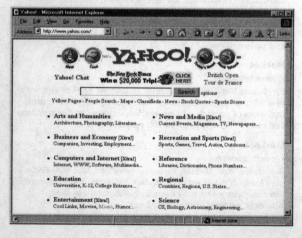

What's On

http://www.whatson.com

> Hosts more than just one essential site. Includes: What's New, the Net's main listing of brand new Web sites; its UK archives, the Internet Directory; a countdown of the top ten sites of the week; the Cool Site of the Day, and a guide to What's On Stage in the UK.

OTHER DIRECTORIES AND SEARCH AIDS

Argus Clearinghouse

http://www.clearinghouse.net

> There are thousands of specialist Web directories, so this selection is hardly exhaustive, but it's meticulously maintained. Crack open the most interesting categories and bookmark anything that might be useful later. You never know.

Ask Jeeves

http://www.askjeeves.com

> Ask questions in plain English for replies that are often more intriguing than useful. Searches several engines, plus its own database simultaneously.

Disinformation

http://www.disinfo.com

> Archives the dark side of politics, religious fervor, new science, and the current affairs you seldom read about in the dailies.

Electric Library

http://www.elibrary.com

> Simultaneously searches databases of newspapers, magazines, newswires, classic books, maps, photographs, and major artworks.

EuroSeek

http://www.euroseek.net

> Multilingual European Web search and directory.

Gopher Searching

gopher://gopher.scs.unr.edu

Find text stored in Gophers using Gopher Jewels or
Veronica. Primarily used by technological retards.

IBM InfoMarket

http://www.infomarket.ibm.com

Searches a wide selection of places that search engines miss
like technical journals, newsletters, newspapers, newswires
and corporate databases. See also NlightN: http://www.nlightn.com

Internet Sleuth

http://www.isleuth.com

Front end to search over 2000 Web and specialist databases,
more than one at a time. However it's usually more efficient
to search each site directly. So use this listing to find it.

Internet Tools

http://www.itools.com

All-in-one search, publicity forms, currency rates, parcel
tracking, dictionaries, pronunciation aids, and you name it.

LookSmart

http://www.looksmart.com

Readers Digest's Web directory. Every link includes a comment.

The Mining company

http://miningco.com

Site directory with purportedly 'expert' guides. Adds a
personal touch.

New Rider's Official Yellow Pages

http://www.mcp.com/nrp/wwwyp/

Online edition of that plump yellow Web guide.

Regional Directories

http://www.edirectory.com

Nearly every country, and for that matter US state, has at
least one Web directory all to itself. You won't find them all
here, but it's still a mighty big list.

Starting Point

http://www.stpt.com

Another general directory which aims at best of genre.

UKOnline

http://www.ukonline.com

The Net's biggest resource for everything British.
Particularly noteworthy for its massive Psion software
archive and superb travel section. Essential reference for
bargain flights and transport timetables.

WebSource

http://www.websource.com.au

Everything Australian on the Internet. see also:
http://www.sofcom.com.au/Directories/

What's New

http://www.whatsnew.com

New sites listed as they're announced. Search archives by
category or country.

Wired Source

http://www.wiredsource.com

Wired's selective directory of essential references.

WWW Virtual Library

http://www.w3.org/vl/

Hotch-potch consortium of subject-specific directories
scattered all over the Web.

WWWWomen

http://www.wwwomen.com

Sites that cater to distinctly female interests.

Yell

http://www.yell.co.uk

A highly professional production from UK Yellow Pages, this
is the biggest UK-specific directory and combines a company
A–Z, film finder, and business phone directory.

Your Personal Net

http://www.ypn.com

Neatly reviewed Web, Gopher, and Newsgroup listings, from
Michael Wolff, publisher of *NetGuide*.

BUSINESS AND PHONE DIRECTORIES

Big Book

http://www.bigbook.com

Lists over 16 million US businesses, plus street maps,
reviews, and free home pages.

Big Yellow

http://www.bigyellow.com

Millions of US business listings, plus links to international
business directories and people finders.

Electronic Yellow Pages

http://www.eyp.co.uk

UK business phone directory.

Switchboard

http://www.switchboard.com

Trace people and businesses in the US.

Telstra Yellow Pages

http://www.yellowpages.com.au

Australian business phone directory. Sydney addresses
include UBD maps. Links to the White Pages for residential
numbers and addresses, and Yellow pages in the UK, US,
Canada, Indonesia, Spain, and Sri Lanka.

World Wide Yellow Pages

http://www.yellow.com

Global business contact directory. Search by name, industry,
and location.

EMAIL SEARCH

As soon as you get an email address, submit it to these directories if you want it made public. Most of their databases are drawn from Usenet visitors, so they're in no way complete, but still worth trying. They also integrate with related services like people finders, free email addresses, and who's online with Internet phones.

Bigfoot
http://www.bigfoot.com

Internet Address Finder
http://www.iaf.net

Four11
http://www.four11.com

WhoWhere?
http://www.whowhere.com

LISTS AND PICKS

100 hot Websites
http://www.hot100.com
> The hundred most visited Web sites each week, overall or by category. Not necessarily accurate, but close enough.

Cool Site of the Day
http://cool.infi.net
> This is such a popular pick-list it's sent some winners enough traffic to crash their servers.

Cruel Site of the Day
http://www.cruel.com
> Something horrid daily.

Internet Chartshow
http://www.emap.com/chartshow/
> Top 10 new sites of the week, as chosen by EMAP Online.

Netsurf Central
http://www.netsurfcentral.com
> Hotwired's Web picks of the day.

Netsurfer Digest

http://www.netsurf.com/nsd/

Subscribe to receive weekly site updates and reviews.

Revolving Door

http://asylum.cid.com/revdoor/revdoor.cgi/

Dynamic, quasi-democratic hotlist maintained entirely by
visitors like you.

Top 50 UK Web Sites

http://www.top50.co.uk/list.htm

The top 50 busiest British sites, maybe.

Useless Pages

http://www.go2net.com/internet/useless/

The sludge festering at the bottom of the Net.

Web100

http://www.web100.com

Reviews and ranks the Web's 100 'top' sites.

MAILING LIST DIRECTORIES

InReference

http://www.reference.com

Search Usenet, thousands of mailing lists, and Web
forums.

Liszt

http://www.liszt.com

Over 70,000 mailing lists to flood your inbox, sorted by
topic.

Publicly Accessible Mailing Lists

http://www.neosoft.com/internet/paml/

Thousands of specialist email discussion groups organized
by name or subject, with details on traffic, content, and how
to join.

Search the Net
http://www.statsvet.uu.se/maillist.html
> List of mailing list directories.

SOFTWARE GUIDES

Archie
http://pubweb.nexor.co.uk/public/archie/servers.html
> Find a file on an FTP site, if you know its exact name.

Browser Watch
http://www.browserwatch.com
> All the latest on browsers and plug-ins.

Cool Tools
http://www.cooltool.com
> Something well worth downloading on a regular basis.

Download.com
http://www.download.com
> The latest notable downloads in all categories, for PC and Mac, from CNET.

FTP Search
http://ftpsearch.ntnu.no
> Powerful, but complex, Norwegian FTP search engine.

InfoMac HyperArchive
http://hyperarchive.lcs.mit.edu/HyperArchive/
> HTML dip into the InfoMac Macintosh software pig trough.

Jumbo Shareware
http://www.jumbo.com
> Mammoth shareware archive for all platforms.

Shareware.com
http://www.shareware.com
> Search several major file archives for all platforms.

Shareware top 20

http://www.clicked.com/shareware/

Top 20 shareware picks in several categories, along with reviews.

Snoopie

http://www.snoopie.com

Zippy searches of a crawler-built FTP database.

SoftSeek

http://www.softseek.com

PC downloads reviewed.

Stroud's Consummate Winsock Applications

http://www.stroud.com

Windows Internet applications posted and reviewed as released.

TUCOWs

http://www.tucows.com

More Windows Internet applications.

The Well Connected Mac

http://www.macfaq.com

Guide to Mac software and resources.

Windows 95

http://www.windows95.com

The latest Windows 95 applications and tutorials.

World Catalog of Software Websites

http://ssrl.rtp.com:443/library/

Hundreds of software archives, lists, and developers, sorted by category.

INTERNET STUDIES

CommerceNet

http://www.commerce.net

Industry consortium which promotes and researches Net commerce.

Forrester Research

http://www.forrester.com

Few research firms are as switched on to new media as Boston-based Forrester. Consequently its views on the Internet don't always come free. Those that do are here.

GVU's WWW User Survey

http://www.cc.gatech.edu/gvu/user_surveys/

The biggest and oldest periodic Web user survey. Its latest results show a marked change in profiles, reflecting the Net's convergence with the mainstream.

MIDS

http://www.mids.org

Examines the composition, content, and users, of the Net and other networks in the matrix of computers worldwide that exchange electronic mail. In graphs, maps, or text.

NUA Internet Surveys

http://www.nua.org/surveys/

Leading Internet survey results as they're announced.

Traveloco Global Node Monitor

http://www.traveloco.com/nodes/

See how far the Internet has spread. One site from every country domain around the world.

Values and Lifestyles

http://future.sri.com

The VALS program is digging deeper into the psychographic profiles of Net users with each new questionnaire. Complete the survey and discover whether you're regarded as an Actualizer, Fullfilled, an Achiever, an Experiencer, a Believer, a Striver, a Maker, or a Struggler. Marketeers, like astrologers and royals, need to class people to help justify their existence.

OTHER INTERNET STUFF

Blacklist of Internet Advertisers

http://math-www.uni-paderborn.de/~axel/BL/

How to deal with electronic junk mail and pesky advertisers buzzing your favorite newsgroups. Plus a list of crafty Net abusers, to discourage you from joining their ranks.

Gamelan

http://www.gamelan.com

Java headquarters. Good for finding innovative sites.

GeoCities

http://www.geocities.com

Build your own free "homestead" in the virtual city that suits your style. Done through forms so you needn't know HTML.

GIF Wizard

www.gifwizard.com

Reduce your Web-bound GIF images instantly.

HTML Converters

http://union.ncsa.uiuc.edu/HyperNews/get/www/html/converters.html

Convert almost any document to a Web page.

Name Registration

http://www.internic.net

http://www.netnames.com

http://www.namesecure.com

If you'd like to register your own domain name, try Internic first, but if that all seems too hard then try a third party specialist. Check here first to see if your choice has been taken. The look-up takes seconds.

Newsgroups in Oxford

http://www.lib.ox.ac.uk/internet/news/

Automatically compiled hypertext list of Usenet groups, FAQs, and reviews.

NewzBot

http://www.jammed.com/~newzbot/

If you're behind a firewall at work or your ISP's Usenet coverage is lacking, try an open news server. This list is generated by a bot that looks for open ports. But if it's open unintentionally, and they notice a marked increase in traffic, they may shut the door. Also provides a way to read Usenet postings via the Web.

Realm Graphics

http://www.ender-design.com/rg/

Pinch these background textures, bullets, icons, buttons, and arty bits and put them on your own Web page.

Silicon Toad's Hacking Resources

http://www.silitoad.org

Crawl through the Net's very underbelly. Hackers, crackers, phreakers, and warez traders – it's business as usual here in Geek Alley.

Scambusters

http://www.scambusters.org

Bulletins exposing the sharks who prey on gullible Net newbies.

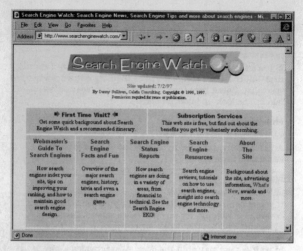

Search Engine Watch

http://www.searchenginewatch.com

Don't believe any search engine's hype about being it the biggest or freshest. Don't even believe what you read in magazines. Here's the truth.

Six Degrees

http://www.sixdegrees.com

Network the Net, by submitting all your friends' email addresses.

URL Minder

http://www.netmind.com

Alerts you when a Web page changes.

World Wide Web Consortium

http://www.w3.org

Read all the hard core technical specs on the Web's next generation.

PART TWO

WEB SITES SUBJECT GUIDE

First off, a disclaimer. This isn't a definitive guide to the best Web sites. That just isn't possible any more: there are too many sites, and besides, it's a matter of taste. However the range here should be broad enough, and each site should contain enough links, to eventually get you where you want to go. So, happy clicking!

ART AND PHOTOGRAPHY

24 hours in Cyberspace
http://www.cyber24.com
Collective output of over 1000 photographers and 100 photojournalists documenting the impact of the digital revolution on 8 February 1996, everywhere from the Sahara to Times Square.

Americans for the Arts
http://www.artsusa.org/clearinghouse.html
US government sponsored index to the arts, focusing mainly on how to get your mitts on the gravy.

Art on the Net
http://www.art.net
Exhibits from all sorts who call themselves artists, from hackers to – potentially – you.

ArtAIDS Link
http://www.illumin.co.uk/artaids/
Internet equivalent of the AIDS patchwork quilt. Upload your own tribute to this ever-growing mosaic of love, loss, and memory.

Big Fire Anime
http://www.bigfire.com/bigfire.htm
Monstrous archive of Japanese cartoon art and software.

Chankstore Freefonts

http://www.chank.com/freefonts.html

Download a new whacked out Chank Diesel display font free each week.

Comics Page

http://www.comics-page.com

Even with a fast, fat connection, reading comics on the Net can be pretty tedious. But if you're into them as a communications medium, or art form, there's ample here.

Computer Graphics

http://mambo.ucsc.edu/psl/cg.html

List of computer-generated art resources.

Core-Industrial Design Resources

http://www.core77.com

Industrial design exhibits, jobs, chat, and tips on how to get yourself seen.

Font Net

http://www.type.co.uk

As with almost everything Neville Brody – uber-designer of *The Face*, *Arena*, and *Actuel* – touches, his Web debut oozes style at every turn. But there's substance as well in the form of various font samples and *Fuse* magazine posters, along with persistent urging to buy FontWorks' type products.

International Clip Art

http://206.17.131.23

Somewhere down the artistic spectrum beneath Pierrot dolls, velvet prints, muzak, and butt photocopies lies clip art. For some reason, this soulless dross is often used to inject life into documents and overhead transparencies. To make your next presentation look thoroughly canned, dig in here.

Kodak

http://www.kodak.com

The beef on Kodak's products, services, and latest
developments, particularly its PhotoCD technology. Plus a
gallery of JPEG and ImagePac stills, and the necessary
viewing software for download.

Life

http://www.pathfinder.com/Life/

View *Life* magazine's picture of the day, then link through to
some of the world's most arresting photographs. Don't expect
to have much change left from an hour.

Ping Datascape

http://www.artcom.de/ping/mapper/

Add to a 3D flight through the Web. Conceived as a TV test
pattern but seems to have come off the rails.

Pitchford's Panoramas

http://www.pitchford.com

QuickTime VR whizzkid Dave Pitchford's 360 degree
snapshots of his jaunts from Sydney to Sarajevo. Straight up
they'll look like regular photos. But just watch what happens
when you drag them around with your mouse. Alas, from
now on your family album's going to look a tad flat.

Production Book Online

http://www.pb.com.au/pb/

More than 18,000 pages of Australian advertising, film, TV,
and multimedia contacts.

Scooter Boy

http://www.iac.co.jp/scooterboy/

Cute interactive Japanese comic.

SITO

http://www.sito.org

Photos, drawings, tattoos, ray-traces, video stills, record
covers, sculpture, art links, and more.

Stereogram pages

http://www.ccc.nottingham.ac.uk/~etzpc/sirds.html

Create your own Magic Eye pictures or download others' spotty 3D creations. Soon you'll induce migraines at will.

Strange Interactions

http://amanda.physics.wisc.edu

Intriguing exhibition of prints, etchings, and lithographs by physicist John E. Jacobsen.

Synergy Grid

http://www.sito.org/synergy/panic-grid.html

Find out how to create collaborative image grids or use the infinite grid selector to tailor a multi-layered psychedelic collage to your favorite of only 12,288,000,000 possible configurations.

UK Multimedia Handbook

http://www.handbook.co.uk

Free contact directory for the UK multimedia industry.

World Wide Art Resources

http://wwar.world-arts-resources.com

Biggest index of everything arty from the mandatory real world galleries, online exhibits and artists' pages to the more obscure tentacles like embroidery, belly dancing, and clock collecting. It's impeccably categorized, mostly reviewed, and maybe all the preparation you need before attempting to wade through a sticky web of slow loading fuzzy pictures.

Writing on the Wall

http://www.gatech.edu/desoto/graf/Index.Art_Crimes.html

Diverse collection of international graffiti art, showcasing the works of youths with little to say, speaking their minds.

BANKING

Many banks will offer Internet banking services soon. Ask around – it might be worth moving your cash, if it's useful.

Advance Bank

http://www.advance.com.au

Bank online in Australia.

Bank of America

http://www.bankamerica.com

Reconcile your books, monitor check clearances, transfer and stop payments, and view your balance, all via your PC. That is, if you're with Bank of America.

Barclays

http://www.barclays.com

As staid as you would expect from the UK's largest banking/stockbroking/insurance conglomerate. In the future it promises serious online features such as credit card applications and a help desk rather than just the leaflets you avoid as you wait in line. If you want online banking you have to do it directly by modem.

DigiCash

http://digicash.com

DigiCash is right on the verge of introducing an acceptable "smart" currency for Net transactions. After years of playing with toy money, real banks are taking interest. Here's where it all started.

First Virtual

http://www.fv.com

Third party clearing house for Net transactions on electronically transferable items such as software, text, and advice. Participating vendors deliver the goods first. If you're satisfied, you instruct First Virtual to pay. Purchases are accrued and charged against your credit card monthly. Since you phone in your credit card details upon joining, no sensitive information ever passes over the Net.

MasterCard International

http://www.mastercard.com

Like Visa, DigiCash, and First Virtual, MasterCard appears well poised to profit from developments in electronic payments, smart cards, and online transactions. You'll get a somewhat biased idea of where it's all heading by delving through these pages, plus whatever MasterCard information you could possibly want other than your balance.

NETBanker

http://www.netbanker.com

Use this as a starting point to shop for a true Internet bank or track down your own bank's site.

Network Payments and Digital Cash

http://ganges.cs.tcd.ie/mepeirce/project.html

Some say paper cash is going the same way as pieces-of-eight, sea shells, and salt. Judge for yourself how close we are to obtaining an alternative global currency or, more urgently, an acceptable method of completing online transactions.

Visa Expo

http://www.visa.com

Will Visa achieve "One World, One Currency – Visa"? Who knows, but they certainly have an edge in electronic banking. As this site drums home.

World Bank

http://www.worldbank.org

The World Bank mainly tries to help developing countries reduce poverty and sustain economic growth. If you're perplexed by how it can give away so much money and still stay afloat, you might come away a little more enlightened, if not positively optimistic for the future.

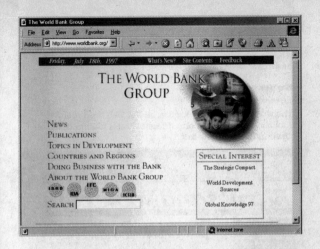

BOOKS AND BOOKSTORES

Amazon Books

http://www.amazon.com

Currently the world's most successful online bookstore,
featuring over 2.5 million US (and to a lesser extent, UK)
published titles, many of them reviewed by visitors, and all
searchable by author, title, and key words. A neat feature is
the choice of gift wrapping. And delivery is swift, both to the
US and internationally.

Atomic Books

http://www.atomicbooks.com

John Waters, director of cult movie classics, *Pink Flamingos*,
and *Hairspray*, frequents this Baltimore shop in search of
"insane books about every kind of extreme." Thanks to a Web
linked storecam you can spy on such sicko clientele as you
order online.

Banned Books Online

http://www.cs.cmu.edu/Web/People/spok/banned-books.html

See which books have been banned or come under attack, and why, by reading the contentious extracts. Many titles are now considered classics.

Barnes and Noble

http://www.barnesandnoble.com

The world's biggest bookseller, on the Web. And it sued Amazon to prove the point. Close to half a million titles, all discounted for online sale.

Blackwells

http://www.blackwells.co.uk

Order online from one of the world's leading academic booksellers.

Bookwire

http://www.bookwire.com

Literary powerhouse charged with bundles of reviews, publishing news, bestseller lists, an author tour calendar, and links to other such nooks Netwide.

Coupland Files

http://thales.yorku.ca/~spiff/coupland/

Douglas Coupland interviews and articles, as well as talk of *Microserfs*, *Generation X*, *Shampoo Planet*, *Life after God*, and other writings. The perennial 20-something's own home page is at: http://www.coupland.com

Dillons

http://www.dillons.co.uk

Excellent academic-oriented UK bookstore, with an emphasis here on computing books.

Educational Texts

http://www.etext.org

Hundreds of thousands of words, ranging from the complete works of Shakespeare to the script of a lost episode of Star Trek. Plus links to similar archives of religious, political, legal, and fanzine text.

Eland Books

http://www.travelbooks.co.uk

Read short extracts from Eland's travel narratives, then order the remainder.

Elsevier Science

http://www.elsevier.nl

Elsevier claims to be the world's leading supplier of scientific information. On board is an exhaustive list of its journals, publications, and multimedia products, plus news, reviews, and ordering channels.

Future Fantasy Bookstore

http://futfan.com

Order fantasy, horror, science fiction, and mysteries, by email.

The Internet Public Library

http://ipl.sils.umich.edu

Links to thousands of online books, magazines, and newspapers.

Kaiser Books

http://kbc.com

Books or magazines, on or off the Net, you'll find a way to get them from here. If not in the book and magazine marketplace, then maybe amongst the hundreds of links, or from a shop in the secondhand bookstore directory.

Laissez-Faire Books

http://www.lfb.org

Libertarian titles from the likes of Ayn Rand, P.J. O'Rourke, and Adam Smith.

Literary Kicks

http://www.charm.net/~brooklyn/LitKicks.html

Shrine to the Beats with a mass of fine audio and text on Kerouac, Corso, Ginsberg, Cassady, and all who came into their Beat orbit.

Loompanics

http://www.loompanics.com

Get your hands on some subversive, strange, and sometimes downright nasty gems of anarchic and alternative writing.

Macmillan USA

http://www.mcp.com

Goes further than most publishers, putting searchable contents pages and full chapter samples for many of its thousands of books online. What's more, you can download copies of any software included with computer titles, here or from its FTP site.

Online Books

http://www.cs.cmu.edu/Web/books.html

Complete texts lie tucked away in obscure archives all over the Net. Here's an index of about a thousand titles as well as links to almost 100 specialist repositories.

Online Bookshop

http://www.bookshop.co.uk

Close to a million titles available from a myriad of publishers.

All books are cross-referenced by subject, with brief synopses and links to related material.

Outpost:Culture

http://www.lb.com/~outpost/

Another zippy book/bookstore/publisher finder, this time from US small press distributor, Inland Book Company.

Penguin Books

http://www.penguin.com   http://www.penguin.co.uk

What's new, and catalogues, from Penguins on both sides of the Atlantic. Featured books include extracts and everything can be ordered direct.

Poetry Society

http://www.poetrysoc.com

UK halfway house for budding poets and their victims.

Project Gutenburg

http://promo.net/pg/

Fifty years or so after authors croak, their copyrights pass into the public domain. With this in mind, Project Gutenburg is dedicated to making as many works as possible available online in plain vanilla ascii text. Not all the books are old, however – some, such as the computer texts, have been donated. As great as that sounds, in practice you might prefer the convenience of hard copy.

Pure Fiction

http://www.purefiction.com

For pulp worms and writers alike. Packed with book previews, author interviews, and hundreds of links to the sort of stuff you need to get off the ground and punch out your first bestseller. See also: alt.books.purefiction

Thomas Pynchon Home Page

http://www.pomona.edu/pynchon/

Archives of Pynchon-l, the fiery mailing list that inspired the book *Lineland*, plus all the literary fandom you'd expect.

Shakespeare

http://the-tech.mit.edu/Shakespeare/

The Bard's complete works online.

Sun Tzu's The Art of War

http://users.cnu.edu/~patrick/taoism/suntzu/suntzu.html

Discover Sun Tzu's *The Art of War*, with or without a guide.
At 2400 years old, it's believed to be the world's oldest
military treatise. Like other Chinese wisdoms such as the
teachings of Confucius, much of it still rings true and its
adages can be applied to any conflict. So much so, that it
became the Yuppies' surrogate bible. Oh well, battles do
have their casualties.

Tech Classics Archive

http://classics.mit.edu

Searchable archive of hundreds of translated Greek and
Roman classics.

Urban Legends

http://www.urbanlegends.com

Repository for dubious yarns compiled from alt.folklore.urban

Ventana

http://www.vmedia.com

Order online from Ventana's range of popular computer texts,
download programs from its companion disks, and check for
updates. The Internet section carries full text of Net selections,
including Walking the WWW, Official Netscape Navigator 3.0,
Internet Business 500, and HTML Programmer's Reference,
complete with thousands of Web site reviews.

Waterstones

http://www.waterstones.co.uk

Britain's best browsing bookshop chain has the elegant,
content-rich site you'd expect, including a pick of the
newspaper book reviews, archives of W, the Waterstones
magazine, and a rare book search for out of print stock. The
site's search engine is swift and efficient and the database as
big as they come in the UK.

X-RAY

http://x-ray.rocke.com

Home spun sci-fi, horror, and fantasy yarns. Feel free to contribute.

BUSINESS

Advertising Age

http://www.adage.com

Newsbreaks from the ad trade.

Barcode Server

http://www.milk.com/barcode/

Find out how bar codes work, then generate your own.

Business Index

http://www.dis.strath.ac.uk/business/

It may look low key, but start here, and you'll be no more than a few clicks away from almost any business-related site.

Companies Online

http://www.companiesonline.com

Get the score on over 100,000 public and private companies.

Direct Marketing World

http://www.dmworld.com

How to junk mail and influence people.

FedEx

http://www.fedex.com

Federal Express has revolutionized the way carriers haul freight, take orders, and service customers. Now it's moved online, you can book shipping, track parcels, or compare rates with UPS at: http://www.ups.com

Friends and Partners

http://solar.rtd.utk.edu/friends/home.html

US–Russian joint venture to help create a better under-standing between the old foes. There's economics, education,

geography, music, weather, and health, plus a literature
section which contains the full text of *The Brothers
Karamazov* and *Anna Karenina*. It's all meant to encourage
trade.

IBM Patent Server

http://patent.womplex.ibm.com

Sift through US patents back to 1971, plus a gallery of
obscurities. Ask the right questions and you might stumble
across tomorrow's technology long before the media. For UK
patents see: http://www.patent.gov.uk

Internet Magazine's Marketing Hotlist

http://www.internet-sales.com/hot/

UK godfather of new media, Roger Green's one-stop guide to
working the Web like a pro.

Internet Marketing Kiosk

http://www.pport.com/kiosk/kiosk.htm

Fodder for online entrepreneurial thought.

MediaFinder

http://www.mediafinder.com

US media profile and contact directory. Lists newspapers,
magazines, mailing lists, catalogues, newsletters and more,
sorted by subject focus.

MoneyHunter
http://www.moneyhunter.com
How to milk funds for your online white elephant.

Virtual Africa
http://www.africa.com
Inexpensive way to put your feelers out in the now commercially acceptable South Africa.

Who's Marketing Online
http://www.wmo.com
What's new in Web marketing trends, including new site reviews from an ad campaigner's perspective.

COMEDY

Archive of Useless Facts
http://www.undergrad.math.uwaterloo.ca/~tford/facts.htm
Just the sort of stuff you didn't want to know, but are glad you do.

Biggest List of Humor Sites on the Net
http://www.bigron.com
Bit of a lucky dip. Take a link, strike it lucky, and you get to laugh.

Bonk Industries
http://www.telegate.se/bonk/
In a subtle satire of corporate propaganda, Bonk highlights how we're conditioned to accept unethical business practices when they're cloaked in the right language.

Complaint Letter Generator
http://www-csag.cs.uiuc.edu/individual/pakin/complaint/
Someone getting on your goat, but stuck for the right words? Just mince their details through here for an instant dressing down.

Humor Database

http://www.humordatabase.com

Thousands of jokes searchable by age, topic, keyword, or popularity.

HumourNet

http://www.humournet.com/HumourNet/

Home of the HumourNet mailing list. Join to exchange funnies or read the archives here.

Improv Comedy Club

http://www.cummingsvideo.com/home/comedy/standup.htm

Live and archived stand-up routines in Real Video.

LaughWeb

http://www.intermarket.net/laughweb/

Bundles of jokes sorted into categories, and rated by readers. Subscribe to get one sent daily.

Milk Kommunications

http://www.milk.com

Shameful but true stories, anecdotes, and jokes. Don't miss the original name-change press release from the artist formerly named after a dog.

Practical Jokes

http://www.umd.umich.edu/~nhughes/htmldocs/pracjokes.html

Larks and laughs at the expense of others compiled from the Usenet archives of alt.shenanigans

Pythonline

http://www.pythonline.com

Terry Gilliam-illustrated Monty Python mayhem, juvenilia, and humor, plus where they all are now.

Rec.humor.funny Home Page

http://www.clari.net/rhf/

Archives of the rec.humor.funny newsgroup, updated daily.

Surrealist Compliment Generator

http://pharmdec.wustl.edu/cgi-bin/jardin_scripts/SCG

It mightn't make a shred of sense, but hey, at least it's positive.

Uploaded

http://www.loaded.co.uk

Monthly emissions from the icon of British lad culture.

for men who should net better

The Whitehouse

http://www.whitehouse.net

A different parody of the official White House site every time you hit reload.

COMPUTING

Your PC brand will have a Web site where you can download software, get support, and find out what's new. It won't be hard to find. Usually it's the company name or initials between a www and a com. So you'll find Dell at: http://www.dell.com, Texas Instruments at: http://www.ti.com Hewlett Packard at: http://www.hp.com Hitachi at: http://www.hitachi.com and so forth. Consult Yahoo if that fails.

Adobe

http://www.adobe.com

Information, support, and download areas for Adobe's desktop publishing software.

Apple

http://www.apple.com

Essential drop in for all Mac users and developers for the latest product info and system updates.

IBM

(1) http://www.ibm.com   (2) http://www.ibm.net

Key the first address for IBM's corporate world, products,

and international operations. The second for IBM Global
Network contact details, plus a helpful set of tutorials and
links to get you started on the Net.

Inquiry

http://www.inquiry.com

Answerbase for computer professionals. References
thousands of IT journals and product sheets.

Macintouch

http://www.macintouch.com

Specializes in Mac software fixes.

Microsoft

http://www.microsoft.com

If you're running any Microsoft product, and the chance of
that seems to be approaching 100%, drop by here regularly
for upgrades, news, support, and patches. That includes the
latest free tweaks to Windows, Office, and particularly all
that falls under the Internet Explorer program. Grab the lot,
and watch your system directory blossom.

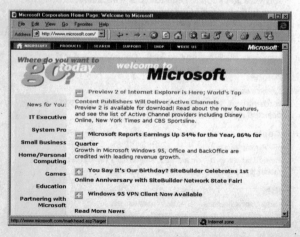

My Desktop

http://www.mydesktop.com

Serious Win95 twiddler's heaven.

Silicon Graphics

http://www.sgi.com

All the corporate and product guff you'd want from SGI,
along with some impressive demonstrations of what its
high-end graphics workstations can do.

Software.net

http://www.software.net

The time can't be far off when it will be standard practice
to ship commercial software via the Net. So far only about
2000 of its more than 20,000 packages are downloadable
here, while the rest are conventionally boxed for Fedex
delivery.

Sun Microsystems

http://www.sun.com

Sun is the Net's biggest hardware player and a major
sponsor in developing new technology, such as the much
hailed Java programming language. Link from here to
any of the company's globally scattered Software
Information and Technology Exchanges, which provide
easy access to public domain software, government info,
product support, and hundreds of innovative projects.

Symantec

http://www.symantec.com

Free software, online updates and support on
Symantec/Norton's award-winning range of virus, disk
management, communications, and Java utilities.

Tidbits

http://www.tidbits.com

Macintosh newsletter, from the author of the pioneering
and enormously useful *Internet Starter Kit*.

Windows 95 Annoyances

http://www.creativelement.com/win95ann/

Fixes and replacements for many Windows 95 "features" and omissions.

Windows95.com

http://www.windows95.com

The transition to Windows 95 isn't always as simple as Microsoft makes out. Here's one of the best independent places to find tutorials, tips, advice, Windows 95 shareware, and remedies for the things the Benevolent Empire neglected.

Yahoo! Computing

http://www.yahoo.com/Computers/

The granddaddy of all computing directories.

ZDNet

http://www.zdnet.com

Computing information powerhouse from Ziff Davis, publisher of PC Magazine, MacUser, Computer Gaming World and several other IT titles. Each magazine provides content such as news, product reviews, and lab test results, plus there's a ton of prime Net-exclusive techno-chow. Good place to research before buying anything even vaguely computer-related.

EMPLOYMENT

America's Job Bank

http://www.ajb.dni.us

Links to over 1800 US State Employment Service offices and 100,000 vacancies. A state project that's free for all.

CareerMosaic

http://www.careermosaic.com

Search for vacancies among a growing field of heavyweight clients, or through Usenet postings. As with most job sites, there's plenty of advice on resumés, career trends, and salaries. Each client outlines its employment conditions and corporate guff. For Asian opportunities see: http://www.careerasia.com

E*Span

http://www.espan.com

Thousands of jobs and seekers frustratingly concealed behind a restrictive search interface.

EagleView

http://www.eagleview.com

Post your details to hundreds of Fortune 500 companies.

Hot Jobs

http://www.hotjobs.com

Technical jobs worldwide. Easier to search than most.

Jobs at Microsoft

http://www.microsoft.com/Jobs/

Join Big Brother's march across the globe.

Monster Board

http://www.monster.com

Search for professional employment in the US and abroad. Like E*Span, the content's there but it's cumbersome.

Price Jamieson

http://www.pricejam.com

Easy to browse international listings mainly in new media, marketing, and communications, updated at least weekly.

Reed

http://www.reed.co.uk

Top-notch service from the UK's largest employment agency, covering such diverse vocations as nursing, computing, catering, accounting, driving, charity, insurance, and project management.

TopJobs

http://www.topjobs.co.uk

Technical positions vacant across the UK and Europe.

Virtual Headroom

http://www.xmission.com/~wintrnx/virtual.html

Post your headshot and resumé and take a shortcut to the stars. It'll cost you to post but not to scout for talent. But then there's the couch to deal with.

ENTERTAINMENT

A Thousand Points of Sites

http://inls.ucsd.edu/y/0hBoy/randomjump1.html

Go blindly where ye have not been before.

Animated Greeting Cards

http://www.greetme.com

Send a card that sings, moves, and talks.

Avenger's Handbook

http://www.cs.uit.no/~paalde/Revenge/

There'll be no more Mr. Nice Guy now you know about this armory of extreme nastiness. Much of it is compiled from the archives of the Usenet group alt.revenge – the definitive meeting place for suburban terrorists. Like vicious programs, things to do before you quit your job, school pranks, and oodles of treacherous anecdotes about getting even. John Steed would never stoop this low.

Build a Card

http://www.buildacard.com

Compete for the tackiest virtual Valentine or greeting card, with this ingenious step-by-step online art studio.

Centre for the Easily Amused

http://www.amused.com

Hundreds of sites where thinking's banned.

Driveways of the Rich & Famous

http://www.driveways.com

Asphalt on the senses.

EventNet

http://www.eventnet.aust.com

Calendar of major Australian conferences, exhibitions, art shows, performances, sporting events and more. Book online.

Events Online

http://www.eventsonline.co.uk

Search or browse UK music, film, stage, arts, TV, kids, and comedy listings.

Famous Birthdays

http://oeonline.com/~edog/bday.html

See who shares your birthday, and estimate how many more you're likely to have.

Hidden Mickeys

http://www.hiddenmickeys.org

Subliminal Mickeys hidden around Disneyland? Must be something in the drinks.

I Ching

http://www.facade.com/Occult/iching/

If the superior person is not happy with their fortune as told by this ancient Chinese oracle, they can always reload and get another one.

Kissogram

http://www.kissogram.com.au

Send not just animated kisses, but wiggling butts, pouting drag queens, hatching eggs and more. Not all in the best taste but then what did you expect?

Lockpicking

http://www.lysator.liu.se/mit-guide/mit-guide.html

They laughed when I told them I was learning to burgle, but when they came home . . .

Miss America

http://www.missamerica.org

It says here to be a modern Miss America you need more

than just long legs and a fancy name like Shawntel. You also have to be a bit of a genius. Thus a panel will toss you topical teasers like whether you approve of this Info SuperHighway thing and how you'd stop kiddies from logging into sites like this to download pictures of swimsuited charity workers. Of course, you'll blitz it in the brains department. So now let's concentrate on your smile.

Net Casino

http://www.netcasino.com

Apply for an offshore debit card, then flush it down the Net.

Peeping Tom

http://www.csd.uu.se/~s96fst/index.html

Spend a night peeping through the Net's many cameras, then rest content that you've sat with pioneers at the very cutting edge of technology. Now, tick that off the list and get on with your life.

Penn and Teller

http://www.sincity.com

While, regrettably, Penn and Teller's input here is fairly minimal, it has enough links to other magic and entertainment sites, including other P&T exhibits, to make it worthwhile.

Say

http://wwwtios.cs.utwente.nl/say/

Enter your profanity, hit return, and it will speak the phrase back for the mirth of all within earshot. Try spelling phonetically for greater success. Or maybe you'd prefer it in morse beeps: http://www.babbage.demon.co.uk/morse.html

Sony

http://www.sony.com

News, service, and support, product blurbs, and colorful allsorts from Sony's huge stable of movies, music, broadcast, publishing, video, Playstation, and electronic toys. It's like ten major sites under one roof, with hundreds of corners to explore. You have to see for yourself.

Tarot Information

http://www.facade.com/Occult/tarot/

Choose from several different packs to find out what your
future holds. For a second opinion, link up to the master site
and try your luck at the *I Ching*, Biorhythm, Bibliomancy,
Stichomancy, or Runes predictions. If you suspect it's all a
great pile of randomly generated nugget, the Cindy Crawford
Concentration exercise will surely set you straight.

The 80s Server

http://www.80s.com

And you swore they'd never come back.

The Postcard Store

http://postcards.www.media.mit.edu/Postcards/

Instead of mailing an actual "e-card" it sends a PIN number,
which is then used to pick up the card.

Ticketmaster

http://www.ticketmaster.com

Book event tickets online.

Trading Card Dealers

http://www.wwcd.com/scdealer.html

Find that elusive baseball, football, or phone card.

UK National Lottery

http://lottery.merseyworld.com

Stats, winning numbers, draw details, numerical analysis: everything you need to know about the UK lottery, except the one thing that matters.

Uri Geller's Psychic City

http://www.urigeller.com

Test your ESP, fail dismally, then find out why you need the services of the champion cutlery curler himself.

Virtual Presents

http://www.virtualpresents.com

Why waste money on real gifts when, after all, it's only the thought that counts?

Voodoo Lounge

http://www.ping.be/~ping2442/voodoo.htm

Send curses by email.

Zodiac Forecasts

http://www.bubble.com/webstars/

Free daily forecasts from the UK *Daily Mail*'s Jonathan Cainer in text or RealAudio. But still no forecast for that controversial thirteenth sign.

EZINES

It's a fine distinction as to what's a Net magazine (ezine) and a magazine posted on the Net; those below are largely the former. The best lists of electronic journals and ezines are the Ezine List: http://www.meer.net/~johnl/e-zine-list/ and Inkpot's Zine Scene: http://inkpot.com/zines/ See also "News, Magazines and Newspapers."

Addicted to: Stuff

http://www.morestuff.com

Quirky ezine where readers share obsessions.

Anorak

http://www.anorak.co.uk

Irreverent daily review of the UK tabloids and broadsheets.

Channel Cyberia

http://www.cyberiacafe.net

Graphic-intense lifestyle e-rag from the original cybercafé, Cyberia London. An ant's nest to navigate but the content's there if you persist.

Erack

http://www.erack.com

Selections and exclusives from UK newsstand titles: *Q*, *Select*, *New Woman*, *FHM*, *Carworld*, *Maxpower*, and *Motorcycle World*.

FiX Magazine

http://www.widemedia.com/fix/

One of London's longest running monthly ezines. Also claims to be the "world's widest." Figure that one out yourself.

Fray

http://www.fray.com

Personal, provocative, and potentially disturbing, Fray melts haunting graphics over strong prose on criminals, drugs, work, and hope.

FutureNet

http://www.futurenet.co.uk

Daily news, plus features from the UK magazine publisher's many titles such as *.net*, *arcane*, *Mountain Biking UK*, *EDGE*, *Comedy Review*, *First XV*, *Total Guitar*, *Total Football*, and the acclaimed *Needlecraft*.

Geek Girl

http://geekgirl.com.au/geekgirl/

Assorted raves compiled by Australian cyberfemme Rosie X.

Giant Robot

http://www.giantrobot.com

Selections from the print popzine that scoops into Asian treats like *Ultraman*, *CYF*, sumo, manga, and larger than average robotica.

Head Space

http://www.head-space.com

Several popular Brixton scene creations under one roof. From the underground angst of *Urban 75* through to *Indie World* and the degree showspace for the Camberwell College of Art, it all shares a sense of community.

J Pop

http://www.j-pop.com

Japanese pop culture features on the likes of manga, anime, games, and Pizzicato 5.

Maxi

http://www.maximag.com

For the woman who doesn't take no for an answer, but then again probably wouldn't ask in the first place.

The Onion

http://www.theonion.com

Satirical newspaper with something that's always funny enough to forward on.

Phrack Magazine

http://freeside.com/phrack.html

The renowned hackers' quarterly. Never far from controversy.

Psyche Journal

http://psyche.cs.monash.edu.au

"An electronic interdisciplinary journal of consciousness research" with all the goss on stuff like vagueness, semantics, the language of thought, delineating conscious processes, and contrastive analysis. Piece of cake.

Salon

http://www.salonmag.com

Daily news and cultural chop-ups with columns from renowned US writers like Camille Paglia, David Horowitz, and James Carville. Sponsors include Apple and Adobe.

Slate

http://www.slate.com

Thoughtful, though dry, news, culture and arts analysis. Read it on the Web, or get it delivered by mail. It's owned by Microsoft, but don't hold that against it.

The Spot

http://www.thespot.com

Glossy cult online soap about the twenty-something residents
of a seven-bedroom Malibu party house. Each day at least one
posts a diary entry and tunes us in. Bed-hopping, tears, and
superbitches. Or your money back.

Student Outlook

http://www.pro-net.co.uk/student/

UK student news, reviews, and opinion.

Suck

http://www.suck.com

Never a kind word for anyone or anything, even itself, every
weekday. It's always worth scanning Suck's jaded jabs at
modern day hubris, if only for the links peppered
throughout the copy.

Swoon

http://www.swoon.com

Dating, mating, and relating. Courtesy of Condé Naste's
Details, *GQ*, *Glamour*, and *Mademoiselle*.

Urban Desires

http://www.desires.com

Modern city stories of technology, food, sex, music, art, performance, style, travel, politics, and more.

Utne Online

http://www.utne.com

Selected articles from the progressive US alternative press digest, *The Utne Reader*, biweekly Web-only content and a busy gender-discriminatory café area for word bashing.

Women's Wire

http://www.women.com

Instantly dispels rumors that the Net's a "man's man's world". But slots in closer to *Elle* than *Riot Girl*: http://www.riotgrrl.com

Z Times

http://www.zpub.com/z/

Monthly time-capsules as viewed from the Web.

Zug

http://www.mediashower.com/zug/

Irreverence, Henry-Root-style email pranks, and a chuckle or two.

FASHION

1-800-SURGEON

http://www.surgeon.org

Well, if it doesn't scrub up in the mirror you can always put a knife to it.

Angel of Fashion Award

http://www.fashionangel.com/angel.html

Unless you have a chubby connection, fancy fashion sites can be pretty frustrating. And if they're not kept up to date, they hardly qualify as fashion. Angel singles out groundbreaking sites for praise and supplies links to many others.

Clothes Care

http://www.clothes-care.com

Point and click image consultancy, stain removal tips, and
soap suds ads.

Designer City

http://www.designercity.com

London fashion and lifestyle monthly with input from *Cosmo*
and *Esquire*.

Elle International

http://www.elle.com

Scraps from the 27 international editions of *Elle*. They barely
resemble their glossy paper counterparts but still sport
enough swish types in bright duds to make you feel
undershopped in any language.

Fashion Internet

http://www.finy.com

Sort your togs, tip to toe, with top tips ranging from the
clueless guy's guide to buying a suit, to Bobbi Brown's
makeup forum for thinking women.

Fashion Net

http://www.fashion.net

More fashion links than you could poke a chapstick at.

Fashion UK

http://www.widemedia.com/fashionuk/

Another minimal, but fresh, vanity monthly out of London.

Is Fashion Silly?

http://www.softeam.it/pittimmagine/

Peephole at the Italian fashion industry.

The Lipstick Page

http://www.users.wineasy.se/bjornt/Lip.html

Cosmetic appliances for fun and profit.

Sneaker Nation

http://www.hardlink.com/~sneaker/

Trainer confessionals and brand reassurance.

FILM AND TV

All Movie Guide
http://allmovie.com/amg/movie_root.html

Colossal, but easy to navigate, sound and screen directory, complete with reviews and synopses.

Beavis And Butthead Extravaganza
http://www.worldramp.net/~pjoiner/bandb/

Interactive Shockwave toy starring MTV's dysfunctional duo.

Capt James T Kirk Sing-a-Long
http://www.loskene.com/singalong/kirk.html

Audio excerpts from William Shatner's bold vinyl masterpiece "The Transformed Man."

Channel 4 TV
http://www.channel4.com

Much-acclaimed Online Magic production with links, contacts, and follow-ups from the UK's adventurous Channel 4. It's particularly strong on sports events such as the Tour de France, which gets a devoted daily site during the race.

Cinemachine
http://www.cinemachine.com

Movie review search engine. Redirects you to the original source.

E! Online
http://www.eonline.com

Daily film and TV gossip, news, and reviews.

Encyclopedia Brady
http://www.primenet.com/~dbrady/

The collected antics of "three very lovely girls," their stepbrothers, and folks.

God of Actors

http://www.geocities.com/
Athens/8907/factor.html

Valuable insight into
the John Woo regular
who makes Arnie look
like Richie
Cunningham. Widely
regarded as the
"coolest man alive."

Hergé and Tintin

http://www.du.edu/
~tomills/tintin.html

The official Tintin site
in English or French.

Hollywood Reporter

http://www.
hollywoodreporter.com

Tinsletown tattle
daily, plus a flick biz
directory.

Internet Movie Database

http://www.imbd.com

You'll be hard pressed to find any work on or off the Net
as comprehensive as this exceptional relational database
of screen trivia from over 100,000 movies and a million
actors. It's all tied together remarkably well – for
example, within two clicks of finding your favorite
movie, you can get full filmographies of anyone from the
cast or crew, and then see what's in the cooker.
Unmissable.

Movie Sounds

http://www.moviesounds.com

Samples and scores from 100 or so films, and links to many
more.

Movies.com

http://www.movies.com

Preview forthcoming Touchstone and Hollywood Pictures. All with short synopses, minute-long sample clips, interviews, stills, and assorted press releases.

Personalized UK TV Guide

http://www.yearling.com

Generate your own UK TV listing from a choice of 60 channels.

Power Rangers

http://ic.www.media.mit.edu/Personal/manny/power/

Save this one for when a noisy junior Power Ranger interferes with your hangover. Point their head this way while you go back to bed. Downloading all the heavy graphics should give you ample time for a kip.

Reel

http://www.reel.com

Claims it's the world's biggest movie store. With more than 80,000 titles for sale and half that for rent, maybe it's right.

Secret Chimps Worldwide

http://digartz.com/link/evorevo.htm

There was a time when it looked like all actors might be replaced by chimpanzees. So, what went wrong?

Shock Cinema

http://members.aol.com/shockcin/main.html

Picking over celluloid scavenged from Mr. Subtlety's dumpster.

The Simpsons Archive

http://www.snpp.com

In barefaced defiance of Fox's "cease and desist" order, fans persist in garnishing the Web with the unofficial sights and sounds of Springfield. Meanwhile, Fox's own at: http://www.foxworld.com/simpindx.htm, hardly compares. Instead, start your Simpsons overdose here.

Les Simpson

http://www.unantes.univ-nantes.fr/~elek/simpson.html

Listen to how our French friends have to hear Homer, El Barto, et al., and maybe you'll go a bit easier on them in future.

Soap Links

http://members.aol.com/soaplinks/

Keep up with who's doing what to whom, who they told, and who shouldn't find out, in the surreal world of soap fiction.

Tromaville

http://www.troma.com

Here's your lucky break. Troma, home of class films like *Toxic Avenger*, *Chopper Chicks* from *Zombie Town*, *Space Freaks from Planet Mutoid*, *Subhumanoid Meltdown*, and *Fatguy goes Nutzoid*, needs acting outcasts and writers for its Troma Army Bizarre productions.

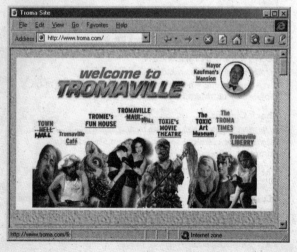

Ultimate TV
http://www.ultimatetv.com

More on everything televisual than is mentally healthy.
Places to vent your gripes, broadcasting addresses,
schedules, job vacancies, and links to fan pages of just
about every show ever made. By the time you get
through this lot, you'll be too plum-tuckered for the neon
bucket itself.

Universal Studios
http://www.mca.com

What's in store from the MCA/Universal movie and music
stable. All sorts of fun promo gimmicks, such as being
able to interview the stars by email and download clips.

X-Links Central
http://www.geocities.com/Hollywood/6050/xfsites.html

The X-Files remains up there with Star Trek in attracting
Net obsessives, despite mockery from respective leading
actors David Duchovny and William Shatner and
copyright bullying from Fox (the network, not Mulder).
Here's a path to at least 800 such X-shrines.

FINANCE

ASX Quote Weblink
http://www.weblink.com.au

Australian stock market quotes and historical charts.

Charles Schwab
http://www.schwab.com

NY brokerage that leads the pack of rats in online money
juggling.

Current Oil and Gas Quotes
http://baervan.nmt.edu/prices/current.html

Get the latest spot and future prices on oil and gas.

Electronic Share Information

http://www.esi.co.uk

UK share quotes and online trading.

Motley Fool

http://www.fool.com

Investment forums, market tipping, quotes and sound advice. Stands above the rabble.

PAWWS, Wall Street on the Internet

http://pawws.secapl.com

Free North American quarter-hourly updated stock quotes, charts, fundamentals, and news. Pay to get more meaty stuff like online brokerage, portfolio management, real-time quotes, research, and all the other services you would expect from a stock shark.

The Privateer

http://the-privateer.com

Entertaining newsletter that's been chronicling the collapse of the US financial system since 1984.

QuoteCom

http://www.quote.com

More free trading data, news and charts, plus a multitude of subscription services.

Shareholder Action Handbook

http://www.bath.ac.uk/Centres/Ethical/Share/

When you buy shares in a public company, you get certain voting rights. By putting the entire text of the Shareholder Action Handbook online, it's hoped you'll exercise those rights to the benefit of your community.

Silicon Investor

http://www.techstocks.com

Outstanding selection of free technology stock quotes, charts, forums, advice, and sentiment surveys. To bet on the Net's success, start your research here.

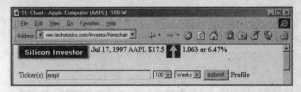

Stockmaster

http://www.stockmaster.com

Quotes, charts, and rankings on major US stocks, funds, and Indices.

Wall Street Journal Interactive

http://www.wsj.com

Not only is this online edition equal to the print, its charts and data archives give it an edge. That's why you shouldn't complain that it's not free. After all, if it's your type of paper, you should be able to afford it, bigshot.

Yahoo! Finance

http://quote.yahoo.com

Business wires, charts, quotes, forex rates wrapped around the Net's mother lode of finance links.

FOOD AND DRINK

All India Food Page

http://www.gadnet.com/foodx.htm

Simple directory of Indian recipes and restaurant sites.

Beer.com

http://www.beer.com

None of the usual beer yarns like waking up in a strange room stark naked with a throbbing head and a hazy recollection of pranging your car. Here, beer is treated with the same dewy-eyed respect usually reserved for wine and trains. You get all the beef down to the specific gravity, bottle color, and alcohol content.

Beershots

http://micro.magnet.fsu.edu/beershots/

Beers of the world put under a microscope. Literally!

Chile-Heads

http://www.netimages.com/~chile/

Dip into chili recipes, chemistry, botanical facts, gardening tips, and general peppering. You can find out what's the hottest pepper, what makes it so hot, how your body reacts, and identify that mystery one in your kebab.

Chocolate Lover's Playground

http://www.godiva.com

Mouth-watering cocoa recipes and meanderings into chocoholism. You can satisfy your cravings online, but only within the US. For even more punishment slide into The Chocolate Club at: http://www.idma.com/chocolate/

Crazy Vegetarian

http://www.crazyveg.com

Light-hearted meatless nutrition raps.

DineNet

http://menusonline.com

Thousands of US restaurant menus, plus maps to aid fulfillment.

Epicurious

http://www.epicurious.com

Web-only marriage of Condé Naste's *Gourmet*, *Bon Appetit*, and *Traveler* magazines, crammed with recipes, culinary forums, advice on dining out around the world, and ways to stave off hunger with panache.

Fillet

http://www.fillet.com

Weekly tales of food snobbery and quiet drunkenness.

Internet Chef

http://www.ichef.com

Over 30,000 recipes, cooking hints, kitchen talk and more links than you could jab a fork in.

Internet Pizza Server

http://www2.ecst.csuchico.edu/~pizza/

Bit of a shame this archetypal online pizza delivery service only belts out graphic facsimiles and not the real McCoy. Maybe you mightn't fancy a piping hot feast of bugs, bolts, kittens, hammers, footballs, and road signs, but it does lay the foundation for a successful fast-food scheme.

Kitchen Link

http://www.kitchenlink.com

Points to more than 7,000 galleries of gluttony.

Mamma's Kitchen

http://www.eat.com

How to fix up Italian bachelor nosh out of a bottle.

Over the Coffee

http://www.cappuccino.com

Enough coffee trivia, mail order firms, reviews, anecdotes,

and links to similarly minded sites to keep you pleasantly
caffeinated for life.

Ribbets

http://www.odyssey.com.au/wtc/ribbets/

How's this for lazy? Just say you're online, in the middle
of a QuakeWorld match, and you need ribs or pizza bad.
If your only phone line's tied up, you could switch to the
Web, buzz Ribbets, and have one in front of you within
half an hour. But you have to get up to answer the door –
and live in Brisbane.

Singapore Unofficial Food

http://www.sintercom.org/makan/

Vibrant guide to eating out in Singapore, plus oodles more
than noodles to cook at home.

Spencer's Beer

http://realbeer.com/spencer/

Here's the place to tune your brew. It carries several
hypertext home-brew recipe books, including the entire Cat's

Meow series. And bottle-spotters will thrill at the gallery of 228 labels in 128 shimmering colors. Real pros might prefer: http://www.probrewer.com or http://www.breworld.com

Tasty Insect Recipes

http://www.ent.iastate.edu/Misc/InsectsAsFood.html

Dig in to such delights as Bug Blox, Banana Worm Bread, Rootworm Beetle Dip, and Chocolate Chirpie Chip Cookies (with crickets).

Tea Time

http://www.teatime.com

Types of tea, tried and tasted, and a turnpike to all that's tea taken truly.

Tokyo Food Page

http://www.twics.com/%7erobbs/tokyofood.html

Where and what to eat in Tokyo, a sushi decoder, plus a few recipes and tips like how to detect parasites in your uncooked mullet. From the author of "What's What in Japanese Restaurants."

Wine Net

http://www.wineguide.com

Slick directory of wineries, retailers, publications, and general grape gratification.

GAMES

For more on online gaming, see our **Online Gaming** chapter (pp.169–175).

Atmospheric Heights

http://www.xs4all.nl/~delite/

Know someone who grizzles on about old school arcade games like Pleides, Lunar Rescue, Donkey Kong, and Xevious? Sentence them to ten minutes here.

Connect 4

http://www.pobox.com/~pomakis/c4/

Challenge the beast to connect four, or any number for that matter. For tips on how to beat the system, read Victor Allis's masters thesis on expert play.

Crime Scene

http://www.crimescene.com

Help two detectives analyze forensic evidence and track down suspects in an ongoing murder investigation. Move along folks, nothing to see here.

Fred

http://langevin.usc.edu/Fred/

Network Doom prototype in Java. More of a curiosity than a playable game.

Frogger

http://speech.ee.yeungnam.ac.kr/htdocs/lsw/Java/applet/froggie/

Play the classic arcade game in your browser.

Games you can play on the WWW

http://www.happypuppy.com/games/w3games.htm

Pit your wits against the computer or remote opponents on a whole variety of games.

Imperial Nomic

http://www.mit.edu/people/achmed/inomic/

You'll take ages to figure out this strange Web game. It's not that it has no rules. On the contrary, the object is to make them up. If they're accepted, your score changes in a way you won't be able to understand until you've spent some considerable time here. Confused? That's the general idea.

Kasparov vs Deep Blue

http://www.chess.ibm.com

If Kasparov ever takes on Deep Blue again, here's where to watch it live. Apart from that, it chronicles the historical triumph of machine over mortal with links that will tickle any serious chess aficionado. Or if you're up for a game yourself, head straight to: http://www.ichess.com

PC Game Finder

http://www.pcgame.com

Top games search engine that intelligently splits results by reviews, cheats, demos, and required hardware. Indexes most of the leading game lairs.

Playsite

http://www.playsite.com

Play chess, checkers, reversi, or backgammon against online opponents.

The Riddler

http://www.riddler.com

Use your Web scavenging, lateral thinking, literary, trivia, and other skills to compete across the Net for prizes.

Sega

http://www.sega.com http://www.segasoft.com

Product news, tips, and support plus games to play online
and a few PC demos like Virtual Fighter and Sega Rally to
download.

The Talker

http://ss002.infi.net/broadcast/login/

Choose an icon, alias, and attitude and bluff your way
through this virtual party. Bear in mind that whoever else
you meet must also have little else to do.

Virtual Vegas

http://www.virtualvegas.com

Showgirls, VRML slot machines, Shockwave blackjack, Java
poker, shopping, and a chat-up lounge. VVbucks are virtual,
but occasionally the prizes are real.

You Don't Know Jack

http://www.toasted.com

This wacky trivia quiz computer game was all the rage a
couple of years back. Now you can download the software
free and compete against other players over the Net for cash.

PC Games

For reviews, news, demos, hints, patches, cheats, downloads,
and other PC game necessities try:

Games Center

http://www.gamecenter.com

Games Domain

http://www.gamesdomain.com

Games Mansion

http://www.gamesmansion.com

Gamespot

http://www.gamespot.com

Happy Puppy

http://www.happypuppy.com

Online Gaming Realm

http://www.ogr.com

PCME

http://www.pcme.com

GOVERNMENT

The British Monarchy

http://www.royal.gov.uk

Official drone of the House of
Windsor. Way more larks at:
http://www.royalnetwork.com

CCTA Government Information

http://www.open.gov.uk

Here's where to find any UK
government authority. Just open this colossal directory, scan
down the list, make your choice, and before long you'll be
nodding off, just as if you were actually there.

Central Intelligence Agency

http://www.odci.gov/cia/

Learn about the CIA's role in international affairs, its
intelligence cycle, history and real estate. But that's not what
you're after is it? You watch TV and read the *Weekly World
News*. You want to know about political assassinations, arms
deals, Latin American drug trades, spy satellites, conspiracy
theories, phone tapping, covert operations, government-
sponsored alien sex cults, and the X-files. This must be
another CIA.

Declassified Satellite Photos

http://edcwww.cr.usgs.gov/dclass/dclass.html

Here's what you've been expecting from the Net: the first spy
pictures taken from satellites, then dropped to earth by
parachute. They're freshly declassified and plenty more will
follow. Look closely and see Soviets knitting socks in
preparation for a bleak winter.

FedWorld

http://www.fedworld.gov

Locate US federal government servers, contacts, and
documents.

Camilla's Diary
Spring 2045

Her Majesty's Treasury

http://www.hm-treasury.gov.uk

Another spine-tingler. Read press releases, ministerial speeches, minutes, economic forecasts, and the budget, and decide whether your tax pounds are going to worthy causes.

Palestinian National Authority

http://www.pna.net

Official mouthpiece of Palestine on the Net with regular "progress" reports on the settlement process.

US Census Bureau

http://www.census.gov

More statistics on the US and its citizens than you'll ever want to know. Search the main census database, read press releases, view the poster gallery, check the projected population clock, listen to clips from its radio broadcasts, then link to other serious info-head sites.

US Federal Government Servers

http://www.fie.com/www/us_gov.htm

Get to any US Fed department.

The White House

http://www.whitehouse.gov

Slick Willy might not really be at his PC when you choose to "speak out" through the White House's official suggestion form, but you never know, something just might filter through. It's easy to be cynical about this PR exercise, particularly the moribund guided tour, but it does show the doors of democracy are at least ajar.

HEALTH

Achoo

http://www.achoo.com

Like a Yahoo of health and wellbeing sites. Drill down until you get your medicine.

Alternative Medicine

http://www.pitt.edu/~cbw/altm.html

Part of the Net's ongoing research function is the ability to
contact people who've road-tested alternative remedies and
can report on their efficacy. Start here and work your way to
an answer.

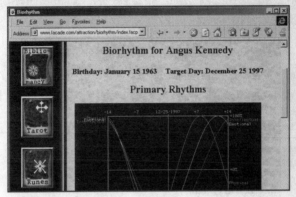

Biorhythm Generator

http://www.facade.com/attraction/biorhythm/

The Skeptic's Dictionary says biorhythms are a con. Generate
your own and put it to the test.

Dr Squat

http://www.ipf.com/fredhome.htm

Avoid getting sand kicked in your face through deep full
squats. There's more in the Weightlifting FAQ at:
http://www.imp.mtu.edu/~babucher/weights.html

The Drugs Archive

http://www.hyperreal.com/drugs/

Articles, primarily accumulated from the alt.drugs
newsgroup, that provide first-hand perspectives on the
pleasures and dangers of recreational drugs. See also:
http://www.paranoia.com/drugs/

First Aid Online

http://www.prairienet.org/~autumn/firstaid/

Advice that could save a life.

Health on the Net

http://www.hon.ch

Medical search engine.

Healthfinder

http://www.healthfinder.gov

US Government-funded directory pointing to a qualified selection of health resources. Search by ailment, for a Web address or phone number.

HealthWorld

http://www.healthy.net

Health megasite styled as a cybervillage with its own university, library, nutrition clinic, self-help center, marketplace, and newsroom. Aimed at practitioners and patients alike with a healthy balance of the conventional to the alternative.

Interactive Patient

http://medicus.marshall.edu/medicus.htm

Determine whether you're really cut out for the quackhood with this doctor/patient simulation. First fire a few questions, make an examination, x-ray, diagnose, and prescribe a remedy. Then send a hefty bill, turn on the answerphone and shoot off to get blotto at the golf course.

Medscape

http://www.medscape.com

While this medical forum is primarily aimed at health pros and med students, it's equally useful to anyone concerned with their general well-being.

NursingNet

http://www.nursingnet.com

Springboard to medical discussion groups, professional bodies, and other nursing resources.

Online Birth Center

http://www.efn.org/~djz/birth/birthindex.html

Support for midwives and parents, especially anxious expectant mums.

Pharm Web

http://www.pharmweb.net

Pharmaceutical Yellow Pages.

Poisons Information Database

http://vhp.nus.sg/PID/

Directory of plant, snake, and animal toxin cures, information centers, and practitioners.

Reuters Health

http://www.reutershealth.com

Medical newswires, reviews, opinion, and reference.

Smart Drugs and Nootropics

http://www.damicon.fi/sd/

If nootropics really make you smarter, how can we afford not to take them? Read all sides and decide whether it's money well spent at offshore pill barns like: http://www.smart-drugs.com

The Virtual Hospital

http://indy.radiology.uiowa.edu/VirtualHospital.html

Patient care and distance learning via online multimedia tools such as illustrated surgical walkthroughs.

The Visible Human Project

http://www.nlm.nih.gov/research/visible/

These unappetizing scans were once the talk of the Net. Namely because, though not mentioned here, the thinly sliced fillets came from the frozen body of an executed serial killer. And now the visible woman, interactive knee, and virtual colonoscopy appear on the menu.

Yoga

http://www.timages.com/yoga.htm

Stretch yourself back into shape with a personalized routine.

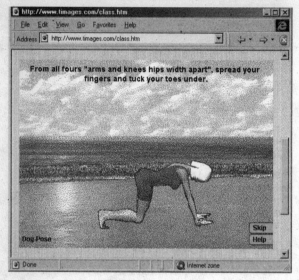

KIDS (MOSTLY)

Animal Information Database

http://www.bev.net/education/SeaWorld/

Tune in to the Web cams at the right time and you'll catch J.J. the grey whale being fed, or any of thirty-two species of sharks doing the kind of big fish chomping stuff that makes surfers shiver. After that there's games, teaching guides, and quizzes about such other adorables as dolphins, dugongs, gorillas, lions, tigers, and walruses.

The Asylum's Lite-Board

http://asylum.cid.com/lb/

This is fun. Insert colored pegs into a board, one color at a time, to create a pretty picture. Then call it something clever, pin it up in the gallery, and hunt for a buyer. Hours of gainful employment.

The Bug Club

http://www.ex.ac.uk/bugclub/

Creepy crawly fan club with e-pal page, newsletters, and pet care sheets on how to keep your newly-bottled tarantulas, cockroaches, and stick insects alive.

Carlos' Colouring Book

http://www.ravenna.com/coloring/

Select a picture segment, choose a color and then shade it in. You don't need to be Leonardo.

Children's Literature Web Guide

http://www.ucalgary.ca/~dkbrown/

Critical roundup of recent kids books, and links to texts.

Club Girl Tech

http://www.girltech.com

Encourages smart girls to get interested in technology without coming across all geeky.

Disney.com

http://www.disney.com

Guided catalog of Disney's movies, books, theme parks, records, interactive CD Roms and such. For a richer experience, try its commercial online service: http://www.dailyblast.com If you're with MSN, it's free, otherwise you can trial it for two weeks and then decide whether to pay.

Everything Cool

http://www.everythingcool.com

Budding ezine written by under 18s for under 18s.

Fractal Explorer

http://www.vis.colostate.edu/~user1209/fractals/

A fractal is a complex self-similar and chaotic mathematical object that reveals more detail as you get closer. Explore a famous example, the Mandelbrot set, by zooming in on the image and changing the color palette. But you needn't understand the complex iteration to generate some funky graphics.

Kids Web

http://www.npac.syr.edu/textbook/kidsweb/

Explore a heap of stuff from 20 main educational subject categories.

Kids' Space

http://www.kids-space.org

Free hideout for kids to swap art, music, and stories with new friends across the world.

Learn2

http://learn2.com

Figure out how to do all sorts of things from fixing a zipper to spinning a basketball. While the interests aren't strictly for kids, there's nothing here that's too hard for a whippersnapper.

Make a Map

http://ellesmere.ccm.emr.ca/wnaismap/naismap.html

Tailor-make your own Canadian map. Specify all sorts of multiple constraints, layers, and relief projections, like political boundaries, geological provinces, and even the grizzly bear range.

Math Magic Activities

http://www.scri.fsu.edu/~dennisl/CMS/activity/math_magic.html

Card, rope, and calculation tricks that require no mirrors or sleight of hand, just a basic understanding of maths.

Mr. Edible Starchy Tuber Head

http://winnie.acsu.buffalo.edu/potatoe/

Create your own, customized Mr. Potato Head.

White House for Kids

http://www.whitehouse.gov/WH/kids/html/kidshome.html

Follow Socks through the White House to uncover its
previous inhabitants, including the kids and pets. Then,
write to the resident moggy and get the goss on what goes
down in DC after dark.

Yahooligans

http://www.yahooligans.com

Kid-friendly Web guide intuitively organized into subject
groups like dinosaurs, hobbies, and homework answers. Like
big brother Yahoo, but without the dodgy and heavy stuff.

The Yuckiest Site on the Internet

http://www.nj.com/yucky/

Crawl behind the walls with Rodney the Roach, get all the
dirt from Wendell the Worm Reporter, mouth off in Strong
Words, or kick with the New Jersey Youth soccer team.

LEGAL

Advertising Law

http://www.webcom.com/~lewrose/home.html

How far you can push your products has always been an iffy
end of the law. And on the Internet, where any snake-oil
merchant can set up shop for next to nothing, many business
precedents are yet to be set. Here's help in finding the fine
line between puffery and lies.

Bentham Archive of British Law

http://www.ndirect.co.uk/~law/bentham.htm

Independent synopsis of Criminal, Roman, European, and
property law, plus UK legal threads and essential lawyer jokes.

Law Crawler

http://www.lawcrawler.com

Search the Web for legal info worldwide. Then try Findlaw:
http://www.findlaw.com

The 'Lectric Law Library

http://www.lectlaw.com

Legal repository aimed at both laypeople and pros. Archives reams of legal references plus guides to legal forms, phrases, software, law schools, business formalities, and professional bodies, as well as the latest case news.

Seamless

http://www.seamless.com

Exceptional local content plus a directory which seems to adequately span the broad ambit of legal carrying-ons.

West's US Legal Directory

http://www.westpub.com

Accused of grand theft, arson, or murder one? Then whip through this database of over half a million US lawyers who'd rather see you go free than go without their fee.

MUSEUMS AND GALLERIES

A-Bomb WWWMuseum, Hiroshima

http://www.csi.ad.jp/ABOMB/index.html

Fiftieth anniversary commemoration of the Hiroshima and Nagasaki bombs, interviews with survivors, and exhibits from the Hiroshima Peace Park and Museum.

Andy Warhol Museum

http://www.warhol.org/warhol/

Not all the Pop auteur's works are here online but you can virtually tour the Pittsburgh gallery and see what's left out. Then order the book, postcard set, and T-shirt. It certainly saves on the travel.

Central Intelligence Museum

http://www.inch.com/~dna/CIMWelcome.html

Spy toys and an active imagination on parade.

Glass Eye Stash

Microfilm (Minox 8x11 mm) is coiled inside glass eye. Film

The Exploratorium

http://www.exploratorium.edu

Museums generally haven't translated to the Web too successfully but this showing from San Francisco's Exploratorium is a notable exception. Some of its 650-odd interactive exhibits have adapted quite well, making it an engaging and educative experience, especially for children.

Expo Ticket Office

http://sunsite.unc.edu/expo/ticket_office.html

Jump aboard a virtual bus to tour exhibits of the Vatican, Soviet archives, European exploration of the Americas, Dead Sea Scrolls, Museum of Paleontology, and the city of Spalato. After all that, you're dropped off at the Expo Restaurant for a feed of French tucker.

Field Museum of Natural History, Chicago

http://www.bvis.uic.edu/museum/

Page through the eras in the DNA to Dinosaurs exhibit, downloading movies and sound bites. Or get caught in the spell of Haitian Vodou art. More for the kids.

Museum of Modern Art NY

http://www.moma.org

If you only ever visit one modern art museum ... here's a sample of what to expect when you get there.

Museums Around The World

http://www.icom.org/vlmp/world.html

Directory of Web museums sorted by country.

The Natural History Museum

http://www.nhm.ac.uk

London's Natural History Museum was one of the Web's pioneering sites. It has a few science galleries that could be classed as exhibits in their own right, but most of the elaborate content simply teases. It won't save you a visit but it might convince you it's worth the trip.

UCMP Time Machine

http://www.ucmp.berkeley.edu/help/timeform.html

Jump aboard the University of California's Museum of Paleontology's time machine for a rocky ride through the geological eras.

Vatican Library

http://www.ncsa.uiuc.edu/SDG/Experimental/
vatican.exhibit/exhibit/Main_Hall.html

Stroll though virtual rooms in the Vatican, each with its own specialty such as literature, music, nature, archeology, humanism, biology, and mathematics.

WebMuseum

http://lot49.tristero.com/wm/

Famous art from Gothic right through to Pop, plus classical music samples, special exhibitions of medieval art, Cézanne, and more to come, complete with commentary courtesy of the *Encyclopaedia Britannica*. Used to be called Le Louvre, until the French lawyers stepped in.

MUSIC

Music is becoming one the Web's strongest selling points and the myriad band, label, and fan sites are fortunately well served by directories like Unfurled (see p.282). Our selections should be seen as little more than starter options. Before you check in grab the RealAudio player – http://www.real.com – so you can listen to music samples.

Addicted to Noise

http://www.addict.com

Monthly news and reviews with a heavy bias towards the alternative rock end of the spectrum.

Algorithmic Music Stream

http://www.stg.brown.edu/~maurice/

Streaming RealAudio music generated on the fly by an algorithm. Not exactly melodic, but not unlistenable either.

All Music Guide

http://www.allmusic.com/amg/music_root.html

Massive music database spanning most popular genres, with bios, reviews, ratings, and keyword crosslinks to related sounds, sites, and online ordering. It's well-researched, sufficiently critical, and surprisingly comprehensive, though appears limited to US releases.

Are Oh Vee

http://www.areohvee.com

Music videos using the Vivo Active plug-in. Similar to Real Video in that they play while downloading, but again the quality hardly compares to TV.

Audio Review

http://www.consumer-review.com/audio/audio.shtml

Audio equipment reviewed by end users. A fine concept but somewhat flawed by extreme opinions. Still, if you're not satisfied here, there's more than enough alternatives off the links page.

Aus Music Guide

http://www.amws.com.au

Massive directory of all that's shakin' down under.

Blackmail Mail Order

http://www.blackmail.co.uk

One of the better British mail order music stores,
particularly strong on 70s stuff, from prog to punk.

Canonical List of Weird Band Names

http://home.earthlink.net/~chellec/

Just be thankful your parents weren't so creative.

CDnow!

http://cdnow.com

CDnow! is everything you've ever wanted from an
entertainment megastore – but online. Alongside a vast
range of CDs, it has reviews, press clippings, and RealAudio
clips, plus it sells movies, clothes, and magazines, and
accepts international orders, which, in some cases, could
work out cheaper than buying locally. Compare prices with
SongSearch: http://www.icorp.net/songsearch/ and CD Universe:
http://www.cduniverse.com

Cerberus Digital Jukebox

http://www.cdj.co.uk

It's more the eclectic selections from labels like Ninja Tune,
Moving Shadow, and On U Sound, than magnitude, that rates
this as a visit. Download the player, flip through the free
samples, and decide whether you'd be willing to pay for more.

Chaos Kitty

http://www.chaoskitty.com

Bachelor beats from the easy listening new school that's
rising from the ashes of the loungecore fad. See also:
http://www.ultralounge.com

Classical Music on the Net

http://www.musdoc.com/classical/

Gateway to the timeless.

The Dance Music Resource
http://www.juno.co.uk

New and forthcoming dance releases, UK radio slots, and a
well stocked link directory.

Digital Dream
http://www.openworld.co.uk/staff/dd/

Amateurish CD reviews conveniently searchable by
genre, rating, and title. Covers the overlapping spectrum
of techno, ambient, and drum'n'bass. Astound your too-
cool disco pals with your new-found fluency in chill,
ambient, trance, and trip hop, without ever having to buy
an album.

Digital Jams
http://www.digitaljams.com

Internet music pirating has caused quite a stink. Not
surprisingly when you can download full CD quality tracks
compressed in MP3 format. Bear in mind while it's legal to
store them on your hard drive for 24 hours, after that you
might breach copyright. Here's just one example of what to
expect. For more, see: http://pw2.netcom.com/~the-fly/

Dirty Linen
http://kiwi.futuris.net/linen/

Excerpts from the US folk, roots, and world music magazine.
Includes a US gig guide.

dotmusic
http://www.dotmusic.com

UK and worldwide charts, gossip, contacts, and profiles from
top industry rags *Music Week*, *Record Mirror*, *MBI*, and
Gavin.

ECM
http://www.ecmrecords.com

Sound samples and online ordering from the German-based
jazz and contemporary classical label, home to the likes of
Keith Jarrett, Jan Garbarek, Pat Metheny, and Arvo Part.

The Ever Expanding Web Music Listing
http://www.columbia.edu/~hauben/music/web-music.html

Monolithic directory split into academic, non-academic, user-maintained, geographically local, and artist-specific sites. Comes close to the impossible task of completely indexing the Net's music content.

Firefly
http://www.firefly.com

Rate and slate a hundred or so records and films and have your taste buds diagnosed. Once processed, it can recommend selections you're likely to adore or abhor, and hook you up with your peers.

Folk Roots
http://www.cityscape.co.uk/froots/

UK equivalent to *Dirty Linen* (see p.275) delivers on British and American folk roots, and Celtic music, with a sublime ear for the best in global sounds.

Fused
http://www.fused.com

Chill out, drum'n'bass, techno, downbeat, and house, reviewed with the odd clip to boot.

Global Electronic Music Market
http://gemm.com

One point access to nearly two million record titles from over 900 sources.

The Grateful Dead
http://www.dead.net

Official place to speak no ill of the Dead. Thanks, Jerry – RIP.

Juan Luis Guerra
http://www.nd.edu/~rvillaro/JLG/

Clips from the Latin superstar plus English and Spanish lyrics, FAQs, interviews, and links to other Merengue and Dominican Republic music pages.

Hyperreal

http://hyperreal.com

One-stop rave shop. Find out what's hip, where it's at, what's going down, and what's the best nourishment.

Independent Underground Music Archive

http://www.iuma.com

Get in touch with hundreds of unsigned and indie-label underground musicians. All provide samples, biographies, and contacts. It's hard work, but you never know what you'll hit.

Michael Jackson Internet Fan Club

http://www.fred.net/mjj/

All you want (and more than you need) to know about little Mr. Epaulettes and his troops.

Jazz Central Station

http://www.jazzcentralstation.com

Bulging global jazz multimedia digest in English or Japanese.

Junglematic 747

http://www.mbinter.com/ss7x7/

Mix your own ambient, jazz, and breakbeat tracks instantly with this astounding Shockwave toy.

Kraftwerk Infobahr

http://www.cs.umu.se/studenter/kraftwerk/

Demos, live out-takes, MIDI files, interviews, lyrics, and the discography of pioneering Krautrockers, Kraftwerk.

Live Concerts

http://www.liveconcerts.com

Major gigs live in RealAudio.

London Techno Events

http://www.sorted.org/london/

What's spinning around London's techno circuit.

Lyrics Server

http://www.lyrics.ch

Search a massive lyrics database by title, artist, or text. Everyone from Aaron Neville to 999.

MIDI Farm

http://www.midifarm.com

Thousands of synthesized debasements of popular tunes, TV themes, and film scores. Cheesy listening at its finest.

Mozart's Musical Dice

http://lecaine.music.mcgill.ca/~dawkins/html/waltz.html

Anyone can write music. Even you. Just by rolling a dice. Well that's what Mozart reckoned anyway. See for yourself. Or be like U2 and toss a coin.

MTV

http://www.mtv.com

What's ironic about MTV's official home on the Web is it's all just a bit too much hard work. Maybe it's not really fair to complain, after all the content's there: news, charts, vid clips, interviews, reviews, and great ladles of its trademark popcultural blancmange. Only you're forced into reading, waiting, and worse, having to think – and surely that's not part of the grand plan.

Music Festival Finder

http://www.festivalfinder.com

Daily-updated listings of more than 1500 forthcoming
Portaloo installations across North America. Covers all
musical genres.

NME

http://nme.com

Weekly soundclipped record reviews, charts, features, news,
gigs, demos, archives, and live chats from the world's most
influential indie/pop tabloid.

Obsolete

http://www.obsolete.com

Mine down from here for
underground labels,
artists, and ezines from
the ilk of Ninja Tune,
B12 and Metalheadz.
Also home to Nicholas
Saunder's ecstasy
education resource.

Offbeat

http://www.neosoft.com/~offbeat/

Monthly music news,
directories, dates, and
jazzy sounds fresh out of
Louisiana.

Polyester Records

http://www.polyester.com.au/PolyEster/

Large Australian indie selection for email order. Ships
internationally, but Australia's no cheap port.

Rap.Org

http://www.rap.org

Videos, sound clips, lyrics, clothes, gossip, and links to just
about every other hip hop haven.

The Residents

http://www.residents.com

The world's strangest neo-classical ensemble has
performed anonymously, wearing giant eyeball heads,
for a quarter of a century, so efficient at subterfuge that
even their most avid fans remain bewildered. Take this
one for instance.

Resonance Records

http://www.netcreations.com/resonance/

Fast-moving eclectic house/techno/drum'n'bass mail
order catalog with recommendations and the occasional
sample.

Rolling Stones

http://www.stones.com

Originally set up to promote the Stones' Voodoo Lounge
album, with ongoing video feeds, loads of sound files,
interviews, and pictures. Carved its place in history by
hosting the first live Internet concert broadcast which,
although not a critical success, was a turning point in the
Net's evolution from research tool to lifestyle accessory.

The Rough Guide to Rock

http://www.roughguides.com/rock/

What can we say? The world's coolest rock encyclopedia
online? It's certainly the most democratic, having been
developed on the Web, using fans as contributors, for the
1100-plus entries. At time of writing, the Rough Guide is set
to kick into a new incarnation with weekly updates of
albums and biographies, new bands, forums for the neglected
and ignored, and more. All entries are also due to link
through to CD ordering, in case you feel moved to explore
lost gems from Slapp Happy or Brainticket, or the latest from
Radiohead.

Shareware Music Machine

http://www.hitsquad.com/smm/

Tons of shareware music players, editors, and composition
tools, for every platform.

Sites and Sound Links

http://www.servtech.com/public/koberlan/

Links to musicians' resources.

Sonic Net

http://www.sonicnet.com

Big name live cybercasts and chats, plus news and reviews.
Something fresh daily.

Sounds Online

http://www.soundsonline.com

Preview loops and samples, free in RealAudio. Pay to
download studio quality.

Spice Hut/Shack/Slap/Abuse

http://www.kig.co.uk/spice/hut/

http://spicegirls.ukonline.co.uk

http://www.head-space.com/Urban75/spicebelt.html

http://privatewww.essex.ac.uk/~tchand/abuse.html

Follow the spice route downhill.

Stereolab

http://www.maths.monash.edu.au/people/rjh/stereolab/

All the gas on the British front-runners in the Moog and
strings revival.

Streetsound

http://www.streetsound.com

Warren of urban
sound and style,
ranging from the
latest electro clips to
a series of streetwear
forums where hip-
hop label lemmings
disclose what brands
they wouldn't be
seen shot dead in.

Sub Pop Records

http://www.subpop.com

Try and buy from the original house of grunge.

Supersonic Guide

http://www.supersonic.demon.co.uk

Links to Britpop and UK indie band sites, labels, and mailing lists.

Taxi

http://www.taxi.com

Online music A&R service. And guess what? You and your plastic kazoo are just what they're looking for.

The Ultimate Band List

http://www.ubl.com

Don't give up if your favorite pop ensemble, music mag, or record shop isn't stowed in here. While it's probably the most professional effort at an all-encompassing music directory, it's nowhere near complete. Still, if you're after something artist-specific, it's generally ace.

Timecast

http://www.timecast.com

What's new on the RealAudio airwaves. Get a sound card, download RealAudio, and visit this site regularly.

Trouser Press

http://www.trouserpress.com

This encyclopedic guide covers alternative rock from the 70s to the present. It features excellent, no-nonsense biographies of the cool and obscure, plus pretty comprehensive discographies, linked through to *CD Now* for order fulfillment.

Unfurled

http://www.unfurled.com

Yahoo/MTV search engine collaboration that points to some 80,000 music sites plus reviews, events, and cybercasts.

Wav Central

http://www.wavcentral.com

Loads of TV/Film audio clips and sound effects. Fun for
assigning to computer events like mail delivery. That is until
they drive everyone around you up the wall.

WorldWide Music

http://worldwidemusic.com

Online music store with close to a half million thirty-second
sound samples from over fifty thousand artists across most
popular genres.

NATURE

Australian Botanical Gardens

http://155.187.10.12/anbg/anbg.html

All the gear on Canberra's Botanical Garden's projects,
flora, and fauna. Like tourist guides, flowering calendars,
biodiversity studies, bird and frog call sound files, and
even the fire procedures. It's a bit like stumbling into a
government office to reams of papers strewn across the
floor in unrelated piles – but in this case substance beats
style.

British Trees

http://www.u-net.com/trees/home.htm

Apparently there are only 33 native British trees. Find out
all about them here, though they might be easier to
recognize if the site included some pictures!

Chocolate Toxicity in Dogs

http://www.netpet.com/articles/choc.tox.html

How to pop off a greedy mutt with household ingredients.

Cool Dog Site of the Day

http://www.st.rim.or.jp/~ito/d/dogmark.html

You really have to wonder about someone who loves dogs this
unconditionally.

Dog Index

http://dogindex.com

Delve a dedicated database for industry doings deep in
American doggiedom.

The Electronic Zoo

http://netvet.wustl.edu/e-zoo.htm

Directory of fauna information that will lead you way up the
virtual garden path before you find what you're looking for.
Despite its name, it's not a virtual zoo with animations and
recordings of animal sounds. However, when one arrives,
you'll be sure to find it here.

The EnviroWeb

http://envirolink.org

Claims to be the largest online environmental information
service on the planet.

Environmental Organization Directory

http://www.webdirectory.com

Primary production and green minded sites sorted by focus
and with comments.

Gardening.com

http://www.gardening.com

Includes an illustrated gardening encyclopedia, a problem
solver to debug some 700 horticultural ailments, and a guide
to hundreds of other ground breaking sites.

The Hamster Page

http://www.tela.bc.ca/hamster/

Definitive guide to online
hamsters and their
inevitable obituaries.

MooCow

http://www.moocow.com

Living under the influence
of cattle as lifestyle
accessories.

Natural History Bookshop

http://www.nhbs.co.uk

Browse or search the world's largest environmental bookshop.

NetVet

http://netvet.wustl.edu/vet.htm

A certain way to anything animal-oriented. Choose from
the NetVet Gopher, Electronic Zoo, Veterinary Medicine
page of the WWW Virtual Library, or one of the several
specialist directories.

Planet Ark

http://www.planetark.org/new/worldnews.html

Daily environmental news from Reuters.

The Virtual Garden

http://www.pathfinder.com/vg/

Splendid horticultural digest – a nibble of Time Warner's
megalithic Pathfinder complex – that provides the most
fulsome online guide to gardening. Includes several
plant society and gardening magazines, databases, book
excerpts, plant directories, and an electronic
encyclopedia which helps pick the best plants for your
patch.

NEWS, NEWSPAPERS, AND MAGAZINES

Now that almost every newspaper in the world is
teething on the Net, it's beyond this guide to list more
than a scattering of the majors, the pioneers, or the
worthies. For comprehensive listings check
AJR/Newslink, Crayon, Ecola's Newsstand, MediaInfo or
the Ultimate Collection of News links (see p.291). See also
our "Ezine" and "Music" listings.

ABC News

http://www.abc.net.au

24-hour news as it breaks from the Australian Broadcasting
Commission.

AJR/Newslink

http://www.newslink.org

American Journalism Review features and a well-stocked directory of newspapers, magazines, broadcasters' and journalists' resources.

Blender

http://www.blender.com

Grab the issue, install it, then fire it up online. If you've seen the CD version, it's more of the same. A fairy floss skim across the surface of pop culture cynicism, with brainless games, trivialities, and interactive tricks, all cushed up in that retro Jetsons' look.

Christian Science Monitor

http://www.csmonitor.com

Daily print news and opinion, plus live and archived audio feeds from Monitor Radio.

Clarinet News

http://www.clarinet.com

High-quality subscription news service with a toe-hold into such big guns as Reuters, Associated Press, and Newsbytes. A single-user subscription costs about $40 per month, or cheaper if shared across a site. If your access provider subscribes, you'll get the clari. series free in Usenet or via this Web address. It also bolsters Newspage's industrial news: http://www.newspage.com

CNET

http://www.cnet.com

Daily technology news and features (some in RealAudio), plus reviews, games, and downloads, along with schedules, transcripts, and related stories from CNET's broadcasting network. Worth reading weekly as a lightweight way to keep up with what's what in computing.

CNN

http://www.cnn.com

Up-to-the minute US and world news, weather, sports, showbiz, technology, food, and health updates as only CNN does it.

Crayon

http://www.crayon.net

Create your own custom paper from hundreds of local, national, and international online sources, such as newspapers, site reviews, sports bulletins, weather reports, comics, and much more. It grabs the headlines. You click to retrieve the story. Looks a bit like the future of news. Try it – you'll be hooked.

Drudge Report

http://www.drudgereport.com

Drudge's knack of leaking stories (though not always true) by email bulletin, before the major press makes this a worthy free subscription. This front page also makes a bookmark and search engine to many of the best news sources on the Net.

Ecola's Newsstand

http://www.ecola.com/news/

Only paper-printed newspapers or magazines with actively
updated English-language content and free access qualify for
this list – that's over 4000. Search, browse, or check what's new.

The Economist

http://www.economist.com

Politics and business commentary, plus a small slab of the
magazine free. The lot if you subscribe.

The Electronic Daily Telegraph

http://www.telegraph.co.uk

Generous daily doses of news, sports, finance, entertainment,
and pictures.

Electronic Newsstand

http://enews.com

Directory of over 2000 magazines' home pages, plus home to
another 200 or so, with sample articles and subscription
facilities.

The Guardian Online

http://www.guardian.co.uk

Selections from the UK *Guardian*'s Thursday Online liftout,
snippets from the broadsheet, the entire weekly edition, jobs,
and cultural bits you won't find anywhere else. High quality,
but not as yet a daily replacement.

The Hindu

http://www.webpage.com/hindu/

Daily online edition of India's national newspaper.

HotWired

http://www.hotwired.com

Part of the *Wired* magazine family, now focusing firmly on
the techie future. The site has delayed archives of the
magazine plus Wired News – an exceptional source of
breaking news of the new electric frontiers. Also a collection
of distinct ezines on Web design, Net culture, jobs, music,

and travel, including the full text of several Rough Guides.
Subscribe to the daily email bulletins, or have them pushed
through PointCast, to see what's new.

InfoSeek Personal
http://personal.infoseek.com

Live personalized news, stock quotes, comics, stars, weather,
movie, and TV updates. Specify which topics, companies,
people, sports, etc, you want to monitor and it will look after
the rest. All the major search directories maintain something
similar. You'll feel flooded.

MediaInfo
http://www.mediainfo.com/edpub/

Switched-on Net publishing news, commentary, and advice
from *Editor & Publisher* magazine. Also maintains an
exceptional online newspaper list.

Multimedia Newsstand
http://mmnewsstand.com

Probably as good as anywhere to lodge subscriptions to any
of over 600 popular magazines or to order videos. Little in
the way of content though.

NewsHub
http://www.newshub.com

Technology headlines from several sources, updated every
quarter hour. Click on the headline to go direct to the
original story. Saves flipping through several sites.
NewsLinx: http://www.newslinx.com is more selective, and
delivers by email, but not as fresh.

NewsWorks
http://www.newsworks.com

Aggregates the top stories from some 200 US newspapers.
Like Crayon, except you're not in control of the content.

New York Times Syndicate
http://nytsyn.com

Link down to *New York Times* daily publications such as

the *Boston Globe*, *Tennis Online*, and naturally, the *Times* itself as well as its syndicated columns on computers and health.

PA NewsCentre

http://www.pa.press.net

24-hour live UK news, parliamentary proceedings, weather, sports, broadcast listings and ball-by-ball cricket.

Pathfinder

http://www.pathfinder.com

Whoah, this one from Time Warner's a monster, with something for everyone. With publications like *Time*, *People*, *Sports Illustrated*, *Life*, *Money*, *Fortune*, *Entertainment Weekly*, and *Vibe*, plus CNN, to draw from, that's to be expected. But it's not all rehashed features and samples. It's a publishing venture in its own right and more like what you'd expect from an Online Service. And not a bit like Crapfinder: http://c3f.com/crapfind.html

PM Zone

http://popularmechanics.com

Popular Mechanics has been showing us "the easy way to do hard things" since the turn of the century. It provides a generous selection of stories, retrospectives, movies, Web tools, home improvement projects, and much more.

South Polar Times

http://205.174.118.254/nspt/home.htm

Whenever the temperature falls below 100 F, the gallant South Polars first squeeze into a 200 F sauna, then charge out into the snow starkers from the socks up. That's what they do for fun, in case you've ever wondered.

Sydney Morning Herald

http://www.smh.com.au

Streamlined news, columns, sports, computers, and the Metro, on the Net before the *Herald* hits the street. Plus archives, opinion polls, and links to the *Financial Review* and Melbourne's *The Age*.

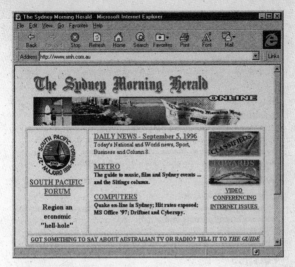

The Times of London

http://www.the-times.co.uk http://www.sunday-times.co.uk

The full *Times* and *Sunday Times* newspapers, on the Net, before breakfast. Threatens to make print look redundant.

Ultimate Collection of News links

http://pppp.net/links/news/

Broad selection of magazines and newspapers.

USA Today

http://www.usatoday.com

News, sport, money, life, and weather from the US national daily.

The Voice of America

http://www.voa.gov

Listen to audio clips of the day's news in various languages as you browse the staid megabroadcaster's other info.

PERSONAL

Match.com

http://www.match.com

Browse for a perfect match. All entries come from the Net.
Dip out here, then try: http://www.date.com

Single Search

http://nsns.com/single-search/

Don't stay at home alone playing on your computer. Just
submit your interests – beer, curry, Nukem, footy, engine
numbers, and speed metal, say – and sit back and wait.
Before long, you'll be Dukematching by candlelight.

Web Personals

http://www.webpersonals.com

Generally harmless free cyberdating and friendship service
with an anonymous remailer for the coy.

POLITICS

Amnesty International

http://www.amnesty.org

"If you think virtual reality is interesting, try reality," says
Amnesty International, global crusaders for human rights.
Discover how you can help in its battles against militant
regimes and injustice.

Australian Political Parties

http://www.liberal.org.au

http://www.npa.org.au

http://www.alp.org.au

http://www.democrats.org.au

Liberal, National, Labor, and Democrat parties' sites
respectively, with news, history, policies and contacts
(although few by email). Expect a flurry of fresh content as
elections loom.

British Political Parties

http://www.labour.org.uk

http://www.libdems.org.uk

http://www.conservative-party.org.uk

Now that the hustings are over, and the reality's set in, all's left is for Labour to deliver. Though it's unlikely you'll see much happening on any of these pages in the near future, they're still a good source for contacts to badger.

Noam Chomsky Archive

http://www.worldmedia.com/archive/

The works of Noam Chomsky, MIT Professor of Linguistics and outspoken critic of US foreign policy. He might change the way you read the world.

Conspiracies

http://www.turnleft.com/conspiracy.html

Create your own conspiracy theory.

DeathNet

http://www.islandnet.com/~deathnet/open.html

A side-effect of DeathNet's euthanasia campaign was the media's predictable focus on the Net as a medium for encouraging suicide. Consequently a large slab of this "right to die" library is dedicated to examples of the press's propensity to dramatize.

Feminist Activist Resources

http://www.igc.apc.org/women/feminist.html

Hundreds of links to feminist forums, articles, political
action groups, legal documents, news items, women's
organizations, counseling services, and spare-rib tickling
humor.

Free Burma

http://freeburma.org

A good example of the kind of international campaign that
the Net can promulgate. And there are few better causes
than this push against Burma's tyrannical military
government.

Friends of the Earth

http://www.foe.co.uk

Find out about Friends of the Earth's latest campaign, your
nearest group, results of environment studies, or how to join
forces.

The Gallup Organization

http://www.gallup.com

About 20% of Gallup's online visitors fill out its
questionnaires and opinion polls. Not a bad response
compared to say, Barclays' callers requesting credit card
flyers. It also supplies results of past surveys, so you can
keep up to date with trends and ratings such as the fickle
swings of Slick Willy's popularity.

Gay and Lesbian Alliance Against Defamation

http://www.datalounge.com/glaad/glaad.html

Campaigning against homophobia in the media and beyond.

Greenpeace International

http://www.greenpeace.org

Apparently the happy ending starts here.

Intelligence Watch Report

http://www.awpi.com/IntelWeb/

Brief updates on political disturbances, terrorism, and

subterfuge worldwide, plus intelligence directories and jobs for spies. And a mirror of the Secrecy and Government Bulletin, published by the Federation of American Scientists, which challenges excessive government secrecy in the US. But maybe it's just a diversion.

One World

http://www.oneworld.org

Crisis news, submitted by a who's who of NGOs and charities, along with their plans. All sortable by country, date, and theme. Plus, daily archived RealAudio news from several short-wave broadcasters.

Spunk Press

http://www.cwi.nl/cwi/people/Jack.Jansen/spunk/Spunk_Home.html

All the anarchy you'll ever need organized neatly and with reassuring authority.

Trinity Atomic Test Site

http://www.envirolink.org/issues/nuketesting/

See what went on, and what went off, fifty years ago, then file into the archives of high-energy weapon testing, and read who else has been sharpening the tools of world peace.

United Nations Development Program

http://www.undp.org

Daily news of the United Nations' involvement in international affairs.

US Party politics

http://www.democratic-party.org

http://www.townhall.com

The digital Democrats link to a couple of dozen senators, and other party strands. You can't actually register to vote online, but you can order the paperwork. The Republican Townhall – the sassiest, dirtiest Republican site – is a pretty fascinating meeting place for Newt's own party reptiles.

RADIO

Looking for live Net radio? Download RealAudio first from:
http://www.real.com, then check http://www.timecast.com for the
latest broadcast listings.

Audio Net

http://www.audionet.com

RealAudio broadcasts from over 175 radio and television
stations, live sports and music, thousands of CDs on demand
and more in the vaults.

BBC

http://www.bbc.co.uk

Becoming the broadcasting blockbuster online it is on the
airwaves. That makes it somewhat daunting, but worth the
exploration. Dig in and you'll find BBC TV, radio and World
Service program mini-sites of varying quality, some with full
length RealAudio archives. Take Radio 1, for example. If you
miss Pete Tong, John Peel, or its swinging technology
special, the Digital Update, you can catch them all online,
anywhere in the world. Whatever you expect from the Beeb,
be it education, news, sport or music, it's surfacing here.

BRS Radio Directory

http://www.radio-directory.com

Radio stations around the world with Web sites and, in many cases, live or archived audio feeds.

Phil's Old Radios

http://www.accessone.com/~philn/

If you've ever drifted to sleep bathed in the soft glow of a crackling Bakelite wireless, Phil's collection of vacuum-era portables may instantly flood you with childhood memories.

Radio Station WXYC

http://sunsite.unc.edu/wxyc/

Live broadcasts from freestyle radio WXYC, the first real-time station on the Net.

Real Time in RealAudio

http://realtime.cbcstereo.com

You'll need a sound card and RealAudio to listen to this Net radio's broadcasts on your PC or Mac. Unlike real radio, it's not quite live. Choose from a menu of pre-recorded specials.

Shortwave Radio Catalog

http://itre.ncsu.edu/radio/

If it's not on the Net, maybe it's crackling over the airwaves. Find out what's on what frequency, and get the latest station ID clips, maps, news, satellite info, propagation reports, sunspot readings, spy station sitings, and much more.

Veronica FM Kits

http://www.legend.co.uk/~veronica/

Build your very own clandestine radio station for less than the price of a PC, and join ranks with:
http://www.0171.com/fullweb/pirates.html and http://www.frn.com

Virgin Radio

http://www.virginradio.co.uk

Tune into London's Virgin FM live via RealAudio.

REAL ESTATE

Home Scout
http://www.homescout.com

Scan several US real estate databases at once.

International Real Estate Directory
http://www.ired.com

For the rare times in your life when you'll actively seek
the attentions of a real estate hawker. Wherever you
want to live, this site will have you sheltered in a flash.

Mortgage Calculators
http://www.mi-mls.com/calc.html

Figure out your monthly payments or what you can't
afford.

Pike Net
http://www.pikenet.com

Reviews and rates commercial real estate sites in over 250
market areas and 42 categories.

UK Property Warehouse
http://www.uk-property.com

Well-organized, searchable warehouse of mostly UK
properties for sale or rent. Also links to mortgage
companies, removal firms, and everything else for
moving home.

REFERENCE

Acronyms
http://www.ucc.ie/info/net/acronyms/acro.html

Before you follow IBM, TNT, and HMV in initializing
your company's name, make sure it doesn't stand for
something blue by searching through these 12,000
acronyms.

alt.culture

http://www.altculture.com

Witty, digital A–Z of Nineties pop culture. Coupland meets *Encyclopaedia Britannica*. Fun to browse, maybe even enlightening, though don't blow your cool by admitting it.

Director John Woo instructs his favorite star, Chow Yun-Fat.

Alternative Dictionary

http://www.notam.uio.no/~hcholm/altlang/

Insult your foreign pals in their mother tongue.

AT&T's 1-800 Information

http://www.tollfree.att.net

Find those elusive 1-800 numbers and cut your phone bill. That is, if your online charges don't contra the savings.

Bartlett's Quotations

http://www.columbia.edu/acis/bartleby/bartlett/

Searchable database of smart remarks.

Britannica Online

http://www.eb.com

Buying this bulky set was never that practical, nor cheap. And it's not likely you'd ever read it all. So it makes more sense to leave it on a server where you can get at it as you need it, and leave it to EB to keep fresh. However, it's only free for a week. After that you or your masters will have to fork out.

Computing Dictionary

http://wombat.doc.ic.ac.uk

In theory, this concise glossary should unravel some of that fuzzy PC barrow boy jargon. However, sometimes you just end up getting more of the same.

Globalink

http://www.globalink.com

Translate documents, including Web pages, between English and French, Spanish or German, in seconds. Run it back and forth a few times and you'll end up with something that wouldn't look out of place on a kitsch Japanese T-shirt.

Jeffrey's Japanese/English Dictionary Gateway

http://www.wg.omron.co.jp/cgi-bin/j-e/

Translate English to Japanese and vice versa. View the output in plain English text or in Japanese characters either as images or via a Japanese character enhanced browser. It takes a while to get started, but there's plenty of help along the way.

LOGOS Dictionary

http://dictionary.logos.it/query/query.html

Searchable a multilingual database which returns translations and example literary passages.

One Look

http://www.onelook.com

Search more than one hundred online dictionaries at once.

Online Dictionaries

http://www.bucknell.edu/~rbeard/diction.html

Linked to more than 330 dictionaries of over 100 different languages.

Rap Dictionary

http://www.columbia.edu/~hauben/music/web-music.html

Hip-hop to English. Parental guidance recommended.

Rhyming Dictionary
http://www.cs.cmu.edu/~dougb/rhyme.html

Find words that rhyme perfectly, just with the last syllable, or sound alike but are spelt differently, sorted by proximity in meaning to another word.

Roget's Thesaurus
http://www.thesaurus.com

The bible of big words finds life anew in hypertext. But it's still useless.

School Sucks
http://www.schoolsucks.com

College plagiarist's paradise. See also:
http://www.ivyessays.com

Skeptics Dictionary
http://wheel.ucdavis.edu/~btcarrol/skeptic/dictcont.html

Punch holes through a bunch of popularly accepted superstitions and pseudo-sciences with this terse dinner party deflator.

Study Web
http://www.studyweb.com

Ideal school research aid with thousands of leads split by topic.

Strunk's Elements of Style
http://www.columbia.edu/acis/bartleby/strunk/

English usage in a nutshell.

United States Postal Services
http://www.usps.gov

Look up a Zip code, track express mail, sort out your vehicle registration or just get down and philatelic.

What's in your name?
http://www.kabalarians.com/gkh/your.htm

According to the non-profit Kabalarians, who've been doing this stuff for over 60 years, names can be rendered down to a numerical stew and served back up as a character analysis. Look yourself up in here and see what a duff choice your folks made. Then blame them for everything that's gone wrong ever since.

What is?

http://whatis.com

Internet terminology unraveled.

RELIGION

Anglicans Online!

http://www.anglican.org/online/

Gentle introduction to what Anglicans believe, with links to parishes, groups, and resources worldwide.

Bhagavad Gita

http://www.cc.gatech.edu/gvu/people/Phd/Rakesh.Mullick/gita/gita.html

To view these PostScript Sanskrit pages of the Bhagavad Gita, the most sacred of Vedic literature, you'll need a program like GhostScript or a PostScript printer. However, if your Sanskrit is not up to scratch, you may find the English summary and translation easier going.

The Bible Gateway

http://www.calvin.edu/cgi-bin/bible/

Search the Bible as a database by textual references or passage. Or turn scripture references into hyperlinks in your own documents by referring to the gateway in your HTML code.

Catholic Information Network

http://www.cin.org

Scripture, liturgy, early writings, Vatican documents, papal encyclicals, pronouncements, books, and other Catholic high-jinks.

Chick

http://chick.com

Hard-core Christian pornography.

Comparative Religion

http://weber.u.washington.edu/~madin/

Multifaith directory for religious academics.

The Global Hindu

http://www.hindunet.org

Hindu dharma – the philosophy, culture and customs.

Hell – The Online Guide

http://webpages.marshall.edu/~allen12/

This lot has never enjoyed good press. If they're ever taken seriously it's only to be accused of some heinous crime against humanity, like backmasking racy slogans into heavy metal tracks, inciting suicide as a fashion statement, or killing the Czar and his ministers. According to this galah, Satanism is a bona fide religion whose followers do not worship the devil, but follow their Darwinian urges to disinherit the meek of the earth.

The Holy See

http://www.vatican.va

Official Vatican showpiece. It's flashy, in six languages, and has to be said, boring beyond description.

Homosexuals and the Church

http://www.qrd.com/QRD/religion/

Collection of links that reflect the church's attitude to sexuality.

Islamic Resources

http://latif.com

Links to Islamic FAQs, announcements, conferences, and social events, Qu'ran teachings, Arabic news, and the Cyber Muslim guide.

Magick

http://www.student.nada.kth.se/~nv91-asa/magick.html

Tunnels to alternative spiritualist groups, strange orders, superstitions, soothsayers, and mystical literature. All stuff you should know better than to believe in, though it still makes compulsive reading. Get to the Freemasons, Rosicrucians, Temple of the Psychic Youth, and Builders of the Atydium, as well as works on Voodooism, Druidism, divination, astrology, alchemy, and so much more – it casts an eerie light on the human condition.

Maven

http://www.maven.co.il

Fattest directory of Jewish/Israeli links on the Net.

Table of Faiths

http://www.servtech.com/public/mcroghan/religion.htm

Links to info on various world religions, along with their principal saints, scriptures, and sects.

Universal Life Church

http://ulc.org/ulc/

You're already a member, just not aware of it yet. Ordain yourself a minister within seconds online and print out the certificate to frame for your bedroom wall.

The Witches' Voice

http://www.witchvox.com

Expresses a burning desire to correct misinformation about witchcraft, a legally recognized religion in the US since 1985.

SCIENCE

The Braintainment Center

http://www.brain.com

Start with a test that says you're not so bright, then prove it by buying loads of self improvement gear.

Cabot Science Library

http://www.fas.harvard.edu/~cabref/

Harvard University's library makes an ideal jumpstation for scientific research. Apart from the library's catalog and policies, it links to several Harvard scientific publications, external databases, and useful journals.

CICA Projects

http://www.cica.indiana.edu/projects/

These bods at the Center for Innovative Computer Applications are always up to something tricky. Whether it's stirring up Siamese Fighting Fish with animated challengers or weighting dices into four dimensions, they're not exactly sitting around watching the darts.

Documentation and Diagrams of the Atomic Bomb

http://neutrino.nuc.berkeley.edu/neutronics/todd/nuc.bomb.html

Gee whiz, how to make an atomic bomb. Let's hope this doesn't fall into the wrong hands.

Earth Viewer

http://www.fourmilab.ch/earthview/vplanet.html

View the Earth in space and time via this nifty simulator. Maps in real time to show the current positioning, lighting, and shadows.

Earthquake Information

http://www.civeng.carleton.ca/cgi-bin/quakes

Stats and maps of the most recent quakes worldwide. For greater detail on the latest big one see: http://www.gps.caltech.edu/~polet/recofd.html

Entomology Image Gallery

http://www.ent.iastate.edu/imagegallery/

If lice, ticks, mosquitoes, and potato beetles get you frisky, you'll sure leave this area feeling mighty aroused.

Interactive Frog Dissection

http://curry.edschool.virginia.edu/go/frog/

This step-by-step frog disembowelment was one of the Web's best loved sites in its early days. Not because it's educational, interactive, and finely detailed. Nah, because it's so gruesome. All you have to do is pin down a frog, grab your scalpel, and follow the pictures. That's all very well, but what next – serve it up for lunch?

Jungian Personality Test

http://sunsite.unc.edu/jembin/mb.pl

Confirm what a beast you really are. Skeptics insist it's simply a psychological parlor game.

Mars Pathfinder Mission

http://mpfwww.jpl.
nasa.gov

Get a bit more red dirt live from NASA's space safari microrover before you stake out your first plot at: http://www. marsshop.com

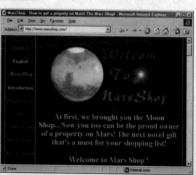

306

MIT Media Labs

http://www.media.mit.edu

If you've read *Being Digital* or any of Nicholas Negroponte's *Wired* columns, you'll know he has some pretty tall ideas about our electronic future. Here's where he gets them.

NASA

http://www.nasa.gov

Top level of NASA's mighty Web presence. Its projects, databases, policies, missions, and discoveries are strewn across the Net, but you can find them all from here, if you persist. If you saw the first moon missions in the late 60s, it's sure to bring back vivid memories of mankind's greatest step.

Net Telescopes

http://deepspace.physics.ucsb.edu http://www.telescope.org/rti/
http://inferno.physics.uiowa.edu

Probe deep space by sending observation requests to remote telescopes.

New Scientist

http://www.newscientist.com

Full features, daily bulletins, and scientific miscellany from the superlative science weekly. A truly excellent site.

Northern Lights – Aurora Borealis

http://www.uit.no/npt/homepage-npt.en.html

If you're ever lucky enough to see the aurora borealis during a solar storm, you'll never be able to look skyward with the same nonchalance again. It will challenge your paradigm of the visible universe and its relative stasis. This Norwegian planetarium does a commendable job in explaining a polar phenomenon that very few people understand. Except maybe these chaps: http://www.geocities.com/CapitolHill/1606/akhaarp1.html

PopSci

http://www.popsci.com

What's new in cars, computers, home technology, science, and electronics, from the editors of *Popular Science* magazine.

Rocketry Online

http://www.rocketryonline.com

Admit it, you've always wanted to build a rocket. Well, get to it.

Skeptics Society

http://www.skeptic.com

The Skeptics Society, a private organization of the intellectually curious and the perennially unconvinced, investigates the pseudosciences, paranormal, and claims of fringe groups. Subscribe to its magazine, order books and tapes, read newsletters, and find out what's new in the world of scientific inquiry.

Space Calendar

http://newproducts.jpl.nasa.gov/calendar/calendar.html

Guide to upcoming anniversaries, rocket launches, meteor showers, eclipses, asteroid and planet viewings, occultations, and happenings in the intergalactic calendar.

Space Environment Laboratory

http://www.sel.bldrdoc.gov

If you're into long-distance radio or aviation, you'll know all about solar activity. Otherwise, you may be baffled by all this. The Space Environment Agency provides current space weather, sunspot levels, solar images, research information, and a brief explanation of its purpose.

Stars and Galaxies

http://www.eia.brad.ac.uk/btl/

Take a multimedia tour through the stars. Find out how they behave, how they generate energy, where they come from, and why they burn out.

Volcano World

http://volcano.und.nodak.edu

Monitor the latest eruptions, see photos of every major volcano in the world, virtually tour a Hawaiian smoky, or shop in a Volcano Mall.

Web-Elements

http://www.shef.ac.uk/~chem/web-elements/

Click on an element in the periodic table and suss it out in depth.

Weird Science

http://www.eskimo.com/~billb/weird.html

Free energy, Tesla, anti-gravity, aura, cold fusion, parapsychology, and other strange scientific projects and theories.

Why Files

http://whyfiles.news.wisc.edu

Twice-monthly features on the science behind current news topics.

SHOPPING

Shopping on the Net is still a pickle. Don't get too worried about someone pinching your credit card number – be more concerned about from whom you're buying. Just like any mail order dealing. A secure server is the first sign they're taking business seriously. But then again it might not be a bargain. It's pretty hard to tell you where to start browsing such an enormous storefront. InfoSeek's UltraShop's not a bad place to begin: http://204.183.199.77 or try InfoSeek's regional mirrors under Shopping to search in the UK, France, Italy, Germany, or Japan. Again, like every section, the following is only meant to get you off the ground. Within two clicks, you could be anywhere. See also our "Books" and "Music" sections for book and CD stores.

All Internet Shopping Directory
http://www.all-internet.com

All cashed up and nowhere to go? Then step into one of these cybermarkets for quick relief.

Barclay Square
http://www.itl.net/barclaysquare/

With Barclay's Bank and UK high-street names like Argos, Toys 'R' Us, Sainsbury's, Blackwells, Debenhams, and Eurostar in the aisles, this dull, under-publicized mall was intended to convince British shoppers that the Net was officially open for trading. So what went wrong?

Catalog Mart
http://catalog.savvy.com

Why hunt through lists of catalogs, then join each separately when you can do it in bulk? Just choose the product category, send your details, and Catalog Mart will look after the rest.

Catalog Select
http://pathfinder.com/CatalogSelect

Another catalog ordering service, this time courtesy of Time Warner.

CatalogSite

http://www.catalogsite.com

Not every major US mail order house, but not far off it. Some offer online ordering but most simply another way to order their catalog.

CompUSA

http://www.compusa.com

US computer megastore's online catalog. It ships anywhere and international buyers might find the prices particularly cheap.

Condom Country

http://www.ag.com/Condom/Country/

The mail order condoms, sex aids, books, and jokes are pretty harmless, but the mere mention of the penis size ready reckoner may prove disquieting to some. You'll find more of the same by wedging your favorite brand names between www and com

Conran Shop

http://www.conran.co.uk

Score a flash sofa online without having to suffer the indignity of sitting in it first.

Downtown Anywhere

http://www.awa.com

Compact directory of online shops, galleries, libraries, museums, sports sites, and more.

Floaty

http://www.floaty.com

The world's neatest tilt-and-something-nifty-happens pens and watches.

Highland Trail

http://www.highlandtrail.co.uk/highlandtrail/

Fine Scottish produce such as malt whiskies, smoked salmon, kippers, oysters, and smoked venison delivered to your doorstep.

Interflora

http://www.interflora.com

Punch in your credit card number, apology, and delivery details, and be back in the good books before you get home.

Internet Mall

http://www.internet-mall.com

With well over 27,000 stores, Meckler Media's mall directory is as close to definitive as you're likely to find. Each entry includes a brief review.

Jarred's Wonderful World of Free Stuff

http://www.oberlin.edu/~jmcadams

Here's that magic word again. Stuff your mailbox for life.

Kellner's Fireworks

http://www.kellfire.com/fireworks.html

Mail order light explosives.

Khazana

http://khazana.com

Indian and Nepalese collectables purchased direct from the artisans and artists, with a "fair trade" policy of payment.

Lakeside Products

http://wholesalecentral.com/Lakeside/

Order the gags and novelties you could never afford when you really needed them. They're all here. Whoopee cushions, X-ray specs, itching powder, joke buzzers, and coffin piggy banks, ripped straight from the pages of your childhood comics. And, it's still the same company selling them.

Loot

http://www.loot.co.uk

British trash, real estate, and assorted classifieds.

Macys

http://www.macys.com

Order essentials like shirts and stockings online, or email a personal assistant to stock your entire wardrobe.

MarketNet

http://mkn.co.uk

Shop for flowers, insurance, chocolate, books, shares, travel and legal services, and more via a secure link to this nonsense-free UK cybermall.

Marrakesh Express

http://uslink.net/ddavis/

Come my friend – I'll show you something special. If you've been pestered to the end of your tether by Moroccan carpet dealers, maybe this will breathe new life into those rugs you tried to avoid. Susan Davis, a Californian anthropologist, has presented this online souk in such an educative manner it might tempt you to buy a carpet or kilim online.

Mind Gear

http://www.mind-gear.com

There's a theory that if you bombard yourself with light and sound of a certain frequency you'll be bludgeoned into a higher state of consciousness. Mind Gear sells various such devices, tapes, and potions to fine-tune your mind.

Mondo-tronics Robot Store

http://www.robotstore.com

Build machines that do exactly what they're told. Exterminate, exterminate!

New and Kewl

http://www.new-kewl.com

Jump site for new and nifty gadgets on sale around the Net.

Newsclassified

http://www.newsclassifieds.com.au

Classifieds from Murdoch's Australian papers.

The Shopping Expressway

http://shopex.com

Ever wondered where else you can get those revolutionary products advertised on TV, usually late at night when you're most receptive to hypnotic gesturing? Wonder no more, because a large section of this exploding cybermall has been cordoned off for all those money-back guaranteed miracles that were designed to be sold rather than used.

Sorcerer's Shop

http://www.sorcerers-shop.com

Attract love and fortune using bottled potions rather than charm and skill.

Speak to Me

http://www.clickshop.com/speak/

Want a swearing keychain, sneezing salt shaker, flirting birthday candle, rapping Christmas tree, or some other talking novelty? Order it, or preview the sound files, here.

Spy Base

http://www.spybase.com

Get to know your neighbours better.

Used Software Exchange

http://www.midwinter.com/usox/

Search for used software by type, price, currency, and platform. Works like a classified listing. You contact the vendor directly.

Yacht Broker

http://www.yachtbroker.com

Scan through the list of yachts on offer, find something in your price range, and then access a staggeringly detailed description complete with pictures of the craft. Once you've narrowed it down to two or three, you can email or phone to arrange a viewing. Theoretically, it can arrange delivery anywhere in the world.

SPORT

Abdominal Training

http://www.dstc.edu.au/TU/staff/timbomb/ab/

Get "abs like ravioli."

Charged

http://www.charged.com

How to get extremely dirty, wet, cold, or gravel rashed, without complaining afterwards.

Cric Info

http://www.cricket.org

Cricket is some bizarre Zen thing. A test match can span five days in the blazing Faisalabad midsummer sun. Often without result. Yet buffs ponder every ball, awaiting the birth of some new statistic. But the ultimate indulgence is following such a match on the other side of the world, ball by ball, over the Internet, while periodically checking Cricinfo's stat tables during tea breaks. Ommm ...

Cybernude

http://www.cybernude.com

Struggling to keep up with fashion? Then join the growing

ranks of the nude. All undressed and nowhere to go? Fret not – here's advice, news, and a roundup of spots to hang out with other naked fun seekers.

ESPN Sportzone

http://espnet.sportszone.com

Live news, statistics, and commentary on major US sports pushed to your desktop.

Faith Sloan's Bodybuilding Site

http://www.frsa.com/bbpage.shtml

Galleries of the grimacing human form pushed to near-illogical extremes, as well as competition results, videos, fan mail addresses, workout advice, and links to vanity pages.

Golf.com

http://www.golf.com

When it comes to golf, this one has the lot. Like international course maps, pro-golf schedules, golf tips, golf publications, golf merchandise, golf properties, golf travel, golf weather, and, uhh, more golf.

Instant Sports

http://www.instantsports.com

Live Major League baseball play and statistics, either in text or via the animated Instant Ballpark.

Internet Disc Shoppe

http://www.digimark.net/disc/

Why risk your fingernails in a rough sport like rugby or strain your back over a croquet stick when you can fling one of these blighters back and forth? They're totally foolproof and available where all good ice cream is sold.

Manchester United Football Club

http://www.sky.co.uk/sports/manu

Manchester United – the world's most popular and sublime football team – has more Web pages than any other club. This one's updated daily, with match reports, comments from the manager, and all the latest on Giggsy and the lads. For a good unofficial site, try the Red Devils Unofficial Home Page: http://www.iol.ie/~mmurphy/red_devils/mufc.htm

NBA.com
http://www.nba.com

Official NBA site with loads of pro basketball news, picks, player profiles, analyses, results, schedules, and highlight videos.

Pure Web Soccer Pages
http://www.justwright.com/rss/pureweb.html

Links to most of the English and European, US, Brazilian, and Japanese clubs. Plus tables, fixtures, results, news, and all sorts of soccer chat. And don't miss: http://www.soccernet.com

Rugby League
http://www.arl.org.au http://www2.eis.net.au/~chrisc/bronco97/

Read how 26 men bash themselves senseless, push each other's faces into the dirt as they're rising, and then meet for a drink afterwards. First, the official ARL page with results, news, tipping, and anti-Super League sentiments. Second, the fanatically maintained unofficial home of the Brisbane Broncos, and one-eyed Telstra Cup analysis. Just follow the links to the international club of your choice.

Sailing Index
http://www.sailingindex.com

Neat directory of links to sailing resources like racing authorities, regatta bulletins, commercial suppliers, weather reports, cruising destinations, and clubs.

SkiCentral
http://www.skicentral.com

Indexes more than 4,000 ski related sites. Like snow reports, resort cams, snowboard gear, accommodation, and coming events in resorts across the world.

Sky Sports

http://www.sky.co.uk/sports/

Regular soccer, cricket, and rugby scores and updates.

Sportsline

http://www.sportsline.com

Daily US sports news, scores, gossip, and fixtures, including live play-by-play baseball action.

Stockdog Server

http://www.stockdog.com/stockdog/stockdog.htm

Keep up with who's who in the stockdog trials. Where the only two mammals with any mutual affection collaborate to corner a very stupid animal into an enclosure. This ambush is appraised by the dominant species while the subordinates inspect each others' equipment. Also includes some sturdy shots of startled sheep, if that's your scene.

SurfLink

http://www.surflink.com

Regionally sorted links to the sort of dude stuff that real surfers live for. Like how to forecast waves, where El Niño's at, surfboard shops, Dick Dale riffs, and surf-cams. And keeping in mind that tough guys don't read in public, there's also a stonking great gallery of cracking breakers to call up for when that Kombi van pulls up in the driveway unexpectedly.

The Virtual Flyshop

http://www.flyshop.com/

Meeting point to trade tips and generally exaggerate about aquatic bloodsports. Don't let this one get away.

When Saturday Comes

http://www.wsc.co.uk/wsc

Britain's original football fanzine produces a self-described "half-decent web page", with the daily news stories from the tabloids and a bit more besides.

WrestleNet

http://www.wrestlenet.com

Vent the frustration of helplessly watching your boofhead heroes being piledriven, suplexed, and moonsplashed, by spilling some hardway juice virtually.

Yahoo Sports

http://www.yahoo.com/Recreation/Sports/

Yahoo's Sports arm is undoubtably the fattest bag of sports links you'll find. If you can't get to your healthy obsession within a couple of jumps from here, it probably doesn't exist.

SUPPORT

Adoption.com

http://www.adoption.com

Disturbing photos and descriptions of children from all over the world seeking adoption.

Bastard Nation

http://www.bastards.org

Parent search advice, campaigns, and support with a tinge of humor.

National Center for Missing and Exploited Children

http://www.missingkids.org

Indispensable tool in the search for missing children and abductors. Search a database by a variety of parameters. Success rate to date has been about one in seven. That's more than 30,000 children. So be aware it exists and call if you can help.

Psychological Self-Help Resources

http://www.gasou.edu/psychweb/resource/selfhelp.htm

Many psychological disorders can be self-cured. For some, it's the only solution. The answer usually comes through finding others who've overcome the same anxieties or neuroses and taking their advice. The Net is the perfect medium for this sort of interaction as it's easy to make contact and still maintain your privacy. This site lists hundreds of resources for such support.

Queer Resources Directory

http://www.qrd.org/qrd/

AIDS support, legal news, attitude trends, clubs, publications, broadcasts, images, political action, community groups, and assorted gay links.

Silent Witness

http://www.getnet.com/silent/

Become a bounty hunter for the Phoenix police department. Just take the brief, get on the case, find your quarry, and call the toll-free number to claim your booty.

Vietnam Veterans

http://www.vietvet.org

Lest we forget.

Weddings in the Real World

http://www.theknot.com

Preparation for the big day.

TELECOMMUNICATIONS

Free Fax Service

http://www.tpc.int

Transmit faxes anywhere in the world via the Internet for the price of your connection. In practice, coverage is limited and subject to delays. But give it a shot anyway.

J-Fax
http://www.jfax.co.uk/

Provides a unique phone/fax number in many cities that
forwards your incoming faxes and voicemail as email
attachments. Plus you can send faxes the same way. Costs
less than Internet access.

World Time
http://www.whitepages.com.au/time.htm

International dialing info from anywhere to anywhere,
including current times and area codes.

TIME

28 hour Day
http://www.kaplan.com/cellar/28hours.html

Living by a 28-hour day, 6-day week regime has a number of
benefits, according to Mr. Mike Biamonte. No more Mondays
for one.

EarthTime
http://www.starfishsoftware.com/products/et/activeet/activeet.html

Active X control that displays the times in your choice of
eight cities. But that's just the start. It can synchronize your
PC clock with an atomic clock across the Net, show the Sun's
path across the Earth and perform a mindboggling range of
measurement conversions. All that and it's free.

Freeminder
http://www.cvp.com/freemind/

Send yourself a timely email reminder.

Time Zone Converter
http://www.cilea.it/MBone/timezones.html

Link to either of two time zone converters. One is simple –
you just click on a region to find its time. The other converts
from one time zone to another at any time and date, not just
the present.

TRANSPORT

Aircraft Shopper

http://aso.solid.com

Troubled by traffic? Rise above it, with something from this
range of new, used, and charter aircraft. And if you can't fly,
then sign up for training or flight simulation.

All-In-One British Timetables

http://www.ukonline.co.uk/UKOnline/Travel/contents.html

Form access to timetables of leading UK carcass haulers like
BA, Eurostar, British Rail, and National Express coaches
plus links to just about everything else that moves across the
Isles. Beats waiting on the phone.

Aviation Safety Records

http://www.faa.gov/asafety.htm

Way more goes wrong up in the air than you realize. Here's
why you should be terrified to fly.

DealerNet

http://www.dealernet.com

Locate, browse, compare specs, and read reviews of the latest
new and used cars, boats, and specialty vehicles from trusty
US dealers.

European Railways Server

http://mercurio.iet.unipi.it/home.html

Timetables, news, and groovy liveries created by ardent loco
locos. Some are faithful reproductions depicting national
color schemes, while others are fantasy sketches conjuring
up futuristic engines.

Exchange and Mart

http://www.ExchangeAndMart.co.uk

Choose from over 50,000 used British bangers. As you can
filter it down by locality, make, model, price, color, and more,
it's actually superior to the print edition.

General Railroad Index

http://www.rrhistorical.com/nmra/nmralink.html

Locophilial banquet of railroad maps, databases, mailing
lists, transit details, and hundreds of shunts all over the Net.

Layover

http://www.layover.com

Long wide loads of essential truckin' stuff, plus special
features like the diary of a lonely trucker's wife and an
Internet guide for prime movers and shakers.

Paramotor

http://cyberactive-1.com/paramotor/

According to this source, paramotors are the among the
smallest, yet safest, aircraft. They require no license, weigh
less than 65 pounds, can be lugged about in a backpack,
assembled in under five minutes, and can soar to heights of
10,000 feet at up to 500 feet per minute. At less than
$10,000, what are you waiting for?

Piaggio

http://www.piaggio.com

50 years have ticked away since Piaggio unleashed its first
two-wheeled peepy-horned menace onto safe European roads.
Yet even today many modern young nostalgics and potential
kidney donors reckon the Vespa scooter remains the absolute
quintessence of cool. You won't find disagreement here but
you will learn more about its origins and what's yet to grace
the piazza.

TRAVEL

Travel is another huge area of the Net – and set to become
one of its commercial successes as folks gain confidence to
book flights and car rental online, and maybe travel with
laptops to browse travel guides and and what's on listings.
Site selections below are only the tip of the iceberg. For
impressive wads of links, check City.Net and Yahoo! Travel.

Abandoned Missile Base

http://www.xvt.com/users/kevink/silo/

Missile bases aren't generally the sort of places you'd open to
the public. Consequently your best and safest chance to see
inside one is through this surreptitious photo tour.

Adventurous Traveler Bookstore

http://www.gorp.com/atbook.htm

No matter how far you're heading off the track, this store
has the guides, maps, and videos to help you on your way.

AESU

http://www.aesu.com

Reserve discounted US air departures.

Air Traveler's Handbook

http://www.cis.ohio-state.edu/hypertext/faq/usenet/
travel/air/handbook/top.html

Now that this FAQ-style travel cookbook has been converted
to hypertext, it's quite easy to find your way around. It aims

to wise you up to the tricks of the travel trade, help you beat the system, save you money, and get you home in one piece.

Amsterdam
http://clix.net/clix/amsterdam/

Certain people drool pavlovially at the mere mention of Amsterdam. Must be all the tulips or something. Whatever, the Dutch capital is most definitely wired.

Arab Net
http://www.arab.net

A bulging omniscient resource of rare detail comprising thousands of pages on North Africa and the Middle East, their peoples, geography, economy, history, culture, and, of course, camels. See also: http://www.arabiaonline.com http://www.1001sites.com and http://www.i-cias.com

Art of Travel
http://www.artoftravel.com

25 chapters of advice on how to see the world on $25 a day.

Asia World
http://www.asiaworld.co.uk

Book an Asian holiday online or just use it for inspiration.

Athand

http://www.athand.com

PacBell's guide to more than a million Californian businesses.
With detailed maps, reviews, and contact details, plus a sharp
way to shop for a shack.

Bargain Holidays (UK)

http://www.bargainholidays.com

Want to go somewhere, anywhere really, say tomorrow even,
if it's cheap enough? See what you think of these fares.

Bermuda Triangle

http://orion.it.luc.edu/~tgibson/triangle/tri.html

Dispels myths about the infamous Caribbean vortex.

British Foreign Office Travel Advice

http://www.fco.gov.uk

Use this service in conjunction with the US travel warnings
when planning your next holiday in Afghanistan or Chad,
but don't rely on it as a sole source: it's often hopelessly brief,
or out of date, and tends to recommend that you contact the
local consul.

Cheap Flights

http://www.cheapflights.co.uk

Scouts the travel market for the best deals on flights
worldwide from UK airports, supported by ample links to
airlines and agents.

CIA World Factbook

http://www.odci.gov/cia/publications/pubs.html

Encyclopedic summary of every country's essential stats and
details. Like geographical boundaries, international disputes,
climate, geography, economy, demographics, government,
communications, and defense. Perfect for a school project
though not quite enough for a military takeover.

City.Net

http://www.city.net

Regionally sorted digest of links to community, geopolitical,

and tourist information from all around the globe. Choose a
locality directly or zoom in from a larger region.

Currency Converter

http://www.oanda.com

Convert between a choice of over 160 daily updated
currencies.

Electronic Embassy

http://www.embassy.org

Directory of foreign embassies in DC plus Web links where
available.

Fielding's Danger Finder

http://www.fieldingtravel.com/dp/

So you didn't make the army? Cheer up, life's not over until
your next holiday.

Hotel Net

http://www.u-net.com/hotelnet/

Find, appraise, and reserve European hotels. Not many
choices but what's covered is well documented.

How far is it?

http://www.indo.com/distance/

Calculate the distance between any two cities.

International Student Travel Confederation

http://www.istc.org

Where to get an international student identity card and what
it's good for.

Internet Travel Services

http://www.itsnet.co.uk

UK travel cybermall and directory, most notable for its late-
booking search. Often a source of bargain fares.

J-Links

http://www.islandtel.com/j-links.html

One of the better Japanese link banks – in English, anyway.
If you're up to reading Japanese, you can't do better than

Yahoo Japan at: http://www.yahoo.co.jp Catch is you'll also need a Japanese browser. But that's merely a download from Netscape or Microsoft away.

Journeywoman

http://www2.journeywoman.com/journeywoman/

Smart magazine-style guide for sassy sisters on the road with regular features like gal-friendly city sites, holiday romances, and where to shop 'til you drop.

London Calling

http://www.london-calling.co.uk

More to see in London when you've done the trundling from the waxworks to the Tower in an open-top double decker bus and you're up for the markets and arts.

London Pubs Reviewed

http://www.cs.ucl.ac.uk/misc/uk/london/pubs/

Find out why Londoners practically live in their locals. You can even add your own, if it's not already there.

Lonely Planet Guidebooks

http://www.lonelyplanet.com.au

Good for summaries of every country in the Lonely Planet series along with basic info and health precautions. But better for it's the wealth of first-hand tales posted by backpacking survivors. Find travel partners, advice, and ideas for your next stint away from the keyboard.

MapBlast!

http://www.mapblast.com

Key in US, and soon European, addresses to generate local maps.

Maps On Us

http://www.mapsonus.com

This is a brilliant US map site. You can punch in any US address and generate a local map or key in two for maps and directions on how to get from one to the other. But even more impressive is that, since it's jacked into the

Yellow Pages, you can key in a business name and get full details (and map), or go the other way, for example, finding all the bars within ten square miles of a nuclear reactor.

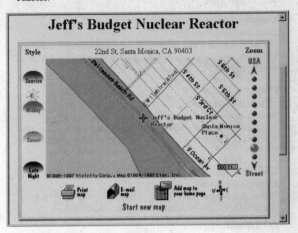

MCW International Travelers Clinic

http://www.intmed.mcw.edu/ITC/Health.html

Not much more than token preparation for the bugs that await your alimentary displeasure, but its links should help, if not entirely dissuade. These include the American Society of Tropical Medicine, the AMSTMH directory of Travel Clinics & Physicians, and the International Society of Travel Medicine. Like the consular warnings, it's all bad news, so be prepared for the worst. See also http://www.tripprep.com

Moon Travel Guides

http://www.moon.com

Read excerpts, and in some cases the full text, of Moon's acclaimed travel books. Or catch Travel Matters, its thrice-yearly newsletter, published in full online.

Netfind Travel

http://netfind.aol.com/aol/Reviews/Regional/Travel/index.netfind.html

Decent bundle of travel links. Sorted, rated, and reviewed courtesy of AOL.

Outside Online

http://outside.starwave.com

Current and back issues of *Outside* magazine, spanning all kinds of outdoor hands-grubbying from cycling the Alps to saving Botswanan fleabags from extinction.

Paris

http://www.paris.org

Virtual tour of popular Parisian museums, cafés, monuments, shops, railways, colleges, and such. All in the comfort of English – or, if you want to punish yourself, French.

PCTravel

http://www.pctravel.com

Check timetables, book a flight, then get yourself a bed, directly through the Apollo reservation system.

QuickAddress

http://www.qas.com/demoindex.html

Reconcile UK postcodes and streets.

Roadside America

http://www.roadsideamerica.com

Guide to the strange attractions that loom between squished animals on US highways.

Rough Guides

http://hotwired.com/rough/

http://roughguides.com

The top address is Rough Guides on HotWired, with full text from our USA, Australia, India, Canada, Mexico, Europe, Hong Kong guides, and more to follow. It's free, searchable, and will soon be linked to reviewed sites and establishments, from small jazz clubs to hotels. The second address is a

Rough Guides information site, with features from each of the 100 print titles, plus readers' updates, menu decoders, and – under construction – a critical directory of world travel links.

Sidewalk

http://www.sidewalk.com

MSN's complete personalized entertainment guides to major US cities.

Telstra Springboard

http://springboard.telstra.com.au/australia/

Launchbase to everything Australian.

Time Out

http://www.timeout.co.uk

Fish through *Time Out*, London's weekly listings guide's site, and you'll find no excuse to stay at home in not just London, but also Amsterdam, Berlin, Edinburgh, Madrid, New York, Paris, Prague, Rome, San Francisco, Sydney, Tokyo, and more to follow. With fortnightly updated tourist guides to each city, classifieds, postcard stores, city maps, sample features and, of course, the highlights of what's on.

The Trip

http://www.thetrip.com

Reservations, flight tracking, airport maps, ground transport strategies, hotel reviews and more. Aimed specifically at the frequent business traveler.

Tourism Offices Worldwide

http://www.mbnet.mb.ca/lucas/travel/tourism-offices.html

Locate tourist offices around the world, and if there's a Web presence, link to it. It's a pretty low-fi affair but it's another place to look.

Traffic and Road Conditions

http://www.accutraffic.com

Live traffic updates in various US cities.

Travel Window

http://www.seaforths.com

Flight and hotel reservation through Galileo, as used by thousands of travel agents worldwide.

Travelmag

http://www.travelmag.co.uk/travelmag/

Several intimate travel reflections monthly.

TravelWeb

http://www.travelweb.com

Flight and hotel booking service with a special late notice weekend hotel bargain finder.

UK Travel Guide

http://www.uktravel.com

Three part insight into the British way of doing things, comprising an A to Z of traveling within and from the UK, an interactive UK map leading to regional pics and sites, and a beginners guide to the "world's most cosmopolitan city." Plus more at: http://www.visitbritain.com

US Travel Warnings

http://travel.state.gov/travel_warnings.html

Essential information if you're planning to visit a potential hot spot, but not necessarily the last word on safety. It only takes an isolated incident with a foreign tourist to start panic, but years to settle the fear. Don't ignore these bulletins, but seek a second opinion before postponing your adventure.

Virtual Tour of Jerusalem

http://www.md.huji.ac.il/vjt/

After you've taken this pleasant tour through the old city of Jerusalem, scout around the rest of Israel by selecting each region from a contact-sensitive map.

The Virtual Tourist

http://wings.buffalo.edu/world/

Click on the atlas interface to zoom into the region of your choice. Once you're down to country level, choose between a

resource map, resource list, or general country information.
Could ultimately link you with any server in the region.

World's Largest Subway Map

http://metro.jussieu.fr:10001/

Pick from a selection of major cities and choose a starting
and finishing destination to estimate the traveling time. It's
relatively entertaining but not really practical – after all, how
many rail networks run this smoothly?

The World Traveler Books & Maps

http://www.travelbookshop.com

Order from a wide range of travel literature, online.

Xerox PARC Map Viewer

http://mapweb.parc.xerox.com/map/

Build your own maps showing rivers, roads, rail lines,
borders, and other information, by specifying a location.
From none other than the inventors of the GUI (Graphical
User Interfaces), the mouse, and Ethernet.

Yahoo Travel

http://www.yahoo.com/Recreation/Travel/

Yahoo's travel section is one of its best stacked areas, with
links to thousands of travel and regional sites. Most have
one-liners, rather than reviews, but they'll give you some
idea of what to expect. It's broad, but uncritical.

WEATHER

Intellicast

http://www.intellicast.com

International weather and half-hourly satellite feeds in a
sleek shell.

National Severe Storms Laboratory

http://www.nssl.uoknor.edu

These guys aren't put off by a bit of drizzle spoiling their ball
game, they're out whipping up lightning rods on mountain
peaks, trying to attract the big stuff. If tornadoes, blizzards,

flash floods, thunderstorms, hurricanes, and cyclones are your idea of prime time viewing, you'd better read the bit on responsible storm chasing. It may just temper that Pavlovian frenzy for the car keys the next time a distant rumble snaps you from your post-prandial stupor.

The Daily Planet

http://www.atmos.uiuc.edu

Meteorological maps, satellite images, and pointers to sources of climatic data, courtesy of the University of Illinois Department of Atmospheric Sciences.

World Meteorological Organization

http://www.wmo.ch

UN division that monitors global climate. Links to national bureaus worldwide.

Yahoo Weather

http://weather.yahoo.com

Five-day weather forecasts, charts, reports, and satellite photos for hundreds of cities worldwide.

WEIRD

Active Most Wanted and Criminal Investigations

http://www.gunnyragg.com/crimes.htm

Compendium of fugitive listings including the FBI's top ten most wanted, the US State Department's Anti-Terrorism Unit, and a war criminal directory.

Aetherius Society

http://www.aetherius.org

When the Cosmic Masters from the Interplanetary Council need to give their message to Earth, Sir George King, their chosen Primary Terrestrial Mental Channel, must enter a Positive Yogic Samadhic Trance. Sort of like when Ramjet takes his protein pills.

Anders Main Page

http://www.student.nada.kth.se/~nv91-asa/

Immense and diverse digest that sways toward the occultish side of spirituality, with a fair helping of transhumanism, mad science, discordia, illumination, magic, and blatant onanism.

The Ants are my friends

http://www.mcs.com/~bingo/lyrics/

Do you know someone who butts in all the time with "I thought you said..." and then laughs? It's a pathological disorder called Mondegreenism. The good news is you can legally have them put down.

Astral Projection

http://www.lava.net/~goodin/astral.html

Don't go out of your mind, go out of your body. Here's how to do it, and land back on your feet.

Blue Dog Can Count

http://hp8.ini.cmu.edu:5550/bdf.html

Give the blue dog an equation and hear her bark the answer.

Church of the Subgenius

http://sunsite.unc.edu/subgenius/

Pipe-puffing Bob's three-fisted surreal preaching. Beyond description.

Clonaid

http://www.clonaid.com

Thanks to the Raelians, we now know all life on earth was created in extraterrestrial laboratories. Here's where you can buy genuine cloned human livestock for the kitchen table. Ready as soon as the lab's finished.

CNI Angel Gallery

http://www.cninews.com/CNI_Angels.html

Leading authorities point to evidence that angels may be alien frauds. Backed up at: http://www.mt.net/~watcher/

Derm Cinema

http://www.skinema.com

Adds a whole new meaning to the term "skin flick."

Exploding Heads

http://www.mit.edu:8001/people/mkgray/head-explode.html

Worried your head might explode? These tips identify early symptoms.

Faking UFOs

http://www.strw.leidenuniv.nl/~vdmeulen/deeper/Articles/UFOfake.html

Create your own crop circles to amuse new-agers and the press.

FlyPower

http://www.flypower.com

We have the technology. We can build a bionic blowfly.

Fortean Times

http://www.forteantimes.com

Highlights and news from the print monthly that takes the investigation of strange phenomena more seriously than itself.

Gallery of the Absurd

http://www.nlci.com/users/
royal/absurd.htm

Strange ways to sell strange stuff.

Geek Site of the Day

http://www.owlnet.rice.edu/~indigo/gsotd/

Further proof that geek is très hip. Each day, a new
obsessive. Always entertaining.

George Goble's Page

http://ghg.ecn.purdue.edu

Engineer George demonstrates the power user way to light a
BBQ.

Great joy in great tribulation

http://www.dccsa.com/greatjoy/index.html

Biblical proof that Prince Chuck is the Antichrist and key
dates leading to the end of the world. For more
enlightenment, including how to debug the pyramids, see:
http://members.aol.com/larrypahl/lpahl.htm

Hutt River Province

http://www.wps.com.au/hutriver/hut1.htm

Leonard Casley got such a raw deal on his 1969 wheat
quota he officially seceded his 18,500-acre property from
Western Australia. The whole thing got so tied up in
colonial red tape that, to this day, no-one has marched in
to reclaim the territory. Consequently HRH Prince
Leonard thinks it's a quite a lark to hand out passports,
driver's licenses, and honors to anyone who asks. Just
fill out the forms.

Hyper-Weirdness

http://www.physics.wisc.edu/~shalizi/hyper-weird/

Links to some of the Web's most impassioned wells of
weirdness. You name it: UFOs, cults, political action groups,
extropians, fringe science, fantasy, and drugs. Water always
seems to find its own level.

Infamous Exploding Whale

http://www.xmission.com/~grue/whale/

Easy. Take one beached whale carcass, add half a ton of
dynamite, turn on the video, and run. In this case not all
went as planned.

Klingon Language Institute

http://www.kli.org/klihome.html

With multimedia language tutorials like this, it's a wonder Klingon isn't more widely spoken. In fact, if Captain James T. Kirk had a better grip on it perhaps the Enterprise would be still in one piece. Oh, and don't miss *Hamlet* restored to the Bard's native tongue.

Lunch is Served

http://zing.ncsl.nist.gov/greg-bin/lunch/

See what's for grub. Hit refresh to send it back.

Mrs. Silk's Cross Dressing Magazine

http://www.cityscape.co.uk/users/av73/

Mrs. Silk can furnish you with a variety of products to ensure that when you do step out of the closet, it's with style.

News of the Weird

http://nine.org/notw/

Chuck Shepard's syndicated column of bizarre news. Get it here, or subscribe to have it delivered direct to your mailbox, weekly.

Steps in Overcoming Urges

http://www.moonmac.com/Mormon_masturbation.html

Having trouble leaving it alone? Here's timely advice.

Strawberry Poptart Blow Torches

http://www.cbi.tamucc.edu/~pmichaud/toast/

Insert Poptart, depress lever, aim, fire! How to turn an innocent kitchen appliance into a deadly incendiary device. But, so long as you adhere to strict laboratory procedures, no-one need get hurt, save the odd marshmallow bunny: http://www.pcola.gulf.net/~irving/bunnies/

Tango

http://www.tango.co.uk

Subliminal inducements to drink orange Tango embedded in pages and pages of entertaining nonsense.

Toilet-train Your Cat

http://www.rainfrog.com/mishacat/

How to point pusskins at
the porcelain. Literally.

Vomitus Maximus
Museum

http://www.vomitus.com

Take heed. Steve Connett's
gallery of surreal sadism
is not in particularly good
taste. Although it's one of
the most popular galleries
on the Net, it's also the
one most likely to invoke a
strong reaction. Don't say
you weren't warned.

WearCam

http://www.wearcam.org

Steve has a Netcam fixed to his head. You see what he sees.
But that won't stop him having fun.

Weird World

http://monkey.hooked.net/m/chuck/

If you like what you see, you're in luck because Chuck's keen
to sell it off. But what exactly will you do with the likes of
David Koresh's business card or copies of Pee Wee Herman's
arrest report? And for the most disturbing real-life horror
story you'll ever read, try the ill-fated Shuttle Challenger's
final transcript.

Why Cats Paint

http://www.netlink.co.nz/~monpa/

New paintings by emerging feline artists, how to spot fakes,
updates from the Museum of Non-primate Art, moggy
masters caught on video, and merchandise including, and
inspired by, the best-selling book of the same name.

A Guide to Newsgroups

Whatever you're into – hobbies, sports, politics, music, philosophy, business, and a thousand other pursuits – there's sure to be a Usenet Newsgroup devoted to it. In fact, you might be surprised how many others share your interests. Usenet Newsgroups provide a forum to meet like-minded people, exchange views, and pose those perplexing questions that have bugged you for years. And the groups are as much yours as anyone's, so once you have the feel of a group, jump in and contribute.

We provide the low-down on reading and posting to Newsgroups on p.90. The following pages are brief directories of around 700 of the most interesting groups. That might seem a lot but it's only around three percent of the total. Not that anyone knows exactly, as many are only propagated within a local area and new groups are added daily.

We've excluded the Newsgroups devoted to "adult interests" – sex, mainly, either talking about it or looking at it. If that's your bag, you don't need our help to browse the alt.sex, alt.binaries.pictures or the alt.personals hierarchy. If you do browse the murkier areas of sex Newsgroups – or the rackets discussed in the pirate software (.warez and .cracks), phone tampering (.2600), or other mischief-making groups – be aware that just because this stuff is readily available on the Net doesn't make it legal. So don't put anything on your hard drive, or post anything, you wouldn't like to defend in front of a jury. Oh, and beware pirate programs bearing surprise gifts . . .

NEWSGROUPS DIRECTORY

For ease of reference, we've broken down Newsgroups into the following categories:

Arts, Architecture, and Graphics

ART

alt.artcom	Artistic community
rec.arts.fine	For art's sake
rec.arts.misc	Unclassified arts

ARCHITECTURE

GRAPHICS AND LAYOUT

Authors and Books

REFERENCE

DISCUSSION

Business and Finance

BUSINESS

FINANCE

Buying and Selling

Comedy and Jokes

Comics

Computer games

comp.sys.ibm.pc.games.adventure	PC adventure games
comp.sys.ibm.pc.games.flight-sim	Taking to the skies
comp.sys.ibm.pc.games.marketplace	Games for sale
comp.sys.ibm.pc.games.misc	Assorted PC games
comp.sys.ibm.pc.games.rpg	Role-playing PC games
comp.sys.ibm.pc.games.strategic	War games
comp.sys.mac.games	Macintosh games
rec.gambling	Beating the odds
rec.games.board	Snakes, ladders, and such
rec.games.frp.dnd	Dungeons and dragons
rec.games.frp.misc	Role-playing games
rec.games.mud.misc	Multi-user dungeon games
rec.games.trading-cards.marketplace	Trading cards
rec.games.video.arcade	Coin games

Computer technology

MISCELLANEOUS

alt.computer.consultants	Rent-a-geek
alt.fan.bill-gates	Lovers of the original micro-softie
alt.folklore.computers	Computer legends
comp.ai	Artificial intelligence
comp.ai.fuzzy	Fuzzy set theory
comp.newprod	New computing products

COMPUTER HARDWARE

alt.cd-rom	Optical storage media
alt.comp.hardware.homebuilt	DIY computing
biz.comp.hardware	Commercial hardware postings
comp.dcom.modems	Data communications hardware
comp.periphs.printers	Paper gobblers
comp.sys.ibm.pc.hardware.misc	PC hardware concerns
comp.sys.laptops	Portable computing
comp.sys.mac.hardware	Macintosh computers

comp.sys.powerpc	RISC processor-driven computers
comp.sys.sgi.misc	Silicon Graphics forum
comp.sys.sun.misc	Sun Microsystems forum

COMPUTER SECURITY

alt.comp.virus	Computer vaccines
alt.security	Keeping hackers out
alt.security.espionage	Cyberspies
alt.security.pgp	Pretty good privacy encryption
comp.society.privacy	Technology and privacy
comp.virus	Virus alerts and solutions
sci.crypt	Data encryption methods

COMPUTER SOFTWARE

alt.comp.shareware	Try before you buy software
biz.comp.software	Commercial software postings
comp.binaries.ibm.pc	PC software postings
comp.binaries.ibm.pc.wanted	Requests for PC programs
comp.databases	Data management
comp.sys.mac.apps	Macintosh software
comp.os.ms-windows.apps.comm	Windows comms software
comp.os.ms-windows.apps.misc	Windows software
comp.sources.sun	Sun workstation software
comp.sources.wanted	Software and fixes
microsoft.public.inetexplorer.ie4	Internet Explorer bugs
microsoft.public.office.misc	Microsoft Office support

NETWORKING AND EMAIL

alt.winsock	PC TCP/IP stacks
alt.winsock.trumpet	Tuning Trumpet Winsock
comp.dcom.lans.misc	Local area networking
comp.mail.misc	General discussions about email
comp.os.ms-windows.networking.windows	Link Windows
comp.os.os2.networking.tcp-ip	TCP/IP under OS/2

OPERATING SYSTEMS

Crafts, Gardening, and Hobbies

CRAFTS

GARDENING

HOBBIES

Dance and Theater

Drugs

Education

Employment

Fashion

Food and drink

Health and Medicine

History, Archeology, and Anthropology

International culture

Almost every culture/ethnic group has a soc.culture and/or an alt.culture group. If yours doesn't, start one!

alt.chinese.text	Chinese character discussion
alt.culture	Cultural forum hierarchy
alt.culture.saudi	Arabian might
alt.culture.us.asian-indian	Native American culture
soc.culture	Cultural forum hierarchy
soc.culture.african.american	Afro-American affairs
soc.culture.yugoslavia	All ex-Yugoslav factions
uk.misc	All things British

Internet Stuff

BBS LISTINGS

alt.bbs	Bulletin board systems
alt.bbs.internet	BBSs hooked up to the Internet
alt.bbs.lists	Regional BBS listings

CYBERSPACE

alt.cybercafes	New café announcements
alt.cyberpunk	High-tech low-life
alt.cyberpunk.tech	Cyberpunk technology
alt.cyberspace	The final frontier
sci.virtual-worlds	Virtual reality

IRC

alt.irc	Internet Relay Chat material
alt.irc.questions	Solving IRC queries

NEWSGROUPS

alt.config	How to start an alt Newsgroup
alt.culture.usenet	Finishing school for Usenetsters
alt.current-events.net-abuse	Usenet spamming

SERVICE PROVIDERS

WORLD WIDE WEB

Legal

Movies and TV

rec.arts.movies.reviews	Films reviewed
rec.arts.sf.movies	Science fiction movies
rec.arts.sf.tv.babylon5	Babylon 5 discussion
rec.arts.startrek.current	New Star Trek shows
rec.arts.startrek.fandom	Trek conventions and trinkets
rec.arts.tv	Television talk
rec.arts.tv.soaps	Parallel lives hierarchy
rec.arts.tv.uk	UK television talk
rec.video.production	Making home movies

Music

There are hundreds more specialist groups under the alt.music and rec.music hierarchies.

GENERAL

alt.cd-rom.reviews	Read before you buy
rec.music.info	Music resources on the Net
rec.music.misc	Music to any ears
rec.music.reviews	General music criticism
rec.music.video	Budding Beavis and Buttheads

POP

alt.elvis.sighting	Keep looking
alt.exotic-music	Strange moods
alt.fan.frank-zappa	The late Bohemian cultural minister
alt.fan.rolf-harris	King of the stylophone
alt.gothic	Dying fashion
alt.music.bootlegs	Illicit recordings
alt.music.brian-eno	Eno's worldly activities
alt.music.hardcore	Head banging
alt.music.kylie-minogue	Is she Elvis?
alt.music.lyrics	Spreading the words
alt.music.peter-gabriel	From Genesis to the Real World
alt.music.prince	The artist formerly named after a dog

alt.music.progressive .... Almost modern music
alt.rock-n-roll .... Counterpart to alt.sex and alt.drugs
alt.rock-n-roll.metal .... Heavy, man
alt.rock-n-roll.oldies .... The golden years
rec.music.dylan .... Rolling Stone cover model
rec.music.gdead .... Jerry lives on

INDIE AND DANCE

alt.music.alternative .... Indie talk
alt.music.alternative.female .... Indie women
alt.music.canada .... Canadian indie scene
alt.music.independent .... Alternative pop
alt.music.dance .... Water? E? Okay, let's go
alt.music.hardcore .... Serious punks
alt.music.house .... Repetitive bleats
alt.music.jungle .... Rumble in the bassbin
alt.music.synthpop .... Keyboard capers
alt.music.techno .... Repetitive beats
alt.punk .... The attitude and the music
alt.rave .... Late-night loonies
rec.music.ambient .... Soundscapes
rec.music.industrial .... Metal machine music
uk.music.breakbeat .... Drumming base

WORLD MUSIC AND FOLK

alt.music.jewish .... Klezmer developments
alt.music.world .... Tango to Tuvan throatsinging
rec.music.afro-latin .... African, Latin, and more
rec.music.celtic .... Irish music mostly
rec.music.folk .... Folk/world music/singer-songwriters
rec.music.indian.classical .... Raga sagas
rec.music.reggae .... Rasta nation

COUNTRY

rec.music.country.western .... Both types, C & W

JAZZ

alt.music.acid-jazz ....Smooth movements
rec.music.bluenote .... Jazz and the blues

CLASSICAL

rec.music.classical .... Classical music
rec.music.early .... Early music

MUSIC MAKING

alt.guitar .... You axed for it
alt.music.makers.electronic .... Electric friends
rec.music.makers.guitar .... Six string along
rec.music.makers.synth .... Synthesize your mind

HI-FI AND RECORDING

rec.audio.high-end .... Audiophile equipment
rec.audio.opinion .... Hi-fi reviews
rec.audio.pro .... Professional sound recording

MUSIC UTILITIES

alt.binaries.multimedia .... Sound and vision files
alt.binaries.sounds.midi .... Music making files
alt.binaries.sounds.music .... Music files
alt.binaries.sounds.utilities .... Sound programs

Mysticism and Philosophy

alt.astrology .... Soothsaying by starlight
alt.chinese.fengshui .... Mystical interior design
alt.consciousness .... Philosophical discourse
alt.dreams .... Welcome to my nightmare
alt.dreams.castaneda .... Don Juan yarns
alt.hypnosis .... You are getting sleepy
alt.magic.secrets .... Letting the rabbit out of the hat
alt.magick .... Supernatural arts

alt.meditation .... Maintaining concentration
alt.paranet.paranormal .... Psychic phenomena
alt.paranet.skeptic .... Doubters
alt.paranet.ufo .... It came from outer space
alt.paranormal .... Bent-fork talk
alt.paranormal.channeling .... Cosmic contacts
alt.philosophy.debate .... The quest for truth
alt.prophecies.nostradamus .... Deciphering the predictions
sci.skeptic .... Questioning pseudo-science
talk.bizarre .... Believe it or not
talk.philosophy.misc .... Navel-gazing

Pets

alt.aquaria .... Fishy things
alt.pets.ferrets .... Polecats as toys
alt.pets.rabbits .... Bunnies
rec.aquaria .... Water wonderful life
rec.birds .... Fine feathered friends
rec.pets .... Animals in captivity
rec.pets.alligators .... Tending the swamp
rec.pets.birds .... Birds behind bars
rec.pets.cats .... Kitty chat
rec.pets.dogs.misc .... Canine capers

Politics and Media

CURRENT AFFAIRS/POLITICAL ACTION

alt.activism .... Agitate, educate, and organize
alt.activism.death-penalty .... For and against
alt.current-events.bosnia .... Bosnia-Herzegovinan strife
alt.current-events.russia .... The rise and fall of the KGB
alt.gossip.royalty .... Tabloid fodder
alt.india.progressive .... Indian politics
alt.individualism .... Hanging on to your ego

POLITICAL THEORY

SEXUAL POLITICS

alt.dads-rights	Custody battles
alt.fan.camille-paglia	Flamboyant feminist
alt.feminazis	Feminist flames
alt.feminism	Sisters for sisters
alt.politics.homosexuality	Gay power
soc.feminism	Gender war zone
soc.men	Men wanting more
soc.women	Women wanting more

US PARTY POLITICS

alt.impeach.clinton	Presidential peeves
alt.politics.democrats	Democrat party discussion
alt.politics.usa.congress	US congressional affairs
alt.politics.usa.republican	Republican party reptiles
alt.president.clinton	Spotlight on Clinton

MEDIA

alt.fan.noam-chomsky	Media watchdogs
alt.journalism	Hack chat
alt.journalism.freelance	Unemployed lines
alt.news-media	Don't believe the hype
alt.quotations	The things people say
bit.listserv.words-l	English language mailing list
biz.clarinet	ClariNet newsfeed news
biz.clarinet.sample	ClariNet news samples
uk.media	UK media issues

Psychological support

For more support groups, see also "**Health**."

GENERAL PSYCHOLOGY

alt.psychology.nlp	Neurolinguistic programming
alt.sci.sociology	Human watching
sci.psychology.misc	Troubleshooting behavior

SUPPORT AND EXPLORATION

Radio and Telecommunications

alt.radio.pirate .... Lend your buccaneers
alt.radio.scanner .... Eavesdropping
alt.radio.talk .... Shock waves
rec.radio.amateur.misc .... Hamming it up
rec.radio.broadcasting .... Domestic radio
rec.radio.scanner .... Airwave snooping
rec.radio.shortwave .... Tuning in to the world
uk.radio.amateur .... Best of British hams
uk.telecom .... Fight call timing

Religion

alt.atheism .... Dogma discussed
alt.bible.prophecy .... Learn the exact date of the end
alt.buddha.short.fat.guy .... Waking up to yourself
alt.christnet .... Christian jamboree
alt.christnet.bible .... Bible discussion and research
alt.christnet.christianlife .... Living with Jesus
alt.christnet.dinosaur.barney .... Barney for Jesus
alt.christnet.philosophy .... He forgives, therefore he is
alt.christnet.second-coming.real-soon-now .... Get ready
alt.christnet.sex .... Christian attitudes to fornication
alt.freemasonry .... The brotherhood
alt.hindu .... Indian philosophy
alt.messianic .... Christ and other visionaries
alt.pagan .... Natural deities
alt.recovery.catholicism .... Getting over the guilt
alt.religion.christian .... Followers of Jesus
alt.religion.druid .... Full moonies
alt.religion.islam .... Being Muslim
alt.religion.mormon .... Joseph Smith's latter-day saints
alt.religion.scientology .... Hubbard out of the cupboard
alt.satanism .... Drop in for a spell
alt.zen .... Inner pieces

Science

GENERAL

ELECTRONICS

ENERGY AND ENVIRONMENT

ENGINEERING

sci.engr	Engineering sciences
sci.engr.biomed	Biomedical engineering
sci.engr.chem	Chemical engineering
sci.engr.mech	Mechanical engineering

GEOLOGY

sci.geo.geology	Earth science
sci.geo.meteorology	Weather or not
sci.geo.satellite-nav	Satellite navigation systems

Space and Aliens

alt.alien.research	Identifying flying objects
alt.alien.visitors	Here come the marchin' martians
sci.astro	Staring into space
sci.space.news	Announcements from the final frontier
sci.space.policy	Ruling the cosmos
sci.space.shuttle	Space research news

Sports

alt.fishing	Advice and tall tales
alt.sports.baseball	Baseball hierarchy split by clubs
alt.sports.basketball	Basketball hierarchy split by clubs
alt.sports.darts	Pub sport
alt.sports.football	Gridiron hierarchy split by clubs
alt.sports.hockey	Hockey hierarchy split by clubs
alt.sports.soccer.european	European soccer
alt.sports.soccer.european.UK	British and Irish soccer
alt.surfing	Surfboard waxing
aus.sport.rugby-league	The world's roughest sport
misc.fitness.weights	Body building
rec.climbing	Scaling new heights
rec.equestrian	Horsing around

rec.martial-arts	Fighting forms
rec.running	Running commentary
rec.scuba	Underwater adventures
rec.skiing.snowboard	Snowboarding techniques
rec.skydiving	Jumping out of planes
rec.sport.basketball.pro	Professional basketball
rec.sport.boxing	Fighting words
rec.sport.cricket.info	Stats, scorecards, and cricket news
rec.sport.football.australian	Aerial ping pong
rec.sport.football.canadian	Canadian football
rec.sport.football.pro	Get grid ironed
rec.sport.golf	Driving the dimpled ball to drink
rec.sport.hockey	Hockey on ice
rec.sport.olympics	Sydney 2000, Mogadishu 2004?
rec.sport.paintball	Weekend warriors
rec.sport.pro-wrestling	Advanced cuddling
rec.sport.rowing	Gently down the stream
rec.sport.rugby.league	Fun game with an oval ball
rec.sport.rugby.union	Meet you down the maul
rec.sport.soccer	Some call it football
rec.sport.tennis	Racketeering
rec.sport.triathlon	Multi-event sports
uk.rec.sailing	Vomiting off Blighty

Transport

alt.binaries.pictures.rail	Train snaps
alt.disasters.aviation	Justify your fear of flying
alt.scooter	Love on little wheels
ba.motorcycles	Bay Area easy riders
bit.listserv.railroad	Locophiles' mailing list
misc.transport.rail.misc	Train fancying
misc.transport.trucking	Eighteen-wheelers
rec.autos.4x4	Bush bashing
rec.autos.driving	Elbows in the breeze

Travel

Software Roundup

The easiest way to stack up on Net software is to copy it from the free CDs given away with Internet or PC magazines. But if you want the latest versions as they're released, then go direct to the Net itself. This chapter lists a selection of the most popular and essential programs to get you started. They're all free – at least for a limited time – though some have superior commercial versions.

How to find the software files

We've given **Web locations** to download each program, so you can read about it first, decide if it's what you want, and make sure you get the newest version. If an address doesn't work, run the program's name through a search engine and look for a new address (See "Finding it", p.137). We're assuming you have a **Web browser that supports FTP**. If not, get one first.

It's a good habit to download everything into a **central directory (folder)**. Call it "download" or something appropriate. Once a program's downloaded, copy it to a temporary directory for installation. Once installed delete the contents of the temporary directory and either shift the original file into an archive or delete it. (See p.88 for How to set up your directory structure.)

All these files should **self-extract**, so installation should be as simple as following the prompts. If not, you'll need an archiving program such as **WinZip** or **Stuffit** (see p.87). Once extracted, read the accompanying text files for installation instructions. It's usually a matter of clicking on a file called install.exe or setup.exe in Windows, or on an install icon on the Mac.

Many programs come in **16-bit and 32-bit versions**. If you're running Windows 95, NT, OS/2, or a PowerMac, go for the faster 32-bit versions. These programs will not work with 16-bit operating systems like Windows 3.x or earlier Macs, nor 16-bit TCP/IP stacks like Trumpet Winsock and some old ISP and Online Service connection kits. Ask your provider if you're unsure.

Agents

NEWSMONGER .... PC
http://www.techsmith.com
Emails you when something is mentioned in Usenet.

WEB COMPASS .... PC
http://www.qdeck.com/qdeck/demosoft/webcompass/
Customize and automate your Web searches.

WEBSNAKE .... PC
http://www.anawave.com/websnake/
Off line Web reader and Web/FTP search agent.

Chat

CLEARPHONE .... Mac
http://www.clearphone.com
Talk and send video over the Net.

COMIC CHAT .... PC
http://www.microsoft.com/ie/comichat/
Chat cutely through a cartoon character.

CU-SeeMe .... PC, Mac
http://www.cu-seeme.com
Video/audio Netconferencing. Works better at high bandwidths.

ICQ .... PC, Mac
http://www.mirabilis.com
Alerts you when your friends are online.

INTERNET PHONE .... PC, Mac
http://www.vocaltec.com
Real-time Internet telephony over IRC.

IRCLE .... Mac
http://www.xs4all.nl/~ircle/
Audio-capable IRC client with handy common phrase shortcuts.

Net2phone .... PC, Mac
http://www.net2phone.com
Place calls through the Net to any conventional telephone.

NetMeeting .... PC
http://www.microsoft.com/netmeeting/
Real-time voice, applications-sharing, and multi-user whiteboard. Slots in nicely with the Internet Explorer bundle.

THE PALACE .... PC, Mac
http://www.thepalace.com
Chat and frolic in interactive animated rooms.

VDOPhone .... PC, Mac
http://www.vdo.net
Full-color video telephony even over a modem.

VISUAL IRC .... PC
http://www.megalith.co.uk/virc/
Audio/visual/text IRC client with features to boot.

WEBPHONE .... PC
http://www.netspeak.com
Polished point-to-point Net telephony with encryption
and smart online directory.

ONLIVE! TRAVELER .... PC
http://www.onlive.com/prod/trav/
Join, build, and talk in 3D Net colonies.

File Transfer and Handling

CUTEFTP .... PC
http://www.cuteftp.com
First-rate FTP client.

FETCH .... Mac
http://www.dartmouth.edu/pages/softdev/fetch.html
Multiple connection, drag-and-drop file transfer with
automatic decoding.

INTERNET NEIGHBORHOOD .... PC
http://www.knowareinc.com
Browse FTP sites with Windows 95 explorer.

NETFINDER .... Mac
http://www.ozemail.com.au/~pli/netfinder/
FTP with resume capabilities.

STUFFIT EXPANDER/DROPSTUFF .... PC, Mac
http://www.aladdinsys.com/consumer/
Essential cross platform drag-and-drop decoding/archiving tool.

VIRUSCAN .... PC, Mac
http://www.mcafee.com
Top-notch virus scanner. Check regularly for signature updates.

WINZIP .... PC
http://www.winzip.com/
Must-have PC file compression/decompression utility.

ZIPit .... Mac
http://www.awa.com/softlock/zipit/zipit.html
Zip and unzip for transfer between Mac and PC.

HTML Tools

When looking for HTML editing programs, don't forget that both Netscape and Microsoft have optional in-built editors for their browsers. They're not perfect but they work – a comment that can be applied to most of the specialized programs below. Microsoft's home page (http://www.microsoft.com) has several tools and add-ons for viewing and converting its applications.

ACTIVATOR .... PC, Mac
http://www.noware.com.au
Bottled Java applets.

BBEDIT .... Mac
http://www.barebones.com
Hands-on HTML editor that excels in text manipulation.

BEYOND PRESS .... Mac
http://www.astrobyte.com
Convert Quark to HTML.

DRUMBEAT .... PC
http://www.elementalsw.com
Drag and Drop WYSIWYG editor that does just about
everything.

GIF ANIMATOR .... PC
http://www.ulead.com/products/ga_main.htm
Animate and jazz up your Web graphics.

GOLIVE CYBERSTUDIO .... Mac
http://www.golive.com
Drag and drop, WYSIWYG, and easy to boot, site builder
that works from a DTP perspective.

HOTDOG EXPRESS/PRO .... PC
http://www.sausage.com
Feature-packed, but somewhat slow, raw html editor.

HTML POWERSPELL .... PC
http://www.opposite.com/spell.html
Spell check your HTML.

PAGEMILL .... PC, Mac
http://www.adobe.com/prodindex/pagemill/main.html
The original WYSIWYG HTML editor.

WEBEDIT .... PC
http://www.sandiego.com/webedit/
Powerful, but requires hands-on with the code.

WEBIMAGE/GRAPHX VIEWER .... PC
http://www.group42.com/webimage.htm
Graphic tool aimed at Web page designers.

WEBMODELER PC

http://www.webmodeler.com
Site design and architecture planning tool.

Mail

Be sure to check the browser offerings from Microsoft (http://www.microsoft.com/ie/) and Netscape (http://home. netscape.com) first before shopping for an alternative. However only Internet Mail & News, the IE3.01 companion, is separable from the browser.

ANAWAVE POSTMARK PC

http://www.anawave.com/postmark/index.html
One of the new breed that can send email to pagers.

EUDORA/EUDORA LIGHT PC, Mac

http://www.eudora.com
Popular, powerful, and reliable, but would you pay when you can get the likes of Outlook Express for free?

PEGASUS MAIL PC, Mac

http://www.pegasus.usa.com
Feature-packed and free. A little unintuitive but worth considering.

PUREVOICE PC, Mac

http://www.eudora.com/eudorapro/purevoice.html
Send voice by email.

Newsreaders

Again, unless you feel under-powered or your system can't handle it, you might as well stick to your browser's newsreader. Otherwise, these are among the most worthy alternatives.

AGENT/FREE AGENT .... PC
http://www.forteinc.com/forte/agent/agent.htm
Queues multiple articles and auto-decode binaries. Unrivaled.

GRAVITY .... PC
http://www.anawave.com/gravity/
Fast and powerful, with advanced search functions.

NEWSHOPPER .... Mac
http://www.demon.co.uk/sw15/
Designed primarily for offline use.

NEWSWATCHER .... Mac
http://www.santafe.edu/~smfr/mtnw/mtnewswatcher.html
Free automatic binary-decoding newsreader, with speech recognition.

Plug-ins and ActiveX controls

Plug-ins and ActiveX controls are meant to extend your browser's capacities. **Plug-ins** are more of a Netscape thing, but will usually work with Internet Explorer as well. You have to download and then install them. **ActiveX** controls load automatically into Internet Explorer. Some, like the increasingly essential **RealPlayer**, also have stand-alone versions that can be useful if you don't have the system resources to open a browser. This list is only a small sample. For close to the full range, see: http://www.browserwatch.com

ACROBAT AMBER .... PC, Mac
http://www.adobe.com/Amber/
View Portable Document Files within your browser.

EARTHTIME .... PC
http://www.starfishsoftware.com
World time clock, synchronizer, city facts, and metric
conversions within your browser.

ENVOY .... PC, Mac
http://www.twcorp.com/plugin.htm
View Envoy documents in your browser.

FUTURE SPLASH
http://www.futurewave.com
View vector-based graphic animations.

KOAN .... PC, Mac
http://www.sseyo.com/koandesc.html
Creates live music based on certain parameters.

LIGHTNING STRIKE .... PC, Mac
http://www.infinop.com
View highly compressed images.

LISTENUP .... Mac
http://snow.cit.cornell.edu/noon/ListenUp.html
Use Apple's PlainTalk to activate Web commands by
speech.

QWICKVIEW PLUS .... PC
http://www.inso.com/frames/consumer/qvp/qvp.htm
View over 200 file formats within your browser.

REALPLAYER .... PC, Mac
http://www.real.com
Essential real-time sound and video add-on or stand-
alone.

SHOCKWAVE .... PC, Mac
http://www.macromedia.com/Tools/Shockwave/
View inline multimedia creations. Get it now.

TALKER .... Mac
http://www.albany.net/~wtudor/
Reads Web pages aloud via Apple's text-to-speech conversion.

VIZSCAPE .... PC
http://www.superscape.com
Explore high-res 3D worlds.

VDOLIVE .... PC, Mac
http://www.vdo.net
Impressive live video viewer, but no threat to TV yet.

VIVO .... PC
http://www.vivo.com
Impressive streaming video player.

WIRL .... PC, Mac
http://www.vream.com/3wirl.html
View and create virtual worlds.

Push

If you want more news and whatever than you could ever hope to read **"pushed" at your desktop** in the form of scrolling tickers, screensavers, or bulletins, you might like to investigate some of the programs below. Their appeal will lie in whether you're interested in any of their channels so it's best you go directly to each site and make your decision based on their partnerships. Both Netscape and Microsoft's fourth generation browsers have built-in "push" programs, though unfortunately they're not compatible. **Microsoft** uses technology from **PointCast, BackWeb,** and **Head-liner. Netscape** uses **Marimba** and **Intermind.**

BACKWEB .... PC, Mac
http://www.backweb.com

CASTANET TUNER .... PC, Mac
http://www.marimba.com

FREELOADER .... PC
http://www.freeloader.com

HEADLINER .... PC
http://www.headliner.com

INTERMIND .... PC, Mac
http://www.intermind.com

POINTCAST .... PC, Mac
http://www/pointcast.com

Servers

Setting up a server using your own PC or Mac is easy with the right software. Just read the Help files.

NETPRESENZ .... Mac
http://www.share.com/peterlewis/
FTP, Gopher, and Web server.

PERSONAL WEB SERVER .... PC, Mac
http://www.microsoft.com/ie/
Free Internet Explorer accessory.

QUID QUO PRO .... Mac
http://www.socialeng.com
Free Mac Web server.

SLMAIL/WINSMTP .... PC

http://www.seattlelab.com/prodsmtp.html/

SMTP/POP3 mail server with auto-responders and mailing lists.

WAR FTP .... PC

http://home.sol.no/jgaa/tftpd.htm

Full featured, yet free, FTP server demon.

Sound and Vision

It's useful to keep an armory of audio, graphics, and video players that activate when you click on the file. Netscape and Internet Explorer can play most multimedia types, but dedicated programs provide more power. See also under "Plug-ins and ActiveX controls."

ACDSEE .... PC

http://www.acdvictoria.com

Extraordinarily fast graphics file viewer that integrates sublimely into Windows.

BIGPICTURE .... Mac

http://www3.sk.sympatico.ca/tinyjohn/

View and manipulate most image file types.

COOLEDIT .... PC

http://www.syntrillium.com

Pro quality audio file processor.

HYPERSNAP .... PC

http://www.hyperionics.com

Capture screen images, even in games.

MIDIPLUG .... PC

http://www.yamaha.co.jp/english/xg/

MIDI jukebox and software synthesizer.

NET TOOB .... PC

http://www.duplexx.com
Versatile viewer for MPEG, AVI, and QuickTime movie files.

PAINT SHOP PRO V PC

http://www.jasc.com
For heavy-duty graphics manipulation.

QUICKTIME .... PC, Mac

http://quicktime.apple.com
Play QuickTime (.mov) movie and 360 degree virtual reality files.

SOUND MACHINE .... Mac

http://www.kagi.com/rod/
Play, edit, and convert sound files.

VUEPRINT .... PC

http://www.hamrick.com
Manipulate oodles of image file types, even zipped, coded, and video files.

For more specialist sound software see:
http://www.maz-sound.com and http://www.hitsquad.com/smm/

TCP/IP, Timers, and Dialers

Be sure to regularly check Apple (http://info.apple.com) for upgrades to Open Transport, MacTCP and its operating system. See Microsoft (http://www.microsoft.com) for upgrades to Windows and Dial-up Networking.

FREEPPP .... Mac

http://www.rockstar.com
Use in conjunction with MacTCP to enable PPP connectivity.

GEARBOX .... Mac
http://www.rockstar.com
Internet configuration management, dialer, and diagnostics.

MACPPP TIMER .... Mac
http://ftp.tidbits.com/pub/tidbits/tisk/tcp/
Track online charges.

OPEN TRANSPORT AND OT PPP .... Mac
http://www.info.apple.com
Replaces MacTCP and MacPPP.

MACTCP WATCHER .... Mac
http://www.stairways.com/mtcpw/
TCP/IP testing tools such as Ping and DNS lookup.

NETMEDIC .... PC
http://www.vitalsigns.com
Monitor your connection's wellbeing, and see what's holding things up.

NETSCAN TOOLS .... PC
http://www.nwpsw.com
Ping, Finger, Traceroute, Whois and more. Get it.

RAS PLUS v PC
http://www.lambsoftware.com/dwnshare.htm
Win95 launchpad and time monitor.

TRUMPET WINSOCK .... PC
http://www.trumpet.com.au/wsk/winsock.htm
Reliable TCP/IP socket for Windows 3.xx. Includes Ping, TCPMeter, and Traceroute.

Telnet

Telnet is a powerful tool that enables you to **log into a remote computer via the Net** to run programs or access local data on UNIX servers (common in universities). Although its technology is useful, there's less and less call for it, as services move on to the Web and more tasks become automated – and that's a blessing, as it requires learning a few UNIX commands.

To log on to a remote server, enter the server's address, and then follow the prompts. It may require a log-in and password, which you should presumably have. If you don't, try hitting return instead. If that doesn't work, you'll have to go back to where you got the address and get the log-in details.

PROTERM .... Mac
http://www.intrec.com
Efficient, feature-packed Telnet client.

NETTERM .... PC
http://starbase.neosoft.com/~zkrr01/netterm.html
Supports remote host file editing, Zmodem, and Kermit.

Web Browsers

Even with thirty-odd browsers on the market the choice is really down to two: **Netscape** and Microsoft's **Internet Explorer**. It's largely a matter of familiarity which you prefer to use. Both are as superb as they are problematic and include a whole suite of add-ons that pretty much do everything from Internet telephony to tea making. For an ominous list of failed alternatives see:

http://www.browserwatch.com

MICROSOFT INTERNET EXPLORER .... PC, Mac
http://www.microsoft.com/ie/

NETSCAPE NAVIGATOR/COMMUNICATOR .... PC, Mac
http://home.netscape.com

Various other Tools

BLUE SKIES .... PC, Mac
http://groundhog.sprl.umich.edu/WUnderground/
Hook into The Weather Underground.

NETWORK TIME .... Mac
http://mirrors.aol.com/pub/info-mac/comm/tcp/
Synchronize your clock across the Net.

REMOTELY POSSIBLE .... PC
http://www.avalan.com
Control a Win95 machine over the Net.

TARDIS .... PC
http://www.kaska.demon.co.uk
Synchronize your PC time online.

WEATHERTRACKER .... Mac
http://www.weathertracker.com
Install a global weather station on your desktop.

WETSOCK .... PC
http://www.locutuscodeware.com/
Delivers current US weather data to your Win95 system
tray.

WINSTOCK .... PC
http://www.teleport.com/~magoldsm/winstock/
Stock quotes in a scrolling ticker bar. Just like at the

exchange except delayed.

WINWEATHER .... PC
http://www.webcom.com/igs/
Up-to-date international weather reports, forecasts, and
images via the Net.

But that's not all

For more depth and the very latest, check in to one of
the specialist software guides in our Web Guide's
"Search Tools and Directories" section (see p.198).

PART THREE

contexts

A Brief History of the Internet

The Internet may be a recent media phenomenon but as a concept it's actually older than most of its users; it was born in the 60s – a long time before anyone coined the buzzword "Information SuperHighway." Of course, there's no question that the Net deserves its current level of attention. It really is a quantum leap in global communications, though – right now– it's more of a prototype than finished product. While Bill Gates and Al Gore rhapsodize about such household services as video-on-demand, most Net users would be happy with a system fast enough to view stills-on-demand. Nonetheless, it's getting there. The medium is moving so fast that there's always something new promising to revolutionize the Net and maybe even our lifestyles.

THE ONLINE BOMB SHELTER

The concept of the Net might not have been hatched in Microsoft's cabinet war rooms, but it did play a role in a previous contest for world domination. It was 1957, at the height of the Cold War. The Soviets had just launched the first Sputnik, thus beating the USA into space. The race was on. In response, the US Department of Defense formed the Advanced Research Projects Agency (ARPA) to bump up its technological prowess.

Twelve years later, this spawned **ARPAnet** – a project to develop a military research network, or specifically, the world's first decentralized computer network.

In those days, no-one had PCs. The computer world was based on mainframe computers and dumb terminals. These usually involved a gigantic, fragile box in a climate-controlled room, which acted as a hub, with a mass of cables spoking out to keyboard/monitor ensembles. The concept of independent intelligent processors pooling resources through a network was brave new territory that would require the development of new hardware, software, and connectivity methods. The driving force behind decentralization, ironically, was the bomb-proofing factor. Nuke a mainframe and the system goes down. But bombing a network would, at worst, only remove a few nodes. The remainder could route around it unharmed. Or so the theory went.

WIRING THE WORLD

Over the next decade, **research agencies** and **universities** flocked to join the network. US institutions such as UCLA, MIT, Stanford, and Harvard led the way, and in 1973, the network crossed the Atlantic to include University College London and Norway's Royal Radar Establishment.

The 70s also saw the introduction of **electronic mail**, **FTP**, **Telnet**, and what would become the **Usenet newsgroups**. The early 80s brought **TCP/IP**, the **Domain Name System**, **Network News Transfer Protocol**, and the European networks **EUnet** (European UNIX Network), **MiniTel** (the widely adopted French consumer network), and **JANET** (Joint Academic Network), as well as the Japanese **UNIX** Network. ARPA evolved to handle the research traffic, while a second network, MILnet, took over the US military intelligence.

An important development took place in 1986, when the US National Science Foundation established **NSFnet** by linking five university super-computers at a backbone speed of 56 kbps. This opened the gateway for external universities to tap in to superior processing power and share resources. In the three years between 1984 and 1988, the number of host computers on the **Internet** (as it was now being called) grew from about 1000 to over 60,000. NSFnet, meanwhile, increased its capacity to T1 (1544 kbps). Over the next few years, more and more countries joined the network, spanning the globe from Australia and New Zealand, to Iceland, Israel, Brazil, India, and Argentina.

It was at this time, too, that **Internet Relay Chat (IRC)** burst onto the scene, providing an alternative to CNN's incessant, but censored, Gulf War coverage. By this stage, the Net had grown far beyond its original charter. Although ARPA had succeeded in creating the basis for decentralized computing, whether it was actually a military success was debatable. It might have been bomb-proof, but it also opened new doors for espionage. It was never particularly secure and it is suspected that Soviet agents routinely hacked in to forage for research data. In 1990, ARPAnet folded, and NSFnet took over administering the Net.

COMING IN FROM THE COLD

Global electronic communication was far too useful and versatile to stay confined to academics. Big business was starting to take an interest. The Cold War looked like it was over and world economies were regaining confidence after the 87 stock market savaging. Market trading moved from the pits and blackboards onto computer screens. The financial sector expected fingertip real-time data and that feeling was spreading. The world was ready for a people's network. And since the Net was already in place, funded by taxpayers, there was really no excuse not to open it to the public.

In 1991, the NSF lifted its restrictions on enterprise. During the Net's early years, its **"Acceptable Use Policy"** specifically prohibited using the network for profit. Changing that policy opened the floodgates to commerce with the general public close behind.

However, before anyone could connect to the Net, someone had to sell them a connection. The **Commercial Internet eXchange (CIX)**, a network of major commercial access providers, was formed to create a commercial backbone and divert traffic from the NSFnet. Before long, dozens of budding access providers were rigging up points of presence in their bedrooms. Meanwhile, NSFnet upgraded its backbone to T3 (44,736 kbps).

The Net had established itself as a viable medium for transferring data, but it had one major problem. You could pretty much only find things if you knew where to look. And that process involved knowing a lot more about computers, and the UNIX computing language in particular, than most consumers would relish. The next few years saw an explosion in navigation protocols, such as **WAIS**, **Gopher**, **Veronica**, and, most importantly, the now-dominant **World Wide Web**.

THE GOLD RUSH BEGINS

In 1989, Tim Berners-Lee of **CERN**, the Swiss particle physics institute, proposed the basis of the World Wide Web, initially as a means of sharing physics research. His goal was a seamless network in which data from any source could be accessed in a simple, consistent way with one program, on any type of computer. The Web did this, encompassing all existing infosystems such as FTP, Gopher, and Usenet, without alteration. It was an unqualified success.

As the number of Internet hosts exceeded one million, the **Internet Society** was formed to brainstorm protocols and attempt to coordinate and direct the Net's escalating expansion. **Mosaic** – the first graphical **Web browser** – was released, and declared to be the "killer application of the 90s." It made navigating the Internet as simple as pointing and clicking, and took away the need to know UNIX. The Web's traffic increased by 2500 percent in the year up to June 1994, and domain names for **commercial organizations** (.com) began to outnumber those of educational institutions (.edu).

As the Web grew, so too did the global village. The media began to notice, slowly realizing that the Internet was something that went way beyond propeller heads and students. They couldn't miss it, actually, with almost every country in the world connected or in the process. Even the White House was online.

Of course, as word of a captive market got around, entrepreneurial brains went into overdrive. Canter & Seigel, an Arizona law firm, notoriously **"spammed"** Usenet with **advertisements** for the US green card lottery. Although the Net was tentatively open for business, crossposting advertisements to every newsgroup was decidedly bad form. Such was the ensuing wrath that C&S had no chance of filtering out genuine responses from the server-breaking level of hate mail that they received. A precedent was thus established for **how not to do business on the Net**. Pizza Hut, by contrast, showed how to do it subtly by setting up a trial service on the Web. Although it generated wads of positive publicity, it too was doomed by impracticalities. Nevertheless, the ball began to roll.

THE HOMESTEADERS

As individuals arrived to stake out Web territory, businesses followed. Most had no idea what to do once they got their brand on the Net. Too many arrived with a bang, only to peter out in a perpetuity of "still under construction signs." Soon business cards not only sported email addresses, but Web addresses as well. And rather than send a CV and stiff letter, job aspirants could now send a brief email accompanied with a **"see my Web page"** for more detail.

The Internet moved out of the realm of luxury into an elite necessity, verging toward a commodity. Some early business sites gathered such a following that by 1995 they were able to charge high rates for advertising banners. A few, including the ever-more-crucial **search engines** such as **InfoSeek** and **Yahoo**, even made it to the Stock Exchange boards, while others, like **GNN**, attracted buyers (in their case the Online Service giant, AOL).

But it wasn't all success stories. Copyright lawyers arrived in droves. Well meaning devotees, cheeky opportunists, and info-terrorists alike felt the iron fists of Lego, McDonald's, MTV, the Louvre, Fox, the Church of Scientology and others clamp down on their "unofficial web sites" or newsgroups. It wasn't usually a case of corporate right but of might, as small players couldn't foot the expenses to test **new legal boundaries**. The honeymoon was officially over.

POINT OF NO RETURN

By the onset of 1995, the Net was well and truly within the public realm. It was impossible to escape. The media was becoming bored with extolling its virtues, so it turned to **sensationalism**. The Net reached the status of an Oprah Winfrey issue. New tales of hacking, pornography, terrorist literature, and sexual harassment began to tarnish the Internet's iconic position as the great international equalizer. But that didn't stop businesses, schools, banks, government bodies, politicians, and consumers from swarming online, nor the major **Online Services** – such as CompuServe, America Online, and Prodigy, which had been developing in parallel since the late 80s – from adding Internet access as a sideline to their existing private networks.

As 1995 progressed, Mosaic, the previous year's killer application, lost its footing to a superior browser program for the Web, **Netscape**. Not such big news, you might imagine, but after a half-year of rigorous beta-testing, Netscape went public with the third largest ever NASDAQ IPO share value – around $2.4bn.

Meantime, **Microsoft**, which had formerly disregarded the Internet, released **Windows 95**, a new PC operating platform incorporating access to the controversial **Microsoft Network**. Although **IBM** had done a similar thing six months earlier with **OS/2 Warp** and its **IBM Global Network**, Microsoft's was an altogether different scheme. It offered full Net access, but its real product was its own separate network, which many people feared might supersede the Net, giving Microsoft the sort of reign over information that Coke has over tooth decay. But that never happened. Within months, Microsoft, smarting from bad press, and finding the Net a larger animal even than itself, about-turned and declared a full commitment to furthering the Internet.

BROWSER WARS

As Microsoft advanced on the horizon, Netscape continued pushing the envelope, driving the Web into new territory with each beta release. New enhancements arrived at such a rate that competitors began to drop out as quickly as they appeared. This was the era of "This page looks best if viewed with Netscape." Of course, it wasn't just Netscape since much of the new activity stemmed from the innovative products of third party developers like **MacroMedia** (**ShockWave**), **Progressive Networks** (**Real Audio**), **Apple** (**QuickTime**), and **Sun** (**Java**). The Web began to spring to life with animations, music, and all sorts of new tricks.

While Netscape's market dominance gave developers the confidence to accept it as the de facto standard, treating it as a kind of Internet operating system into which to "plug" their products, Microsoft, an old hand at taking possession of cleared territory, began to launch a whole series of free Net applications. These included **Internet Explorer**, a browser with enhancements of its own, including **ActiveX**, a Web-centric programming environment more powerful than the much lauded Java, but without the same platform independence, and clearly geared to toward progressing Microsoft's software dominance. Not only was Internet Explorer suddenly the only other browser in the race, unlike Netscape, it was genuinely free. And many were rating it as the better product, crediting Microsoft with a broader vision of the Net's direction. By mid-1997, every Online Service and major ISP had signed deals with Microsoft to distribute its browser. At the time of writing, the browser battle continues, but on the home front at least, it appears Microsoft has all but won the war.

FOUND ON THE INTERNET

Skipping back to late 95, the backlash against Internet freedom had moved into full flight. The expression **"found on the Internet,"** became the news tag of the minute, depicting the Net as the source of everything evil from bomb recipes to child pornography. While editors and commentators, often with little direct experience of the Net, urged that "children" be protected, the Net's own media and opinion shakers pushed the **freedom of speech** barrow. It became apparent that this uncensored, uncontrollable new media, could shake the very foundations of democracy. At first politicians didn't take much notice. Few could even grasp the concept of what the Net was about, let alone figure out a way to regulate its activities. The first, and easiest, target was **pornography**, resulting in raids on hundreds of **private bulletin boards** worldwide and resulting in a few much publicized convictions for the possession of child porn. BBSs were an easy target, being mostly self-contained and run by someone who could take the rap. Net activists, however, feared that the primary objective was to send a ripple of fear through a Net community that believed it was bigger than the law, and to soften the public to the notion that the Internet as it stood posed a threat to national wellbeing.

In December 95, at the request of German authorities, **CompuServe** cut its newsfeed to exclude the bulk of newsgroups carrying sexual material. But the groups cut weren't just pornographers, some were dedicated to gay and abortion issues. This brought to light the difficulty in drawing the lines of obscenity, and the problems with publishing across foreign boundaries. Next came the **US Communications Decency Act**, a proposed legislation to forbid the online publication of "obscene" material. It was poorly conceived, however, and, following opposition from a very broad range of groups (including such mainstream bodies as the American Libraries Association), was overturned, and the decision later upheld in the Supreme Court. Several groups including the Family Research Council are presently working on a new version.

Outside the US, meanwhile, more authorities reacted. In **France**, chiefs of three major access providers were temporarily jailed for supplying obscene newsgroups, while in **Australia** police prosecuted several users for downloading child pornography. NSW courts introduced legislation banning obscene material with such loose wording that the Internet itself could be deemed illegal – if the law is ever tested. In **Britain**, in mid-1996, the police tried a "voluntary" approach, identifying newsgroups that carried pornography beyond the pale, and requesting that Providers remove them from their feed. Most complied, but there was unease within the Internet industry that this was the wrong approach. That the same groups would migrate elsewhere and the root of the problem would remain.

But the debate was, or is, about far more than pornography, despite the huffing and puffing. For **Net fundamentalists**, the issue is about holding ground against any compromises in liberty, and retaining the global village as a political force – potentially capable of bringing down governments and large corporations. Indeed, they argue that these battles over publishing freedom have shown governments to be out of touch with both technology and the social undercurrent, and that in the long run the balance of power will shift toward the people, toward a new democracy.

WIRETAPPING

Another slow-news-day story of the mid-90s depicted **hackers** gaining control of networks, stealing money, and creating havoc. It made great reading, but the reality was less alarming. Although the US Department of Defense reported hundreds of thousands of network break-ins, there was little evident damage, just annoyance. And in the commercial world, little went astray except the odd credit card file. Bear in mind that every time you hand your credit card to a shop assistant they would get the same information. In fact, by and large, for an online population greater than the combined size of New York, Moscow, London, and Tokyo, there were surprisingly few noteworthy crimes. Yet the perception was – and still is – that the Net is too unsafe for the exchange of sensitive information like payment details.

Libertarians raged at the US Government's refusal to lift export bans on crack-proof **encryption algorithms**. But cryptography, the science of message coding, has traditionally been classified as a weapon and thus export of encryption falls under the Arms Control acts.

Encryption requires a secret key to open the contents of a message and often another public key to code the message. These keys can be generated for regular use by individuals or, in the case of Web transactions, simply for one session upon agreement between the server and client. Several governments proposed to employ official escrow authorities to keep a register of all secret keys and surrender them upon warrant – an unpopular proposal, to put it mildly, among a Net community who regard invasion of privacy as an issue equal in importance to censorship, and government monitors as instruments of repression.

However, authorities were so used to being able to tap phones, intercept mail, and install listening devices to aid investigations, that they didn't relish giving up their freedom either. Government officials made a lot of noise about needing to monitor data to protect national security, though their true motives probably involve monitoring internal insurgence and catching tax cheats – stuff they're not really supposed to do, but we put up with anyway because if we're law-abiding it's mostly in our best interests.

The implications of this obstinacy go far beyond personal privacy. Business awaits browsers that can talk to commerce servers using totally snooper-proof encryption. Strong encryption technology has already been built into browsers, and approved for use with and between authorized financial bodies, to and from the US. However, at present, it's illegal, or at least questionable, for a US citizen to export the most powerful technology encryption for private use.

THE ENTERTAINMENT ARRIVES

While politicians, big business, bankers, telcos, and online action groups like **CommerceNet** and the **Electronic Frontier Foundation**, fretted the future of privacy and its impact on digital commerce, the online world partied on regardless. If 1996 was the year of the Web, then 1997 was the year the **games** began. Netizens had been swapping chess moves, playing dress-up, and struggling with the odd network game, over the Net for years, but it took id Software's **Quake** to lure the gaming masses online. Not to miss out, Online Services and ISPs took steps to prioritize game traffic, while hard core corporate data moved further back on the shelves.

Music took off, too. **Bands and DJs** routinely simulcast, or exclusively played, concerts over the Net while celebrities like Michael Jackson, Joe Dolce, and Paul McCartney bared their souls in public chat rooms. Web pages came alive with the sound of music, from cheesy synthesized backgrounds to live radio feeds. Many online music stores like **CDNow** reported profits, as did booksellers like **Amazon**.

And then there was the Net as a prime news medium. As **Pathfinder** touched down on Mars, back on Earth millions logged into NASA sites to scour the Martian landscape for traces of life. China marched into Hong

Kong, Tiger Woods rewrote golfing history, Australia regained the Ashes, and Mike Tyson fell from grace, all live on the Net. In response to this breaking of news on Web sites and Newsgroups, hundreds (maybe by now thousands) of **print newspapers** began delivering online versions before their hard copies hit the stands. In 1997, if you weren't on the Net, you weren't in the media.

THE CASUALTIES

Not everyone had reason to party in 1997. **Cybercafés** – touted as the coolest thing in 1995 – tended to flop as quickly as they appeared, as did many small **Internet Service Providers**, if they weren't swallowed by larger fish. And the technology became heavily focused. From over thirty **Web browsers** in early 1996, less than a year later, only two players – Netscape and Microsoft – remained in the game. The also-ran software houses that initially thrived on the Net's avenue for distribution and promotion, faded from view as the two browser giants ruthlessly crammed more features into their plug and play Web desktops. These days, too, every product Microsoft produces, including future versions of Windows, updates itself online, either automatically or with a single click. So much for the software dealer.

Meanwhile, **Web TV** arrived delivering Web pages and email onto home TV screens. It offered a cheap, simple alternative to PCs, but failed to find an immediate audience. Perhaps its day is yet to come.

The whole **Web design media** began shaking up, too. Overnight Web cowboys – without the programming skills to code, the artistic merit to design, or the spelling standards to edit, yet who'd charged through the teeth for cornering the home page design scam – were left exposed by the advent of ActiveX, Java, data processing, and print-standard art. New media had come of age. The top Web chimps reworked their résumés and pitched in with Online Design houses. Major ad agencies formed new media departments, and splashed Web addresses over everything from milk cartons to toothpaste tubes.

Bizarrely, though, 1997's best known Web design team, **Higher Source**, will be remembered not for HTML handiwork, but for publishing their cult's agenda to top themselves off in conjunction with the passing of the Hale Bopp comet. This was the Internet as a major news story in itself. Within hours of the mass suicide, several sites appeared spoofing both its corporate pages as well as its cult, **Heaven's Gate**. Days later, there were enough to spawn four new Yahoo subdirectories.

Back in the real world of **business and money**, major companies have played surprisingly by the book, observing netiquette – the Net's informal code of conduct. The marriage has been awkward but generally happy. Even the absurd court cases between blockbuster sites like **Microsoft Sidewalk v. TicketMaster** and **Amazon v. Barnes & Noble**, did little to convince Netizens that they were witnessing anything more than carefully orchestrated publicity stunts. Indeed, many felt launching a Web site without some kind of legal suit was a waste of free publicity. It just seemed like a bit of fun. And as big money flowed in, **bandwidths** increased, content improved, mums and dads scuttled aboard, and the online experience richened.

Alas, the same couldn't be said for the new school entrepreneurs. Low advertising costs saw **Usenet newsgroups** choked with crossposted get-rich schemes, network marketing plans, and porno adverts. Unprecedented **banks of email** broke servers at AOL, MSN, and scores of smaller providers. Netcom was forced to temporarily bar all mail originating from Hotmail, the most popular free Web email service, and consequent safe haven for fly-by-night operators due to the level of spam originating from its domain. At the same time, in July 1997, a mislaid backhoe ripped up a vital US backbone artery darkening large parts of the Net – something many had presumed impossible – and reducing the worldwide network to a crawl. The Net was nuclear-proof maybe, but certainly not invulnerable.

THE BOTTLENECK

The bigger problem for the Internet is that even when it surges at full health, it is still too slow. It hasn't over-loaded to a standstill as some predicted, but Netizens have been far from satisfied in the past couple of years. Many snapped up the **new modem speeds** – first 33.6 kbps, and soon after 56.6 kbps – only to strike bottle-necks further up the line. As the Internet population grows, Web demands rise, while bandwidth-hungry tech-nologies like Real Audio, Push, and Internet telephony do their bit to push the backbone to capacity. The long-haul wires that comprise the backbone have expanded to meet rising demand, but not enough for comfort.

The **power to upgrade** lies in the hands of those who own the major cables and thus effectively control the Internet. Over the next few years, the global telecom-munication big guns look set to starve the small players out of the market. Then by the new millenium, Internet access will come bundled with household services like telephone and cable TV. The telcos accept that even the fastest modems are inadequate, and ISDN is only mar-ginally better, so they're unwilling to waste money promoting either. And with the emergence of Internet telephony, they're forced to look further down the track at the broader scenario where whoever controls the Internet not only controls data, but voice traffic as well. They recognize that their core business could be eroded by satellite and cable companies. Their choice is to compete on the same level, provide an alternative, or buy them. At the moment all three seem viable.

A BRIGHTER TOMORROW

When Bill Clinton stunned the online world by declaring the Internet a **tax-free zone**, no-one was quite sure if he knew what he meant, especially as the US is not the only tax-collecting country in the network. It was, though, a sign that the Net's commercial significance is underwritten at the highest level. The Net will push on. Whatever obstacles stand in its path, be they technological, geographical, political, or fiscal, they will be overcome.

The big flaw is that the pioneers stand to lose the most money, especially in the high bandwidth stakes. If telcos like AT&T decide to inject **ADSL** into homes and offices, they can instantly supply up to 10 Mbps downstream and 640 kbps upstream over their existing phone lines – ample for audio, and maybe even video on demand. However, to do so would require refitting the exchange side hardware at great expense. **Cable companies** are similarly placed, with high speed pipes ready to go, yet few have taken the plunge seriously. While they promise similar speeds to ADSL, it has to be shared between everyone within a given cable zone – similar to an office LAN.

Meanwhile, their main threat comes from the skies. Apart from existing high speed **satellite** downlink services from DirecPC, expect to see SkyStation's solar-powered stratospheric airships hovering over large cities and beaming down megabits before the end of this century. And by 2002, **Teledesic**, from Gates, Boeing, McCaw, and others, will launch several hundred low-orbiting satellites with the sole purpose of creating an alternative high speed Internet backbone infrastructure accessible from anywhere on earth with a relatively small dish. So the **Information Super Highway** may just be on its way. It's a matter of when, what it will cost and how you'll pay for it. But the big question is, will it be for you?

The answer is, most likely, yes. You may not be able to justify spending on greater bandwidth unless you're earnestly intent on downloading video and high fidelity audio, and since you can already get that free with TV and radio, the decision is whether you're prepared to pay extra to do your own programming. It's already possible to download full CD quality music tracks from the Net. But at high speed, it could be the future of **record shopping**. You'd scan the reviews, listen to a low fidelity clip, then pay by smart card to download the song, an album or a custom compilation derived from your other musical preferences. The same goes for **videos**. In this scenario you might expect the shops to pay for your bandwidth, in the same way they build car parks in the real world. You'd be hoping. But we will soon become blasé about the Net as a medium and focus on its content. As with magazines, it will be about what's in them, not the paper they're printed on.

Likewise, telcos have given in to **Internet telephony**. They see it's about the people at the end of the wires, not what they do with them. They just don't know how to work the bills. How this will pan out is anyone's guess, but the boundaries between email, chat, and voice will blur. Presumably this will mean cheaper long distance phone calls and phone numbers that can move with you. This **new mobility** will induce many to leave their offices and work from home, and just as likely, while they're on holidays. Don't be surprised if freedom from the office means never being able to escape work.

Still, all in all, the future looks bright for the Internet. It might be age thirty, but it's still in its infancy. The problem with such rapid improvement is that our expectations grow to meet it. Be patient, enjoy it for what it is today, and complain, but not too much. You'll look back and get all nostalgic about the days you logged into the world through old copper telephone wires. It's amazing it works at all.

Net Language

The Internet hasn't always been a public thoroughfare: it used to be a clique inhabited by students and researchers nurtured on a diet of UNIX programming, scientific nomenclature, and in-jokes. Meanwhile, in a parallel world, thousands of low-speed modem jockeys logged into independent bulletin board networks to trade files, post messages, and chat in public forums. These groups were largely responsible for the birth of an exclusively online language consisting of acronyms, emoticons (smileys and such), and tagged text. The popularizing of the Internet brought these two cultures together, along with more recently, the less digitally versed general public.

Low online speed, poor typing skills, and the need for quick responses were among the pioneers' justifications for keeping things brief. But using Net lingo was also a way of showing you were in the know. These days, it's not so prevalent, though you're sure to encounter Netty terms in **Internet Relay Chat** (IRC) and, to a lesser extent, in **Usenet Newsgroup** postings. Since IRC is a snappy medium, with line space at a premium, acronyms and the like can actually be useful – as long as they're understood.

Shorthand: Net acronyms

It doesn't take long in IRC to realize that Net acronyms are peppered with the F-initial. It's your choice whether you add to this situation, but if you don't tell people to "f*** right off" in ordinary speech or letters, then FRO is hardly appropriate on the Net, and nor is adding F as emphasis. However, you may at least want to know what's being said. And, BTW (by the way), the odd bit of Net shorthand may be useful and/or vaguely amusing, even if unlikely to make you ROFL (roll on the floor laughing).

AFK	Away from keyboard
AOL	America Online
BAK	Back at keyboard
BBL	Be back later
BD or BFD	Big deal
BFN	Bye for now
BRB	Be right back
BTW	By the way
CUL8R or L8R	See you later
CYA	See ya
FB	Furrowed brow
GAL	Get a life
GDM8	G'day mate
GRD	Grinning, running, and ducking
GR8	Great
GTRM	Going to read mail
HTH	Hope this helps
IMHO	In my humble opinion
IYSWIM	If you see what I mean
IAE	In any event
IOW	In other words
LOL	Laughing out loud
NRN	No reply necessary
NW or NFW	No way
OIC	Oh I see
OTOH	On the other hand

PBT	Pay back time
RTM or RTFM	Read the manual
SOL	Sooner or later
TTYL	Talk to you later
YL/YM	Young lady/young man
|LY| & +LY	Absolutely and positively

Smileys and emoticons

Back in the old days, it was common in Usenet to temper a potentially contentious remark with <grins> tacked on to the end in much the same way that a dog wags its tail to show it's harmless. But that wasn't enough for the Californian E-generation, whose trademark smiley icon became the 80s peace sign. From the same honed minds that discovered 71077345 inverted spelled Greenpeace's bête noire, came the **ASCII smiley**. This time, instead of turning it upside-down, you had to look at it sideways to see a smiling face. An expression that words, supposedly, fail to convey. Well, at least in such limited space. Inevitably this grew into a whole family of **emoticons** (emotional icons).

The odd smiley may have its place in diffusing barbs, but whether you employ any of the other emoticons in use is up to your perception of the line between cute and dorky. All the same, don't lose sight of the fact that they're only mant to be fun :-). Anyway, that's up to you, so here goes:

:-)	Smiling	: =)	Little Hitler
:-D	Laughing	{}	Hugging
:-o	Shock	:*	Kissing
:-(	Frowning	\$-)	Greedy
:-Ō-)	Crying	X-)	I see nothing
;-)	Winking	:-X	I'll say nothing
X=	Fingers crossed	:-L~~	Drooling

:-P ...... Sticking out tongue	@Ñ`-,ÑÑ .... A rose
(hmm)0oo.. :-) ...... Thinking happy thoughts	8:)3= .... Happy girl
(hmm)0oo.. :-(......... Thinking sad thoughts	A few other, mostly Japanese anime derived, work right way up:
0:-) .... Angel	
}:> .... Devil	@^_^@ .... blushing
(_)] .... Beer	*^_^* huge dazzling grin
\V/ .... Vulcan salute	^_^; .... sweating
\o/ .... Hallelujah	T_T .... major tears

If you still want more, try consulting a few unofficial dictionaries on the Web. Use "smiley dictionary" or "emoticon" as a search term at http://www.hotbot.com

Emphasis

Another common way to express actions or emotions is to add commentary within < **these signs** >.

For example: <flushed> I've just escaped the clutches of frenzied train-spotters

< removes conductor's cap, wipes brow >.

More commonly, and more usefully, Netizens also use **asterisks in email** to *emphasize* words, in place of bolds and italics. You simply *wrap* the appropriate word: Hey everyone look at *me*.

Misspellings and intracaps

Some clowns pointedly overuse **phonetic spellings, puns, or plain misspellings** (kewl, windoze, macintrash, etc.) And wannabe crackers like to **intercapitalize**, LiKe tHis. You can safely assume they're either very young and trying to make an impression, total plonkers, or both.

Glossary

A

Access Provider Company that sells Internet connections. Known variously as Internet Access or Service Providers (IAPs or ISPs).

ActiveX Microsoft concept that allows a program to run inside a Web page. Expected to become a standard.

ADSL Asynchronous Digital Subscriber Line. High-speed copper wire connections at up to 6 Mbps downstream and 640 kbps up.

Anonymous FTP server A remote computer, with a publicly accessible file archive, that accepts "anonymous" as the log-in name and an email address as the password.

Altavista Web and Usenet search engine at: http://www.altavista.digital.com

AOL America Online. Presently, the world's most populous Online Service.

Archie Program that searches Internet FTP archives by file name.

ASCII American Standard Code for Information Interchange. A text format readable by all computers. Also called "plain text."

Attachment File included with email.

B

Bandwidth Size of the data pipeline. The fatter the bandwidth, the faster data can flow.

Baud rate Number of times a modem's signal changes per second when transmitting data. Not to be confused with bps.

BBS Bulletin Board System. A computer system accessible by modem. Members can dial in and leave messages, send email, play games, and trade files with other users.

Binary file All non-plain text files are binaries, including programs, word processor documents, images, sound clips, and compressed files.

Binary newsgroup Usenet group that's specifically meant for posting the above files.

Binhex Method of encoding, commonly used by Macs.

Bookmarks Netscape file used to store addresses.

Bounced mail Email returned to sender.

Bps Bits per second. The rate that data is transferred between two modems. A bit is the basic unit of data.

Browser Program, such as Netscape or Internet Explorer, that allows you to download and display Web documents.

C

Client Program that accesses information across a network, such as a Web browser or newsreader.

Crack To break a program's security, integrity, or registration system, or fake a user ID.

Crash When a program or operating system fails to respond or causes other programs to malfunction.

Cyberspace Term coined by science fiction writer William Gibson, referring to the virtual world that exists within the marriage of computers, telecommunication networks, and digital media.

D

Digital signing Encrypted data appended to a message to identify the sender.

Direct connection Connection, such as SLIP or PPP, whereby your computer becomes a live part of the Internet. Also called full IP access.

DNS Domain Name System. The system that locates the numerical IP address corresponding to a host name.

Domain Part of the DNS name that specifies details about the host, such as its location and whether it is part of a commercial (.com), government (.gov), or educational (.edu) entity.

Download Retrieve a file from a host computer. Upload means to send one the other way.

E

Email Electronic mail carried on the Net.

Email address The unique private Internet address to which your email is sent. Takes the form user@host

Eudora Popular email program for Mac and PC.

F

FAQ Frequently Asked Questions. Document that answers the most commonly asked questions on a particular subject. Every newsgroup has at least one.

File Anything stored on a computer, such as a program, image, or document.

Finger A program that can return stored data on UNIX users or other information such as weather updates. Often disabled for security reasons.

Firewall Network security system used to restrict external traffic.

Flame Abusive attack on someone posting in Usenet.

Frag Network gaming term meaning to destroy or fragment. Came from DOOM.

FTP File Transfer Protocol. Standard method of moving files across the Internet.

G

GIF Graphic Image File format. A compressed graphics format commonly used on the Net.

Gopher Menu-based system for retrieving Internet archives, usually organized by subject.

GUI Graphic User Interface. Method of driving software through the use of windows, icons, menus, buttons, and other graphic devices.

H

Hacker Someone who gets off on breaking through computer security and limitations. A cracker is a criminal hacker.

Header Pre-data part of a packet, containing source and destination addresses, error checking, and other fields. Also the first part of an email or news posting which contains, among other things, the sender's details and time sent.

Home page Either the first page loaded by your browser at start-up, or the main Web document for a particular group, organization, or person.

Host Computer that offers some sort of services to networked users.

HotBot Web and Usenet search at: http://www.hotbot.com

HTML HyperText Markup Language. The language used to create Web documents.

HyperText links The "clickable" links or "hotspots" that connect pages on the Web to each other.

I

Image map A Web image that contains multiple links. Which link you take depends on where you click.

IMAP Internet Message Access Protocol. Standard email access protocol that's superior to POP3 in that you can selectively retrieve messages or parts thereof as well as manage folders on the server.

Infoseek Web and Usenet search service at: http://www.infoseek.com

Internet A cooperatively run global collection of computer networks with a common addressing scheme.

Internet Explorer The now-dominant Web browser produced by Microsoft.

Internet Favorites Internet Explorer directory that stores filed URLs.

Internet Shortcut Microsoft's terminology for a URL.

IP Internet Protocol. The most important protocol upon which the Internet is based. Defines how packets of data get from source to destination.

IP address Every computer connected to the Internet has an IP address (written in dotted numerical notation), which corresponds to its domain name. Domain Name Servers convert one to the other.

IRC Internet Relay Chat. Internet system where you can chat in text, or audio, to others in real time, like an online version of CB radio.

ISDN Integrated Services Digital Network. An international standard for digital communications over telephone lines, which allows for the transmission of data at 64 or 128 kbps.

ISP Internet Service Provider. Company that sells access to the Internet.

J

Java Platform independent programming language designed by Sun Microsystems. http://www.sun.com

JPEG Graphic file format preferred by Net users because its high compression reduces file size, and thus the time it takes to transfer.

K

Kill file Newsreader file into which you can enter keywords and email addresses to stop unwanted articles.

L

Latency Length of time it takes data to reach its destination.

Leased line A dedicated telecommunications connection between two points.

Lycos Free Web search service at: http://www.lycos.com

M

MIME Multipurpose Internet Mail Extensions.
Standard for the transfer of binary email attachments.

Mirror Replica FTP or Web site set up to share traffic.

Modem MOdulator/DEModulator. Device that allows a
computer to communicate with another over a
standard telephone line, by converting the digital data
into analog signals and vice versa.

Mosaic The first point-and-click Web browser, created
by NCSA, now superseded.

MPEG A compressed video file format.

Multithreaded Able to process to multiple requests
simultaneously.

N

Name server Host that translates domain names into
IP addresses.

The Net The Internet.

Netscape Popular and influential Web browser – and
the company that produces it.

Newbie Newcomer to the Net, discussion, or area.

Newsgroups Usenet message areas, or discussion
groups, organized by subject hierarchies.

NNTP Network News Transfer Protocol. Standard for
the exchange of Usenet articles across the Internet.

Node Any device connected to a network.

P

Packet A unit of data. In data transfer, information is
broken into packets, which then travel independently

through the Net. An Internet packet contains the source and destination addresses, an identifier, and the data segment.

Packet loss Failure to transfer units of data between network nodes. A high percentage makes transfer slow or impossible.

Patch Temporary or interim add-on to fix or upgrade software.

Phreaker Person who hacks telephone systems.

Ping A program that sends an echo-like trace to test if a host is available.

Platform Computer operating system, like Mac System 7.0, Windows 95, or UNIX.

Plug-in Program that fits into another.

POP3 Post Office Protocol. An email protocol that allows you to pick up your mail from anywhere on the Net, even if you're connected through someone else's account.

POPs Points of Presence. An access provider's range of local dial-in points.

Post To send a public message to a Usenet newsgroup.

PPP Point to Point Protocol. This allows your computer to join the Internet via a modem. Each time you log in, you're allocated a temporary IP address.

Protocol An agreed way for two network devices to talk to each other.

Push Technique where data appears to be sent by the host rather than requested by the client. Email is a type of push.

R

Robot Program that automates Net tasks like collating search engine databases. Also called a Bot.

S

Server Computer that makes services available on a network.

Signature file Personal footer that can be automatically attached to email and Usenet postings.

SLIP Serial Line Internet Protocol. Protocol that allows a computer to join the Internet via a modem and requires that you have a pre-allocated fixed IP address configured in your TCP/IP setup. It's slowly being replaced by PPP.

SMTP Simple Mail Transfer Protocol. Internet protocol for transporting mail.

Spam Inappropriately post the same message to multiple newsgroups.

Streaming Delivered in real time instead of waiting for the whole file to arrive, e.g. Real Audio.

Stuffit A common Macintosh file compression format and program.

Surf To skip from page to page around the Web by following links.

T

TCP/IP Transmission Control Protocol/Internet Protocol. The protocols that drive the Internet.

Telnet Internet protocol that allows you to log on to a remote computer and act as a dumb terminal.

Trumpet Winsock Windows program that provides a dial-up SLIP or PPP connection to the Net.

U

UNIX Operating system used by most service providers and universities. So long as you stick to graphic programs, you'll never notice it.

URL Uniform Resource Locator. The addressing system for the World Wide Web.

Usenet User's Network. A collection of networks and computer systems that exchange messages, organized by subject into Newsgroups.

UUencode Method of encoding binary files into text so that they can be attached to mail or posted to Usenet. They must be UUdecoded to convert them back. Better mail and news programs do this automatically.

V

Vaporware Rumored or announced, but non-existent, software or hardware. Often used as a competitive marketing ploy.

W

Warez Software, usually pirated.

The Web The World Wide Web or WWW. Graphic and text documents published on the Internet that are interconnected through clickable "hypertext" links.

Web authoring Designing and publishing Web pages using HTML.

World Wide Web See Web, above.

WYSIWYG What You See Is What You Get. What you
type is the way it comes out.

Y

Yahoo The Web's most popular directory at:
http://www.yahoo.com

Z

Zip PC file compression format that creates files with
the extension .zip using PKZip or WinZip software.
Commonly used to reduce file size for transfer or
storage on floppy disks.

Zmodem A file transfer protocol that, among other
things, offers the advantage of being able to pick up
where you left off after transmission failure.

Still confused . . .

Then try the Computing dictionary (http://wagner.
princeton.edu/foldoc/); or What is? (http://www.whatis.com)

Further Reading

The best way to find out more about the Net is to get online and crank up a search engine, but sometimes it's more convenient – and maybe more enjoyable – to read about it in a book or magazine. Among Internet mags, good reads include the US-based *Internet World* and cyber-style bible *Wired*, the British-based *Internet* and *.net*, and the Australian *Internet.au*.

Books about the Net are harder to recommend as they date so quickly – it's hardly worth opening one that's more than a year old. This guide should be more than enough to get you started. However, the techie manuals can be handy when you need to check specifics, and don't feel like trawling the Net for them. Following are a few volumes that might prove useful, plus a selection of Net-related tales and discussions.

Techie manuals

Barron, Ellsworth, Savetz et al. *The Internet Unleashed,* (SAMS, US). Quality doorstopper of a techie manual, covering most Internet aspects in reasonable depth.
Adam Engst *The Internet Starter Kit* (Hayden, US). Step-by-step guidance, plus software. For Mac/Windows.

Web-site design

John December and Mark Ginsburg *HTML 3.2 & CGI Unleashed* (Sams, US). Web builder's reference chest.
Molly Holzchlag *Laura Lemay's Web Workshop* (Sams, US). How to use tables, frames, and style sheets.

Joseph Schmuller *Active X – No Experience Required* (Sybex, US). Control design from the basics up.

David Seigel *Creating Killer Web Sites* (Hayden, US). Site layout with DTP savvy.

Special interests

Simson Garfinkel and Gene Spafford *Web Security and Commerce* (O'Reilly, US). Developments in online transactions and hackproofing.

Thomas Mandel and Gerard Van der Leun *Rules of the Net* (Hyperion, US). As if. But a book that, despite its oxymoronic title, is packed with sound advice.

Brian Thomas *The Internet for Scientists and Engineers* (IEEE, US). How to use the Net for scientific research.

Joe Vitale *Cyberwriting* (Amacom, US). Writing copy to sell online.

Peter Wayner *Digital Cash* (AP Professional, UK). New payment methods.

Web directories

Harley Harn *Internet & Web Yellow Pages* (McGraw-Hill). This is arguably the best of the big phonebook style directories of the Web, with a mass of sites sorted by subject and briefly reviewed.

Rositano, Rositano, and Stafford *Que's Mega Web Directory* (Que, US). And if you want a second big print volume on your shelves, look no further: over 18,000 Web sites detailed by subject.

Net culture

Ric Alexander (ed.) *Cyber-Killers* (Orion, UK). Arresting anthology of network terrorism, robot crime, and virtual murder from authors such as William Gibson, Terry Pratchett, and J G Ballard.

Constance Hale *WiredStyle* (HardWired, US). An elegant primer of English usage for techie editors. How should you line-break Web addresses? It's all here.

Michael Hyman *PC Roadkill* (IDG, US). Humorous exposé of computer industry warfare.

Andrew Leonard *Bots: The Origin of a New Species* (HardWired, US). Celebrating a new generation of Wired warriors/online slaves.

Jonathan Littman *The Fugitive Game* (Little Brown, US). Catching super-hacker Kevin Mitnick.

Nicholas Negroponte *Being Digital* (Knopf, US/Hodder, UK). The MIT luminary and *Wired* columnist stabs at the future. A good primer for online thinking.

Neil Randall *The Soul of the Internet* (Thomson, US). The Net, its history, and those who made it happen.

Clifford Stoll *Silicon Snake Oil* (Doubleday, US/Macmillan, UK). Stoll reckons it was better back in the old days. Ever heard that before?

James Wallace *Overdrive* (Wiley, US). How Microsoft stomped its way to the top. To be continued.

Still want more?

The Net, of course, has its own directories of books about itself. Best are The Unofficial Internet Booklist (http://www.eurocube.it/kay/booklist.htm), and the sites run by the US online bookstores, Smartbooks (http://www.smartbooks.com) and Amazon (http://www.amazon.com).

PART FOUR

isp directory

Internet Service Providers

The directories following list major Internet Service Providers (ISPs or IAPs) in Britain, North America, Australia, New Zealand, Asia, and beyond. They are by no means complete and inclusion shouldn't be taken as an endorsement. We've concentrated on the larger, established, providers with multiple dial-in access points, as these are what most users require. There are, in addition, hundreds of local access providers, catering for individual cities and states.

Your first priority is to find a provider with local call access, preferably without paying a higher tariff for the convenience. If you can't find one from our lists, ask around locally, or sign up temporarily, get online, and consult one of these **Net directories**:

  http://www.the-list.com (global)
  http://www.netalert.com (global)
  http://www.cynosure.com.au/isp/ (Australia)
  http://www.emap.com/internet/isp/ (UK)

Unfortunately, these lists aren't anywhere near comprehensive either. Nor do they offer advice. For something more subjective, check out local **computer/Internet publications**; in the UK, for example, *Internet* magazine (http://www.emap.com/internet/) runs monthly performance charts. If you're still having problems, once online, try posting to the newsgroup: alt.internet.services

INTERNATIONAL ISPs

Most providers only operate in one country (or the US and Canada). For truly **international access**, which may be a priority if you plan to use the Net on your travels (see our "On The Road" chapter – p.176), consider one of the following.

Provider	Web address	Points of Presence
AOL	http://www.aol.com	Worldwide
CompuServe / SpryNet	http://www.compuserve.com	Worldwide
IBM Global Net	http://www.ibm.net	Worldwide
Microsoft Network	http://www.msn.com	Worldwide
Netcom	http://www.netcom.com	North America, UK

For phone numbers – and more details – of the above, see our "Online Services" chapter (p.45).

BRITAIN

Provider	Telephone number	Web Address
BT Internet	0800 800 001	http://www.btinternet.com
ClaraNet	0171 647 1000	http://www.clara.com
Demon Internet	0181 371 1234	http://www.demon.net
Direct Connection	0181 297 2200	http://www.dircon.net
Easynet	0171 681 4444	http://www.easynet.co.uk
IBM Global	0990 426 426	http://www.ibm.net

Mercury Internet Dial	0500 200 980 — http://www.mcmail.com
Netcom	01344 395 600 — http://www.netcom.net.uk
Netkonect	0171 345 7777 — http://www.netkonect.net
Prestel Online	0990 223 300 — http://www.prestel.co.uk
SAQ	0800 801 514 — http://www.saqnet.co.uk
U-Net	09125 484 444 — http://www.u-net.net
UUNet (Pipex Dial)	0500 474 739 — http://www.dial.pipex.com
Virgin Net	0500 558 844 — http://www.virgin.net
Zoo Internet	0345 326 326 — http://www.zoo.co.uk

EUROPE

Provider Web address	Telephone number Points of Presence
Algonet http://www.algonet.se	08 5875 8710 Sweden
BitMailer http://www.bitmailer.com	902 386 586 Spain
Centrum http://www.centrum.is	511 7000 Iceland
Deutsches Provider Network http://www.dpn.de	0130 123 441 Germany
Easynet http://www.easynet.fr	01 44 54 53 33 France, UK
Eunet Traveller http://traveller.eu.net	25 countries in Europe, North Africa, USA

| FranceNet | 01 40 61 01 76 |
| http://www.francenet.fr | France |

| GlasNet | 095 222 0990 |
| http://www.glasnet.ru | Russia |

| Ireland Online | 01 855 1739 |
| http://www.iol.ie | Ireland |

| Itnet | 10 6503641 |
| http://www.it.net | Italy |

| NetMedia | 02 6795860 |
| http://www.netmedia.co.il | Israel |

| Pingnet | 01 418 6222 |
| http://www.pingnet.ch | Switzerland, Liechtenstein |

| Scandinavia Online | 22 58 35 30 |
| http://www.sol.no | Norway |

| T Online | 049 59 990 |
| http://www.t-online.de | Germany |

| Telepac | 1 800 200 079 |
| http://www.telepac.pt | Portugal |

| XS4all | 020 3987666 |
| http://www.xs4all.nl | Netherlands |

NORTH AMERICA

| Provider | Telephone number |
Web address	Points of Presence
AT&T WorldNet	800 WORLDNET
http://www.att.net	USA

Brigadoon	800 899 0222
http://www.brigadoon.com	USA
Concentric Networks	800 939 4262
http://www.concetric.net	USA, Canada
EarthLink Network	800 395 8425
http://www.earthlink.com	USA, Canada
GTE Internet	800 GTE 1322
http://www.gte.net	USA
Hookup	800 363 0400
http://www.hookup.net	Canada
IBM Internet Connection	800 455 5056
http://www.ibm.net	USA, Canada
IDT Internet Services	800 245 8000
http://www.idt.net	USA
iStar	888 GO ISTAR
http://www.istar.ca	Canada
MCI Internet	800 550 0927
http://www.mci.com	USA
MindSpring	800 719 4332
http://www.mindspring.com	USA
Netcom	800 NETCOM1
http://www.netcom.com	USA, Canada
PSINet	800 827 7482
http://www.psi.com	USA, Canada
Sprint	800 747 9428
http://www.sprint.com/sip/	USA

| SpryNet | 800 SPRYNET |
| http://www.sprynet.com | USA, Canada |

| Sympatico | 800 773 2121 |
| http://www.sympatico.ca | Canada |

AUSTRALIA

Provider	Telephone number	Web address
Access One	1800 672 395	http://www.aone.net.au
AusNet	1800 806 755	http://www.world.net
Enternet	1800 681 113	http://www.enternet.com.au
GigaNet	1800 686 884	http://www.giga.net.au
IBM Global Network	132 426	http://www.ibm.net
Magnet	1800 809 164	http://www.magnet.com.au
Ozemail	1800 805 874	http://www.ozemail.com.au
Starway	1800 24 2020	http://www.starway.net.au
Telstra Big Pond	1800 655 744	http://www.telstra.net

NEW ZEALAND

Provider	Telephone number	Web address
Clear Net	0800 777 765	http://www.clear.net.nz
Telecom XTRA	0800 BUY XTRA	http://www.xtra.co.nz
Voyager	0800 888 258	http://www.voyager.co.nz

ASIA

Provider Web address	Telephone number Points of Presence
Brain Net http://www.brain.net.pk	42 541 4444 Pakistan
DataCom http://www.magicnet.mn	1 312 063 Mongolia
Global Online http://www.gol.com	03 5341 8000 Japan, USA, Canada
VNSL http://web.vsnl.net.in	22 264 1544 India
Pacific Surf http://www.pacific.net.sg	1 800 872 1455 Singapore
Pinter http://www.pacific.net.id	21 5307830 Indonesia
Jaring http://www.jaring.my	03 966 5000 Malaysia
Thailand http://www.ksc.net.th	662 576 0899 Thailand
Taiwan http://www.hinet.net	2 344 3143 Taiwan

REST OF THE WORLD

Provider Web address	Telephone number Points of Presence
Africa Online (Prodigy) http://www.africaonline.com	617 395 5500 (US) (233 21) 226802 (Ghana) (254 2) 243775 (Kenya) (255 51) 666983 (Tanzania) (225) 21 90 00 (Ivory Coast)
Impsat http://www.impsat.com.ar	01 318 8333 Argentina, Latin America
Cybernet http://web.cybernet.com.br	21 553 5577 Brazil
DataNet http://www.data.net.mx	5 107 5400 Mexico
Egypt Online http://www.egyptonline.com	202 395 4111 Egypt
UUNet Internet Africa http://www.iafrica.com	0800 020 003 South Africa, Worldwide

Acknowledgements

I have a confession. When I wrote the first edition of this pocket book two years back, I had no idea it would be such a success. I figured it would be swamped by all those loud knucklehead guides with light bulb icons, "top tips," and "insider secrets." I certainly didn't expect to see it in the bestseller lists and to find myself producing three updated editions in quick succession. I'd like to think a big part of these sales have come through word of mouth. People often write and tell me they bought it on a friend's recommendation. That's a nice feeling, because it's makes me think we've got something right. I'm not sure exactly what that is, but I know I can't take full credit for it.

As author, I don't get to see all the machinations of who got us where, but I do know that without Henry Iles' flair, Richard Trillo's connections, Susanne Hillen's timing, and Al Spicer's Web mastery, we mightn't have got anywhere at all. Thanks to them, and everyone else at Rough Guides and Penguin who has worked on the book, especially Mark Ellingham, who came up with the original idea, and publicists Simon Carloss in London; Jean Marie Kelly and SoRelle Braun in New York; and Nicole Lyons in Melbourne.

This edition drew me back to London and once more to *Internet Magazine*, which had changed every bit as much as its subject matter. First up from there, I'd like to thank new media godfather, Roger Green, for his ongoing encouragement and generosity; publisher, Ruth Allen, for making me welcome in the office; and editor, Gail Robinson, for letting me pull her out of the network so long as the right flavor wine gums got pulled out at the same time. Working from there meant rocking up some time after lunch and wading through quagmires of Web slush until the sparrows chimed in near dawn. A time only the perennially cheerful Tamsin Hughes was ever up, still twiddling in her BBC sweatshop, ready to explain how to use a thesaurus or offer encouragement (mainly telling me to get on with it).

Also at *Internet Magazine*, thanks to Liz Bailey for sharing her fruit and declaring me sane compared to someone very obviously not; Mike Bracken for flicking me his Memphis beta, costing me days in lost computer hours; Mike Hales whose presence nights and weekends made me feel relatively human; slightly improved Quakefodder, and world-class bloke, Darren Wallace for everything shockworthy; barely improved Paul Bennett for bigtime string-pulling in the travel and entertainment stakes; and easybeat, Craig Lancaster for spinning top tunes and keeping Cass under wraps.

Further lid-dipping is due to the Internet old school, namely: Matt Townend, at UUnet Pipex, for bundling us into record sales; Lisa Hughes in debuting her Internet book for kids; Neil Ellul for pioneering Net access into Saudi Arabia; Sarah Johnstone for translating a German review of our French edition into something complimentary; Dave Pitchford for mad adventures at any excuse and landing me a cool blend of earthmovers, jackhammers and rattling guns to sleep next to; and media geek Garret Keogh for understandably fleeing town to spend less time with his mates and more on IRC after lampooning a certain *MSN News* interview about my unfeasibly large email volume.

Then across the globe, thumbs up to Shelley Ronson for getting me through the worst bit; my father for buying land as an excuse to spot me a ute over summer; my mother for readily embracing email as a way to keep us in touch; Gerry Browne for submitting scores of fascinating URLs and snippets (though none suitable for reproduction); John Hooper for his infectious enthusiasm for large numbers, high voltage and wire in general; Delphine Le Dain for late-night quakey roundtables hooked in through the KL Downtown Paradise eggphone; and Irene Tchaikovsky, Jeff Davis & Teigen Ekedal for making me think LA mightn't be such a bad place to live after all.

And to those who made the whole process more enjoyable. In no particular order, that includes: Marls Ramalingam; Elliot Trudgian & kin; Jo Chichester; John & Carla Little; Greg, Gayle, Katie, & Sedgwick NG; Celeste Withey; Haris Hadzialic; Morgan Sowden; Simon Davies; J T, J Q, & E F MacNamara; Jane Fish; Brian Hickey; Chris Carrigan; Nadine, Kylie & Ben Griffin; Reggie Huybers; Leo Ryan; Sophie Parer; Bouchra Senadji; David Quilty; Sarah Hall; Arthur Daley of West End; Bruce Hutton; the brothers Rodentia and Gallagher; Cooey; Martin & Leanne; Tiffany Thomas; Farrah; Nick Ryan; Anton Lavin; Col Battersby; Alex James; Fiona Macadam; Catrin and Dr Rees; Beaufort Weinburger; Dot Hooper; and Victoria Banfield. And finally, to the memory of an all-time great, Bill Nicklin.

Angus Kennedy
angus@easynet.co.uk

HELP US UPDATE

Trying to keep up with the ever-changing Internet is a near impossible task. So don't be alarmed if you find a few addresses that don't work, or dubious recommendations. It was all correct at time of press. Honest. But it's sure to change. So, if something's not right, or you think we could have explained it better, please let me know via email at: angus@easynet.co.uk and I'll attend to it in the next edition.

In the meantime, keep an eye on:
http://www.roughguides.com/net/

Index

C

D

E

F

I

T

50 things to do with this book

You're online, so where now? Has it all been worth the effort? Listed below, in no particular order, are 50 ideas of things to do on the Net – try a selection and you will be a full-fledged Netizen. The page numbers detailed will direct you to full instructions in this book but with many it's simply a question of keying in the Web address and following prompts.

1.   Look yourself up on the Web
http://www.hotbot.com

2.   Reignite an old flame
See p.134

3.   Publish your own magazine
See p.142

4.   Check a movie star's résumé
http://www.imdb.com

5.   Pretend you're someone else
See p.69 and p.162

6.   Advise the US President
http://www.whitehouse.gov

7.   Flirt with a stranger
See p.157

8. Fall over laughing (FOL)
See p.227

9. Work from the Bahamas
See p.176

10. Sort out your weeds
http://www.gardening.com

11. Battle in QuakeWorld
See p.173

12. Tune in to foreign radio
See p.296

13. Natter by Netphone
See p.165

14. Rekindle your childhood interests
See p.90 and p.125

15. Make your first million
See p.251

16. Get fanatical about football
See p.317

17. Move to Mars
http://www.marsshop.com

18. Confirm you're mad
http://www.mentalhealth.com

19. Plan your next holiday
See p.324

20. Make exotic music
http://bunji.realitycom.com/kilo4-3/

21. Build an atomic bomb
See p.305

22. Witness a whiteout in Tromso
http://www.cs.uit.no/~ken/images/big/weather.jpg

23. Buy a frilly bra
http://www.brasdirect.co.uk

24. Read your hometown's paper
See p.285

25. Stare into space
http://www.telescope.org/rti/

26. Become a master chef
http://www.ichef.com

27. Cast a voodoo spell
http://www.ping.be/~ping2442/voodoo.htm

28. Watch sport at work
See p.315

29. Answer hard questions
See p.90

30. Research anything
See p.125

31. Track down a killer novel
http://www.purefiction.com

32. Fix your computer
See p.229

33. Seek legal advice
See p.269

34. Obey the Interplanetary Council
http://www.aetherius.org

35. Identify a murderer
See p.336

36. Hang with loonies
See p.336–341

37. Clone a companion
http://www.clonaid.com

38. Hunt for a better job
See p.232

39. Agitate, educate, organize
See p.292

40. Show off your baby snaps
See p.65 (email) and p.142 (Web page creation)

41. Immerse yourself in virtual reality
http://www.pitchford.com

42. Ordain yourself
See p.304

43. Indulge in hypochondria
http://www.pharminfo.com

44. Learn to be cool
http://www.geocities.com/SunsetStrip/4160/big.html

45. Chat with a pop star
http://www.sonicnet.com

46. Fish for a compliment
http://pharmdec.wustl.edu/cgi-bin/jardin_scripts/SCG/

47. Argue with experts
See p.72 and p.90

48. Attend a live gig
http://www.liveconcerts.com

49. Preview and then buy one of 250,000 CDs
http://www.cdnow.com

50. Join the Foreign Legion
http://www.specialoperations.com

Backpacking through **Europe**?
Cruising across the **US of A**?
Clubbing in **London**?
Trekking through **Costa Rica**?

Wherever you're headed, **Rough Guides** tell you
what's happening – the history, the people,
the politics, the best beaches, nightlife and
entertainment on your budget

GUIDES

100 destinations worldwide
...to Zimbabwe.

Special Offer

internet *magazine*

Subscribe for just £15 and save over £20

Rough Guide readers can take advantage of a very special price on a year's subscription to Internet Magazine, the UK's biggest and best Internet title. For just £15 you'll get Internet Magazine delivered to your door every month.

The latest **Net news**
Interviews from **the cutting edge**
The newest Net products tried and tested
Your Net **questions answered**
The ultimate Internet **Service Provider tests**

How to subscribe

To take advantage of this very special offer call up the Internet Magazine subscription hotline on (0181) 956 3015 and quote the reference code RG98. For more details on the content of the magazine and for a Net news service updated every working day visit our Web site at www.emap.com/internet

This offer is available to UK residents only

internet *magazine*

SPECIAL OFFER

For all Rough Guide readers